The Capture of Speech and Other Political Writings

michel de certeau

Edited and with an Introduction by Luce Giard

Translated and with an Afterword by Tom Conley

University of Minnesota Press

Minneapolis

London

The University of Minnesota Press gratefully acknowledges financial assistance provided by the French Ministry of Culture for the translation of this book.

Originally published as *La prise de parole, et autres écrits politiques*, © 1994 Éditions du Seuil. Édition établie et présentée par Luce Giard.

Published by the University of Minnesota Press
111 Third Avenue South, Suite 290
Minneapolis, MN 55401-2520

http://www.upress.umn.edu

Printed in the United States of America on acid-free paper

Library of Congress Cataloging-in-Publication Data

Certeau, Michel de.
   [Prise de parole, et autres écrits politiques. English]
   The capture of speech and other political writings / Michel de
Certeau ; edited and with an introduction by Luce Giard ; translated
and with an afterword by Tom Conley.
     p.   cm.
   Originally published as La prise de parole, et autres écrits
politiques.
   Includes bibliographical references and index.
   ISBN 0-8166-2768-1 (hc : alk. paper). — ISBN 0-8166-2769-X (pb :
alk. paper)
   1. Sociolinguistics. I. Giard, Luce. II. Title.
P40.C4413   1998
306.44—dc21   97-43050
                                     CIP

The Capture of Speech and
Other Political Writings

Contents

Contents

Introduction
How Tomorrow Is Already Being Born

Luce Giard

Philosophy is not a body of doctrine, but an activity. A philosophical work consists essentially of clarifications.
    Wittgenstein, Tractatus logico-philosophicus *(1921), § 4.112*[1]

Nothing seemed to predispose Michel de Certeau to feel bonded with the "events" of May 1968, to the point of welcoming this strange, forever enigmatic situation,[2] with as much emotion as marvel:

> Something happened to us. Something began to stir in us. Emerging from who knows where, suddenly filling the streets and the factories, circulating among us, becoming ours but no longer being the muffled noise of our solitude, voices that had never been heard began to change us. At least that was what we felt. From this something unheard of was produced: we began to speak. It seemed as if it were for the first time. From everywhere emerged the treasures, either aslumber or tacit, of forever unspoken experiences. (Chapter 2)

Nothing was preparing him for it, at least according to cursory evidence. By profession a historian, Michel de Certeau had amply paid his dues to erudition and to source studies. He had completed scholarly editions of the works of Pierre Favre and Jean-Joseph Surin.[3] He was clearly nourished as much by philosophy and theology through his advanced studies as he was by a complementary training in the Society of Jesus, which he entered in 1950, on the basis of an adult decision that he never called into question, even though, in his own way, he sought to follow a "road untraveled." He also refused to give over to this religious institution the résumé of his social identity or the refuge of an inner conformism. But in May 1968 he should have chosen to take shelter beneath the high ramparts of knowledge, far

vii

from the crowd, far from the streets ablaze with laughter, far from the songs and the barricades erected by university and high-school students. It would have been logical.

He should have been irritated by the adolescent revolt ("Professors, you're making us senile!"), criticized the utopia of their slogans ("I take my desires for realities because I believe in the reality of my desires!"), and been annoyed by the rhetoric and ignorance that reduced the call to the police by the dean of liberal arts at Nanterre—a former member of the French Resistance and specialist in German studies, who had once narrowly escaped deportation and had recently courageously struggled against the Algerian War—to a call to the Nazi SS.[4]

As did so many others, Michel de Certeau should have been frightened by the general strike, seeing in it ubiquitous signs of Soviet menace or the risk of "havoc." He should have feared a deadly "turmoil" about to sink the nation, its institutions, and its laws.[5] He should have cried out in indignation, deplored, moralized, scolded, or at least stayed put or steered clear of the general chaos by seriously tending to his very serious business while waiting for better days to come, since "youth has to have its day."

Driven by another logic, he made none of these choices. Where did he find the inspiration of an entirely different attitude? Whence came to him this understanding of unspoken things that were welling up, or this respect for such an unthinkable upheaval? From the first days onward, it was indicated by the intense attention given to these questions that were *unheard* and whose answers were *unspoken*, that remained to be sought in what he was designating as a labor of common elucidation whose secret or privilege no individual could hold. A position was taken that aroused irreducible oppositions among his friends and tenacious rancor among his peers. In truth, it was the staging of an action that he was later to call the *founding rupture*.[6]

Most remarkable is that, armed only with the assurance that a need of inner veracity forced him to move ahead, he took to this "road untraveled" without knowing where it would lead him. As he went along, in studies that he first wrote for himself, and then published in *Études* beginning in June, he tried to understand the movement. The analyses that he put together from May to September 1968 (which make up the first part of this volume) betray his desire to go beyond the narrative of a personal experience in order to extend the field of investigation to the social dimensions of the present, by specifying the differences that emerged among the actors, the groups, the spectators, and the authorities, each willingly playing a role on the national scene: "The event cannot be dissociated from the options to which it *gave place*; it is that space constituted by often surprising choices that have modified customary divisions, groups, parties, and communities, following an unforeseen division" (chapter 1).

For Certeau, this reaction was synchronous with the "events," as his writings of the time confirm; it was the consequence neither of revising his views in the aftermath nor of a swashbuckling penchant for grandstanding. I shall attribute to him three reasons, each referring to a level of temporality. The first, a *tradition*, is written in long duration. At stake is the history of Christianity and, specifically, these mystical authors of the sixteenth and seventeenth centuries who had been Certeau's primary subject of historical research and inner meditation. Their mystical texts—which he analyzed on their own grounds on the basis of a speaking subject and its modes of expression (a style, "ways of speaking")—he considered as a "moment" in a sociopolitical context in which a group or a network sharing the same affinities was expressing a disquiet, a hope, or was seeking to invent for itself a "way of being and believing." Reading and rereading these mystics, Certeau discerned the traces of this "power of the weak" through which the violence of the strong would be resisted, if not visibly, at least by inner means, by finding mental protection from their attacks, by shutting themselves off from their injunctions. Certeau saw these infinite resources of a silent and sometimes desperate resistance in the work at once of the seventeenth-century "Christians without a church," of the Amerindians crushed by colonizers since the Renaissance, and of the "man without qualities," our contemporary human beings who are submerged—even in the secrecy of their dreams—by mass consumerism.[7]

The middle term of the three temporalities pertains to the fact of belonging to a certain *generation*. Compared to the mostly adolescent actors in the theater of 1968, Michel de Certeau (born in May 1925) belonged to the generation of fathers whose children, enrolled in undergraduate programs or high schools, were filling the streets. He had this ability to go out and meet young people as might a father without children, since he had formerly freely consented to this privation by accepting the discipline of a consecrated life. He scrupulously tried to prolong this privation of the flesh in the order of the mind. As one of his former students was to remark, he was "the master who wanted no disciples," through a gesture, forever begun over and over again, of lucidity about the exchange of affect and the ties of dependency established between fathers and children, or between masters and disciples, but even more, it seems to me, through a concern for extreme prudence and extreme respect for the freedom of his interlocutor. That cast an incomparable light on his way of relating to others.[8] It was a "style of action." Later, having become slightly less unaware, I recognized the deep and silent mark of Ignatian inspiration, either because it had been confirmed through his experience in the Society of Jesus or because he had been drawn into this order through a secret affinity for this career. It was probably both at once.

What had specifically marked his generation was the common, painful experience of the shock, felt in his adolescence in 1940, when he had to witness — rage pulsating in his veins — the annihilation of the "old country" in resignation, fear, shame, and disorder. He retained its unforgettable lesson, which often returned, through the detours of his conversation, to the effect that no place exists for children to obey their fathers and, even less, to accept the currency of their discourse of value or the code of honor whose celebration that these fathers, in agreement with authorities, are forever ready to perpetuate. To the contrary, he believed in the hard labor of emancipation that everyone had to accomplish on his or her own, by personal means, in solitude, in order to bring to light the ethical need that would have to govern one's life, in the order of the visible and the invisible, that is, to become capable of assuming responsibility in the construction of the social body through a multiplicity of possible accomplishments. He asked no one to be a hero, a paragon of virtue, and even less a sacrificial victim. He bore no illusions about the complacencies and the rewards dissimulated beneath these types of conduct. He abhorred injunctive or instigational speech that called for abnegations for which others alone would reap benefits. He asked of those who have to "pronounce the speech of authority" to be conscious of it, and to instill more modesty and respect for the freedom and suffering of others in each of their acts.

He knew that he was leading this labor of emancipation into a painful phase of sundering, of distance taken from earlier assurances, sometimes to the point of a break without the possibility of return, but for him, none of that ever meant denial or ingratitude. Quite to the contrary, he was a man more than ready to recognize a "debt" to others. But the construction of his autonomy, the removal of the "obviously" received facts of a tradition, a milieu, of a family, meant staying faithful to the inner violence of the adolescent of 1940 who had refused the resignation of the fathers (most of them in power), support for the old marshal [Pétain], the moralizing discourse on the defeat that a sinful France really deserved. He had other goals, and he had dreamed of faraway lands while hiking up mountain paths to transmit messages to the Resistance. From the difficult years of 1940–44 he retained this certitude: no one can ever be absent from the public sphere, because no one can elude his or her political responsibility in what is everyone's struggle. In his eyes, this responsibility played a role in the proof that every life would have to bring forward: critical Reason, moral conscience, national solidarity, Last Judgment, and so on. If he was rarely bothered with establishing proceedings of judgment or with defining the rules that dictate their functions, for him it was absolutely crucial to nourish the fire of a need, the courage of a radicality in which, one day, there would extend a liberty embracing all at once action, speech, understanding, and belief.

The last reason that I shall adduce to shed light on his attitude in May 1968 is placed on a shorter scale of time and bears on the *conjunction of personal circumstances*. He had been beset by a series of deaths in his family (his younger sister prematurely passed away in 1966; his mother died in an automobile accident in August 1967, in which he himself almost died, losing the sight of one eye). A crisis broke out at *Christus*, the journal of the Society of Jesus that appeared three times a year, for which he was the associate director under the leadership of François Roustang. It concluded with Roustang's departure, who changed affiliation and in the autumn of 1967 rejoined the editorial board of *Études*, the monthly that the Society published on culture at large. The completion in 1966 of a labor of several years' duration, the critical edition of Surin's correspondence, had left him uncertain over the future of his research. He hesitated at the threshold of a new direction, he dreamed of unknown connections to be made between history and theology, and psychoanalysis increasingly attracted him as a means of personal elucidation and as a "critical theory of society."[9] He had just returned fresh from the experience of another continent, following a tour of teaching in Latin America. He was no sooner impassioned, indeed given over to a lasting passion, for these young, mixed, bubbling societies in which active minorities of engaged intellectuals and "base" Christian communities sought to put an end to the established disorder, if necessary by resorting to armed struggle.

This first trip to the South American continent—which would be followed by many others—forged numerous ties for him to Brazil, Chile, and, later, Mexico. His texts were translated, recordings of his lectures were circulated, one person made a trip to Paris to write a dissertation under his direction. The perspicacious observer who recognized in him the "master who wanted no disciples" came from Brazil and went back. Despite the difference of situations, these meetings in South America clearly played a determining role in the way that Certeau experienced the crisis of May 1968. He perceived beforehand the mute disquiet that was fomenting the "ennui" of a France that was prosperous but unsatisfied.

Unknowingly, between 1965 and the beginning of 1968 he followed a complete cycle of apprenticeship. He thus learned how to explore these sensitive zones, these "sites of transit" as he would later call them, in which unspoken questions were sought, in which improbable responses were invented.[10] I would add to this cycle of apprenticeship a political valence, even if it incorporated a number of more personal factors. But we must not be mistaken about the meaning of "political." Michel de Certeau never made a career of political analysis, neither at the level of practices nor at that of theories. He was neither the mouthpiece nor the inspiration for a current of opinion, nor was he an adviser, nor an active militant of any party, and he was not a "fellow traveler" in the many organizations that were more or less affiliated with the Communist Party.

But he took with utmost seriousness the political involvements of his contemporaries; he respected militant behavior in the service of social projects (even if he was not affiliated); he closely read, in both German and French, many of Marx's writings (but the epigones were of little interest to him) and meditated with particular delight—for reasons that I still cannot fathom—on *The Eighteenth Brumaire of Louis Bonaparte,* a text crucial to all of his writings on historiography. In the limited part of his work that deals more directly with political matters, its words and themes return as if through a profound scansion. Significant is the fact that they also figure in all of the other writings, whether of historiography, mystics, or the culture of everyday people. From this I gather that the words and themes refer to a conceptual architecture that subtends the movement of his thinking. I shall now briefly indicate three that are indispensable for the reader who will move about the present volume.

There is first a central and nagging question, ubiquitously present in diverse forms, from the very first text he published — and which I have reedited[11] — to the last piece of writing, in his final days, a book review of oral and written literature (songs and pamphlets) that satirized Mazarin.[12] It is a question of *speech,* of its efflorescence, of its free circulation in the social body, and of its circulation in either an oral or a written form.[13] Characteristic of this point of view is the summary he soon provides of the "events" of May 1968: "Everywhere we saw exploding in the form of lyricism, in undefined palavers, an apology for the tidal wave of common speech, what was basically a kind of neutral experience, but of a veracity for each and every person because everyone could discover themselves in a fabric of language, of speech."[14] Speech is what grants entry into the concert of voices where partial, contradictory, or inchoate truths confront, contradict, and complete one another; a medium of elaboration, also of the deployment of veracity, it gives nourishment to every member of the social body. It is a flux that irrigates and instills life. In it are stated the relations of power; conflicts are acted out; the ruse of the weak is insinuated and wins over a space of freedom.[15]

To that he added a razor-sharp consciousness of *differences,* of finding in the plural of diversity what assures a society's vitality and power of invention. But he knew that every social group dreads the proximity of "different people," tending thus to reject the foreigner in order to protect its own coherence. The principal goal of political labor seemed to him to be one of realizing a kind of plural unity, what he had called "union in difference," solely capable of making marked differences sustainable for the one and the other.[16] He assigned a good deal of this task to educators. At the time of the predoctoral seminar in cultural anthropology that he directed at the University of Paris-VII (Jussieu), students asked him to clarify his own practice of teaching.[17] From this time and place that were officially aimed at initiating students into research methodologies, he felt it necessary first to produce a phase of resurgent awareness, then one of an elaboration of differences recognized and taken to exist as such.

> In a group, the experience of *time* begins with the clarification of its plurality. People need to see themselves as different (of a difference that cannot be assailed by any magisterial position, by any particular discourse, by any festive fervor) so that a seminar will turn into a common and partial *history* (a labor on and between differences) and so that speech will therein become

the instrument of a *politics* (the linguistic element of conflicts, of contracts, of surprises, in brief, of "demo-cratic" procedures).[18]

Yet, informed by the study of North American society, he also knew the danger that can issue from a belonging to "minorities" that is maintained and asserted over time. Ostensibly protecting a cultural and social identity, guaranteeing the transmission of a heritage, this belonging can lead to enclosing minorities in as many ghettos, to circulating the stereotypical images of each, to confirming a division of roles and responsibilities, and, finally, to eradicating tradition, which becomes embalmed, set aside from the current forces in society, such that it becomes a deceitful means of "stigmatization" or conservation of every kind of nostalgia, and often both at once. This difficult question (up to what point can the plurality of differences be upheld, and how to ensure their mutual respect and the coherence of a society?) cuts across his entire work, from the first articles written for the readers of *Christus* to the historical research on the labor of linguistic unification undertaken by the French Revolution, from the study of cultural practices to the definition of a scholarly politics on the part of the member states of the Organization for Economic Cooperation and Development (OECD).[19]

A last characteristic of his political writings, and whose continued importance and presence exists, I would like to show, in the entire body of writing, concerns the attention devoted to *places*, to every kind of site, be it real or symbolic, public or private, whose mobile geography maps out the successive figures of a society. Social institutions and milieus, groups defined by affinity or belonging, sites of militancy or debate: they are important for Michel de Certeau because they become so many punctuations of the social body. In other words, he sees in them sites of feeling and intellect. For each there is, first of all, the need to express the identity, the particularity of the place in which it is found. It marks his thoughts on Christianity: "A place is needed if there is going to be a departure, and departure is possible only if it has a site from which it can proceed: the two elements — the *place* and the *departure* — are correlative in that a distancing allows the closure of the initial localization to be perceived, but nonetheless this closure makes possible all new investigation."[20] This clarification is no less indispensable in the act of teaching; it allows students to recognize themselves as different (and here we understand the logic of the "master who wanted no disciples"):

My position would thus preferably be one of specifying my own place (instead of camouflaging it under a discourse presumably apt to include others), and of offering the greatest number of possible effects, both theoretical and practical, in the group discussions, and, reciprocally, of reacting with the participants in an interrogative way that leads them to state their difference and to discover in the suggestions that I can make a means of formulating that difference with greater force. The proposed theoretical "models" are used to mark off *limits* (the specific nature of my questions) and to give rise to *deviations* (the expression of experiences and other questions).[21]

But reference to places also informs his historical works. Analyzing the paths taken in *The Writing of History*, he entitles the first section "Productions of Places." In this part the celebrated chapter titled "Historiographical Operation" also begins with an initial subtitle: "A Social Place."[22] In order to reach their goals, historians must clearly state where they are, without which there would be neither a code of professional ethics nor the realization of the aims of inquiry. "Connecting history to a place is the condition of possibility for any social analysis." Furthermore, "the denial of the specificity of the place being the very principle of ideology, all theory is excluded" (69). Reflection on the place, neither a second thought nor something secondary, is a cornerstone in the act of learning. To neglect it is tantamount to ruining the edification of knowledge. But it is also tantamount to arguing that the knowledge of particularity has something to do with the construction of a scientific order, that the latter does not only involve the expression of universal truth, a daring thesis that Certeau tried to develop in respect to the "arts of making and doing" in everyday life.[23]

On the plurality of places, of speech, of action, of knowledge, of labor, he proposes a dynamic cartography of the same dynamic order as his reading of "differences." He always concentrates on virtual ways of circulating, whether in social networks, in individual voyages begun on the spot, in the way that, in the strategic space of the dominant order, the ruse of the weak is insinuated by subtle and tactical means. Whence the interest in spatial practices, in the person who walks in the city,[24] but also in the way that the "possessed woman" skitters from place to place in her responses to lawyers' cross-examinations, and how she disrupts the logic of their identification of places and names;[25] or still, the astonishing study of the circulation of Surin's story of the meeting with the "young man in the wagon" that yielded from this "illiterate" a marvelous mystical illumination;[26] or finally, Labadie's desperate journey in his impossible quest for a place about the truth of God, of a land of certitude in which the church of "true faith" could be grounded.[27]

Prepared by the crisscrossing of association with a tradition, of belonging to a generation, and through a fate of circumstances affecting his personal life, provided with means of clarification that his interest in speech assured him, by means of differences and the plurality of places grasped in their particularity, in both intellectual and spiritual ways Michel de Certeau happened to be better prepared than his contemporaries to understand the stakes for society in May 1968. The articles that he wrote in May and June — tinted here and there with lyricism or romantic fancy — remain, uncannily, on the mark. He does not write a story of the events, or a discourse that would take a bird's-eye view to state what they are about. In these startling pages, Certeau sought neither to make a memorial work nor to sermonize or prophesy. He simply wanted to take part in a common labor of political clarification to which appeal was made in the new speech circulating in the streets. The hubbub in the streets corresponded to intellectual commotion: discourses of state apparatuses, of political parties and labor unions, were equally incapable of analyzing what was taking place and, furthermore, of making any sense of it.

Hence this first observation: "We have to come back to this 'thing' that happened and understand what the unpredictable taught us about ourselves, that is, what, since then, we have become" (chapter 1). In the "symbolic revolution" or "failed revolution," there occurred — massively, irresistibly, movingly, in lyrical confusion — a *taking of speech*. Everywhere it staged the act of speaking more than it articulated a statement. Hence the impossibility of identifying it with given demands, of assigning it to social places, of knowing its authors and its "leaders." It designated what was fundamentally lacking in institutions, in representations; for that reason, the revolution had no means of knowing how or what to say. Where was the dividing line drawn between the "subjugated" and their institutions, between the beliefs that were assumed about them and their real convictions? Certeau knew no more than anyone else, but among them he had the advantage of recognizing himself in a situation of nonknowledge and of seeking its clarification: "I needed to clarify it. Not in the first instance for others. Rather, because of a need for veracity" (chapter 1). He places this labor of clarification under the sign of history and recognizes in it a natural prolongation of his everyday tasks. It is not through usurpation or an imprudent mix of genres that he studies

May 1968: "The very function of history (of historiography) is probably to constitute—but with lucidity—a discourse that expresses a relation between reason and its 'other,' with events" (chapter 4).

In other words, the labor of "making history" (the celebrated title of one of his articles that subsequently became the first chapter of *The Writing of History*) deals with the present as much as with the past.[28] Because it makes events of the past intelligible in the present in terms of their conditions of possibility, this work consists in a large measure in making possible in the present the birth of the future through the transformation of the social body. In reality, then, at stake is a labor of clarification, both historical and political, that cannot be one without being the other, since it must be associated with action, expression, and understanding. As one historian familiar with Michel de Certeau, and a perspicacious reader of his work, remarked: "The project undertaken by anyone inquiring about the invention of society is above all political."[29]

The essays that follow have been arranged according to a unity of intention and method. Ordered along the chronological line of their publication, between 1968 and 1985, they trace the parabola of an evolution—or, rather, of a deepening—of analysis, but with a handsome cohesion of style in the diversity of moments and aims. What visibly changes in these two decades of ardent work is the breadth of the field of observation and of experience, with the enrichment brought by the trips to the Americas (both North and South) and the distance gained, that is, reflected, vis-à-vis the European context, as a reader will immediately observe in chapter 7 (written in 1975), or in the last part (chapters 14–17, dating from the beginning of 1985).

Chapters 1–6 are devoted to May 1968. They are drawn from the booklet *La prise de parole*, published at the end of October 1968.[30] This booklet, which was published in the autumn months, reprinted (with some modification of detail) articles published in *Études* in June and July (that is the case with chapter 2) and in October (chapter 3 and the "bibliographical appendix" that I have included here as chapter 5). Chapter 4 of the 1968 edition is not included. What was chapter 5 in the first edition is now included as chapter 4. Under the title of chapter 6 I have added an article from *Études* (May 1969) that rounds out and completes the bibliographical findings studied in chapter 5.

For this new edition I have taken the liberty of completing a few references and correcting some typographical errors. I have systematically added the Christian names of people cited in the text. Their omission was understandable when the narrative of the events was present in collective memory, but today it would be baffling to the reader. For the same reason, I have put between brackets a few dates and details. I have added a few supplementary notes indicated by the initials L. G. I have followed the same principles in establishing the text of the other chapters, all having been published separately during the author's life. Their assemblage in a single volume is my responsibility.

After the first part, devoted to May 1968, a second part (chapter 7) deals with the Americas.[31]

The third part takes up the report that we had both prepared for the French Ministry of Culture, under the title *L'Ordinaire de la communication* (Paris: Dalloz, 1983), 167 pp. The readership for whom this piece was written explains why it ends on "Propositions" and in different places adopts an injunctive tone in order to suggest that specific types of action need to be undertaken. It is worth recalling that in 1983 a future seemed possible and that many of us believed that society could be transformed. I have left this text in its original state in order to provide a testimony to the "moment" of our intellectual history and because I saw no need to deny what we believed to be our goals. I have restricted myself to reformulating the subtitles and excising the first chapter of the 1983 text, which was already used for another joint article, "La culture comme on la pratique" (*Le Français dans le monde*, no. 181 [November–December 1983]: 19–24). This article is reprinted as the conclusion to another volume by Michel de Certeau, Pierre Mayol, and myself: *L'Invention du quotidien*, vol. 2, *Habiter, cuisiner*, revised and expanded edition (Paris: Gallimard, "Folio," 1994).[32] I have also removed a part of chapter 4 (1983) that Michel de Certeau had titled "Les revenants de la ville" [The ghosts of the city], published in *Architecture intérieure/Créé*, no. 192–93 (January–March 1983): 98–101. This article is also reprinted in *L'Invention du quotidien*, vol. 2 (new edition), chapter 8. In the report of 1983, our studies were followed by a series of others that we had initiated and directed. Led by young researchers, they were devoted to childhood (Anne Baldassari), immigrants (Philippe Mustar), suburbs (Jacques Katuszewski and Ruwen Ogien), and regional cultures based on the model of Brittany (Fanch Elegoët).

Finally, the last part is based on a report that the OECD had asked Certeau to write for a symposium of experts on the theme "Educational Policies and Minority Social Groups" (January 16–18, 1985). Translated into English by the organizer and circulated in the form of a conference paper, this text was first published in part under the title "L'actif et le passif des appartenances" (*Esprit*, issue titled "Français/immigrés," June 1985, 155–71). After Michel de Certeau's death, the report was published in its entirety as "Économies ethniques," in *Annales ESC* 91 (1986): 789–815. After six years of teaching at the University of California, when he was offered a position at the Écoles des Hautes Études en Sciences Sociales (where he began work in October 1984), Michel de Certeau had asked me what questions called for an intellectual and social investment, in other words, a labor of political clarification of the kind to which this volume attests. In my response, I had indicated two, in my view, that were of primary concern: the problem of immigrants and relations with Germany. He then began to work on these two themes, attending colloquiums, gathering information, establishing various contacts. The report for the OECD was the first beam in the scaffolding on immigration. Ten years later, we lack Michel de Certeau's generous intelligence to advance in this direction. Nonetheless, we know that henceforth this problem will be one of the touchstones of traditional Europe at the dawn of the twenty-first century.

I have tried to assemble this volume of political writings not as a memorial but as a "toolbox" placed before another generation on whom devolves the responsibility of leading, yes, in its own way, the labor of political clarification. A society that would not, with new costs to each generation, take up this reflexive labor would be destined to die. This necessary rethinking is equivalent neither to the oblivion of what preceded nor to the rejection of the tools invented by earlier generations.

In these pages by Michel de Certeau, the reader will discover penetrating analyses, illuminating intuitions, ideas and concepts, new information, and new perspectives. Most valuable, because it is extremely rare, is the chance to watch the work of a powerful and generous intelligence, ready to respect the difference of others, inhabited by a secret tenderness for the anonymous crowd of living beings, never seeking to "take power," but forever to "make possible" the rise of a future liberty, the resurgent growth of an unknown future, the "invention of a society." An intelligence convinced that such was the function of the mind. I believe that this conviction is contagious.

Part I

May 1968

Chapter 1
A Symbolic Revolution

The rains of August seem to have doused the fires of May and flushed their ashes down the sewers. With Paris emptied, the streets, then the walls have been cleaned. This cleansing has also washed our brains and erased our memories. As a wave laps over a sandy beach, the great silence of midsummer has passed over the many speeches and protests of spring. Here we are, back to the "law and order" that a *Walkout of Yesterday* (the announced title of a German film) was supposed to have suppressed and that soon appeared either uniquely compromised or intolerable. The *after* recommences the *before*. Here we are back where we were.

Impossible to Forget

Even if the waste of a failed revolution is thrown into the dumpsters, it still cannot be said that the revolution has been forgotten. Something in us is caught up in it, something we cannot eliminate so easily. The event cannot be dissociated from the options to which it *gave place*; it is that space constituted by often surprising choices that have modified customary divisions, groups, parties, and communities, following an unforeseen division. A new topography has transformed (at least, let's say, a moment), as a function of this place surging up like an island, the official map of ideological, political, or religious constituencies.

Can this past, which is *our* past, also be "cleansed"? Was it merely a dream, or have we fallen back into the sleep from which we awakened last May? Where is the fiction? Where is the real? The link between the "events" and "order" engages the relation that we have with ourselves, both individually and collectively. To let go means choosing and selecting once again, but a choice made in secret. It is tantamount to pronouncing a judgment, but without a trial, cutting into our history in order to make a division between truth on one side and illusion on the other. No, in the aftermath we cannot accept the blind simplicity of a dividing line that would withdraw all meaning from one side of the country and from one side of ourselves. We have to come back to this "thing" that happened and understand what the unpredictable taught us about ourselves, that is, what, since then, we have become.

An abundant literature on the subject has responded to our need to situate ourselves in regard to the events. It attests to very divergent approaches and contrary interpretations, but in that very way it comprises a rich and incoherent dossier for a new debate about what we are and the methods we have for analyzing it. At stake are both nations and human sciences. A disquiet is resurgent everywhere, even in the most categorical affirmations, as soon as we tire of fingering a rosary of facts and documents: what, after all, do we know about a society and the mute agreements on which the contracts of language are based? What does it mean to understand that society? As the wise Épistémon puts it, "with what concepts can this revolt be thought?"[1] Something that had been tacit began to stir, something that invalidates the mental hardware built for stability. Its instruments were also part of what shifted, went awry. They referred to something *unthinkable*, which, last May, was unveiled while being contested: values taken to be self-evident; social exchanges, the progress of which was enough to define their success; commodities, the possession of which represented happiness.

An idea of man inhabited the immense organizational apparatus of society at large. Implicitly recognized or accepted, this secret rule was pulled out of the shadows in which it was keeping an order. From André Glucksmann to Raymond Aron, from Claude Lefort to Épistémon, every one of the authors who reflected on the events has taken up, in his or her own way, what Lenin formerly stated: "What is important in these crises is that they make manifest what had until then remained latent."[2] But, today, what had been made manifest as latent is not a *force* more powerful than the ideological or political powers (from the Marxist perspective, it would be the proletariat), but a sum of principles, essential to the established order, that have *become* an issue. Where, in order to restore this order, can reasons be found that justify what its reason was? Conversely, what references can be substituted that are fundamental for another order? *"In the name of what?"* Pierre Emmanuel had asked long ago. The irruption of the unthinkable is as dangerous for any "specialist" as it is for the entire nation. The survival of the tree is at risk when its roots become exposed.

It therefore no longer suffices to *say* that the "evident truths" of earlier times must become evident once again or that social life becomes impossible from the moment when its roots are exposed to critical view. It does not suffice to live *as if* nothing had happened, as if one had not *viewed,* beneath the assurance of the country, a system of conventions that had become fragile (because they were becoming subject to debate) and the lack of other recourses (capable of upholding or replacing the shaken order). This hole, opened by a society that calls itself into question, cannot be covered over with the massive and normal reaction that has merely refused the void, cast aside a question that was still without an answer, and hastily replaced the need for a better division of goods on the demand, indicated by the crisis, for a restoration or for a veracity in social relations.

It was a question of redefining a social *code,* at the end of a period that had slowly brought about a distortion between a rationalization of society and the system of values that had animated this labor in the nineteenth century, but that is now imposed upon it. Beyond an always unforeseen threshold (because it is always linked to accidents), such a distortion is no longer tolerable. It does not mean that this system can be replaced, much less that it *is* replaced. This system is perhaps so intimately linked to a civilization that it will not survive being scrutinized. Perhaps too, the country, being forced into redefining itself while existing as it is, will no longer have the strength to do so. No matter what happens, if we face these recent "events" that oblige us to interrogate ourselves and that open up an uncertain future, I do not believe (and who indeed could believe?) that it is possible to speak of a revolution said and done. But it is the symptom of a global problem, one that quite possibly characterizes a society on the road to technical rationalization and in which the tensions are all the more searing in that it bears an older tradition and its relation to its past is less frankly elucidated.

A *symbolic* revolution, therefore, either because it *signifies* more than it effectuates, or because of the fact that it contests given social and historical *relations* in order to create authentic ones. After all, the "symbol" is the indication that affects the entire movement, in practice as well as in theory. From the beginning to the end, speech is what has played the decisive role, from that of Daniel Cohn-Bendit to that of Charles de Gaulle. I have lingered on this strange fact (it is a way of approaching it) by believing that it was fundamental and that it engaged the entire structuring of our culture (it is an option).

Symbolic Action

The revolution of May was not explained by any hostility to odious characters or by the destruction of instruments and products of labor. Neither professors nor bosses were directly threatened, and a sort of respect protected machinery and laboratories (in truth, more in the factories than in the universities): workers spent entire nights in keeping their material functioning during the strike; students maintained a defense guard.

The damages—beyond those that inevitably came with the disorder—seemed to have the allure of sacrifices necessary for the *expression* of a demand. Thus, the history of May-June was written in terms of cars, of overturning or maintaining the autonomous machine, at once possessed and possessive, a symbolic vocabulary of a human conduct.

People were killed, but only in spite of extraordinary precautions taken to avoid a loss of life.[3] A return to order was necessary and essential for, suddenly, at the beginning of June, the number of dead victims (who were then considered "normal") to be known and for a newspaper to publish, at the end of the summer holidays, this hallucinating headline: "10,000 deaths predicted..." The May protesters were struggling against helmetted black Martians, an irruption and a sign of power in the streets, whereas, in contrast, the police violence was provoked less by the students—even the "insurgents"—than by their color and, especially, by the red flag (to the point where this reaction extended to everything red!) or by black banners, ultimately visible signs of a threat whose horrific image had been carefully cultivated by the anticommunist training given to armed troops. Were these struggles shadowboxing in which all the players were clashing with their phantoms? Not at all, but they were struggles that were not taken literally. It was a spiritual war or, if one prefers, a *ritual* struggle (not that it was any less real), before being harnessed for political, social, or simply individual ends. The revolt was opposed to a system; it "demonstrated" signs contrary to other signs. It ultimately attacked the *credibility* of a social language. In that way it was already a symbolic action.

It was no less so in its topography, which renewed the classical geography of strikes and riots. First the Sorbonne and, turned toward the Left Bank, the parade toward Denfert-Rochereau, the Arc de Triomphe, the Odéon, the Stock Exchange ("the temple of profit," as one poster proclaimed), the pilgrimage led to Billancourt, and so on (not to mention those that failed to take place, such as the plan to go to the ORTF [French Radio and Television Service], which Alain Geismar called "one of the symbolic places of power") — all these gestures aimed at an effect of language. They were subversive because they were chosen or, in the national idiom, because they took the signs of its articulation *against the grain*. The site of knowledge passed into the hands of its "objects"; a sacred linkage overcame the partition between university students and workers; "blasphemy" desacralized a patriotism; a theater (all of society is one) changed spectators into actors, and the spectacle into a collective creation; the fireworks (always associated with spending beyond calculation) were celebrated right where accounts had measured exchanges according to their monetary worth, and so on. The protests created a network of symbols by taking the signs of a society in order to invert their meaning. This scheme of a vocabulary did not convey, but rather *represented*, a "qualitative" change.

As one sign among many, the barricades also had little meaning in terms of their logistic value. They clearly played a political role in that they drove the enormous governmental machine into taking the dangerous alternative of capitulating in front of these curtains of pebbles, or turning the "insurgents" into innocent martyrs — two ways of losing face. But, on a deeper level, they transformed the fear of the cop into a collective action; they broke the spell of an authority; from a paralyzing atomization they produced the joyous experience of a creatively communal transgression; they disenchanted a social organization by revealing a fragility in the space where force was supposed to reign, and by making possible a power at the very site where the feeling of powerlessness held sway.

No doubt this symbolic weapon is the converse of a strongly anchored ideological power; it threatens by demystifying the "aura" with which that power is credited. It would function less well in a more pragmatic organization, of an American type, for example. If realism is no less in Paris or in Moscow than in New York, it is nonetheless necessary to refer the successive — indeed, contradictory — choices to monolithic doctrinal positions imposed by politics. Hence the impact of gestures that affect the system in the cloudy heavens from which it claims to receive a sense of history. At the outer limit, it was a revolution of humor. Laughter can kill power that plays the role of Jupiter and that thus cannot tolerate it. The Czechs used this weapon masterfully: the heaviest tanks in all of Europe rumbled down the streets of Prague, but the banners inserted in the muzzles of their cannon barrels made a mockery of them.[4] In France, the same humor did not prevail, for there was neither the same assurance nor the same unanimity. Instead of expressing what an entire nation surely knew, the symbolic action was aimed at opening perspectives that, until then, had been forbidden. It was a way out of a heretofore ineffable malaise and of a "repressed voice."

The central place of the symbol in the events has resulted not merely from an analysis of what happened. It has been the object of a reflection that is perhaps, in the style of a tactic, the most original theoretical contribution of this period. In fact, this tactic is defined as a function of what a society *does not state* and of what it tacitly admits to be *impossible*. It therefore has the effect of a dissuasion in respect to an organization of possibilities: the creation of a "symbolic site" is also an action. That students *can* sit in professors' chairs, that a common language *can* assail the division between intellectuals and manual laborers, or that a collective initiative *can* respond to the representatives of an omnipotent system — thus is modified the tacitly "received" code that separates the possible from the impossible, the licit from the illicit. The *exemplary action* "opens a breach," not because of its own efficacity, but because it displaces a law that was all the more powerful in that it had not been brought to mind; it unveils what was latent and makes it contestable. It is decisive, contagious, and dangerous because it touches this obscure zone that every system takes for granted and that it cannot justify. It remains no less "a symbolic place," as the March 22d Movement put it.[5] The exemplary action changes nothing; it creates *possibilities* relative to *impossibilities* that had until then been admitted but not clarified. I see a new and important sociocultural phenomenon in the impact of the expression that demonstrates a disarticulation between what is *said* and what is *unsaid*, that deprives a social practice of its tacit foundations, that ultimately refers, I believe, to a displacement of "values" on which an architecture of powers and exchanges had been constructed and that was still assumed to be a solid base. From this point of view, symbolic action also opens a breach in our conception of society.

It leads us to what might be the essential and most enigmatic quality of a "revolution" characterized by a desire, articulated in terms of "places of speech" that contest silent acceptances. Speech and action become identical in the repetition of the same type of gesture: "Contestation-revolution," declared the March 22d Movement, "the unmasking of something untenable, light shed on the mechanism responsible for this untenable condition, the creation of a place where a mode of speech that rejects and refuses is made possible."

A Revolution of Words

Two quotations among thousands can state precisely the nature of this strange "revolution." Both are taken from the important dossier that Philippe Labro assembled.[6] A young elevator operator from the Samaritaine department store who was being interviewed by a journalist stated: "I really don't know what to say, I don't have any education." A friend who was on strike interrupted him: "Don't say that! Knowledge is finished. *Today, education, well, it's all in what we say!*" For his part, Jacques Sauvageot declared, "Everybody wanted to express themselves, to take matters into their own hands. That's what socialism is all about."

Did speech really redefine education and culture? Is there an equivalence between "taking speech" and "taking matters into one's own hands"? By June 1968 the facts proved the contrary. But the problem became even more serious. Speech that appeals to a change of culture or for socialism surges forth from the untrained world or from those who had been assumed to be irresponsible. What was no longer being stated in the text became a margin. The nonparticipation in the social mechanisms that ought to have assured communication took the form of an exteriority. A contestatory interrogation, aiming at this public institution that is language and that unveils the fragility of its foundations, had as a safety valve nothing more than an *aside* of language.

Speech that had become a "symbolic place" designates the space created through the distance that separates the represented from their representations, the members of a society and the modalities of their association. It is at once everything and nothing because it announces an unpacking in the density of exchange and a void, a disagreement, exactly where the mechanisms ought to be built upon what they claim to express. It escapes outside of structures, but in order to indicate what is *lacking* in them, namely, solidarity and the participation of those who are subjected to them.

No more than becoming conscious, taking speech is neither an effective occupation nor the seizure of a power. By denouncing a lack, speech refers to a labor. It is a symbolic action par excellence that reveals a task that today concerns the totality of our system. To believe it effective on its own would be to take it for granted and, as if by magic, to claim to control forces with words, to substitute words for work. But then to conclude that it is meaningless would be to lose meaning, to put a mechanism in the place of a system of relations, and to suppose, ultimately, that a society can function without human beings.

The reflections that follow are born of the conviction that the "revolutionary" speech of May 1968, a symbolic action, puts language on trial and calls for a global revision of our cultural system. The question posed by my experience as a historian, a traveler, and a Christian, I recognize, and I also discover, in the movement that stirred the inner workings of the country. I needed to clarify it. Not in the first instance for others. Rather, because of a need for veracity. A partisan of what such a fundamental "speech" meant and what it was teaching me, I could neither think nor believe that it could have been exiled to the borders of the country, a prisoner of itself at the same time as it was imprisoned; its absence promised also the death of the society that sought to expel it. A schism between the irreducibility of consciousness and the objectivity of social institutions appeared to me at once as the denounced and unacceptable fact, that is, as the current problem of thought and action. To the challenge that, in May 1968, made clear the givens of an *illegitimate* situation, a wager to be won responds today.

Chapter 2
Capturing Speech

An Event: The Capture of Speech

Last May speech was taken the way, in 1789, the Bastille was taken. The stronghold that was assailed is a knowledge held by the dispensers of culture, a knowledge meant to integrate or enclose student workers and wage earners in a system of assigned duties. From the taking of the Bastille to the taking of the Sorbonne, between these two symbols, an essential difference characterizes the event of May 13, 1968: today, it is imprisoned speech that was freed.

Thus is affirmed a wild, irrepressible, new right, a right that has become identical with the right of being a human, and no longer a client destined for consumer culture or instruments useful for the anonymous organization of a society. This right commanded, for example, the reactions of assemblies that were always prepared to defend it whenever it appeared to be threatened in the heat of debate: "Everybody here has the right to speak." But this right was only given to those who spoke in their own name. The assembly refused to hear whoever was identified with a function or intervened in the name of a group hidden behind the statements of one of its members: to speak is not to be the "speaker" in the name of a lobby, of a "neutral" and objective truth, or for convictions held elsewhere.

A kind of festival (what liberation is not a festival?) transformed the inner workings of these days of crisis and violence—a festival tied to, but not identified with, the dangerous stakes of the barricades or the psychodrama of a collective catharsis. Something happened to us. Something began to stir in us. Emerging from who knows where, suddenly filling the streets and the factories, circulating among us, becoming ours but no longer being the muffled noise of our solitude, voices that had never been heard began to change us. At least that was what we felt. From this something unheard of was produced: we began to speak. It seemed as if it were for the first time. From everywhere emerged the treasures, either aslumber or tacit, of forever unspoken experiences. At the same time that self-assured discourses were muffled, and as soon as "authorities" were reduced to silence, frozen existences melted and suddenly awoke into a prolific morning. Once the metallic carapace of the car was abandoned, and the solitary charm of the living-room television set broken, with traffic snarled, the mass media cut off, consumerism threatened, in a Paris undone and assembled in its streets, wild and stupefied at discovering its face washed clean of its cosmetics, an unknown life surged forth.

The capture of speech clearly has the form of a refusal. It is a protestation. We shall see that its fragility is due to its expression as contestation, to its testimony as negation. Therein, perhaps, lies its greatness. But in reality, it consists in stating, "I am not a thing." Violence is the gesture that rejects all identification: "I exist." Thus, if those who begin to speak deny the norm in the name of which they were declared to be censured, or the institutions that wanted to use a force apparently freed of all ties, then these persons clearly want to declare an affirmation. An autonomous act precedes by far the inscription of autonomy in the program of an academic or trade-union demand. Hence the scandal of seeing this demand replaced by reformist measures of another order. Hence too the scorn for those who do not "speak," but who only express their fear (in the pathos of acquiescence or of overstatement), their political aims (in the rhetoric of "service" or "realism"), or their power (which patiently awaits its time).

This new right is not added to a list that is already long. It is a choice that founds and anticipates other choices, such as a secret reason that would turn reasons around, or else direct every reason any way it wishes. The same goes for what remains. It decides about what remains. And now the first implications of this initial invention are already put into action: the direct experience of democracy, the permanence of contestation, the need for critical thought, the legitimacy of a creative and responsible participation for everyone, the demand for autonomy and collective management, and also the celebration of freedom — the power of the imagination and poetic festivity... We can also sketch out this new region through what it rejects: a "detained" knowledge whose apprenticeship would turn those acquiring it into the instruments of a system; institutions enrolling each of its "employees" in causes that are not its own; an authority devoted to imposing its language and in censuring nonconformity, and so on.

But, first of all, we need not refer to these generalities (indications of problems that are henceforth open) or to the idea of a cultural revolution (which is quite problematic), but to something more simple and even more radical. Although it has been overly localized—and often ill perceived outside of the places in which it was produced— one *fact* is more important than the claims or even the contestation that expressed it in terms prior to the event: a *positive* fact, a *style* of experience. A creative—that is, poetic—experience. "The poet has lit the fuse of speech," stated a flyer at the Sorbonne. It is a fact that we can attest to for having seen and been participants: a throng became poetic. Hidden, perhaps, until then (but that means that it was not alive), speech exploded in the relations that fostered it or that it appropriated, with the joy (or the seriousness?) of shattered categories and unforeseen bonds of solidarity. Everyone finally began to talk: about essential things, about society, about happiness, about knowledge, about art, about politics. A permanent drone of speech spread like fire, an immense therapeutic nourished on what it delivered, contagious with every prescription and every diagnosis. It gave everyone access to every one of these debates that assailed both professional barriers and those of social milieus. It changed spectators into actors, confrontation into dialogue, information or apprenticeship in "knowledge" into impassioned discussions about options involving life itself. This experience happened. It is impregnable; it *cannot be taken away*.

But what does it mean for us?

A Choice

A displacement thus took place, I would not say in our conception of culture, but in the experience that we have of it. This fact interrogates us. Can it be *forgotten*? And if not, with what revisions and what reversals are we engaged? In any event, it is provocative and revealing. It involves and it requires a choice.

Even if this moment has not been a moment of truth, even if it lifts the lid of repression and is the explosion of a long frustration, even if it is a time of madness (madness sometimes heralds the coming of new forms of reason), even if a hangover came on the heels of the drunken frenzy of speech and the disenchantments of the aftermath that returned to the days before (everything, fortunately, remaining subject to discussion), a question has been put to us. *It must not be lost.* But now it risks being lost, either by being smothered after too much excess or too much fear, in the play of forces that mobilized and propelled its irruption, or by being forgotten in the reforms it inspired, or by being drowned in the more "serious" objectives of unionized, academic, or political readjustments.

The establishment and analysis of these reforms, the history of movements that have allowed or organized them, will be taken up elsewhere. They are necessary. But, however satisfied we are with the benefit that society will have reaped from the events, we cannot bracket away the provocative question that summons society itself. We cannot admit that only a few improvements need to be made in the structures of teaching or in the salaries of workers (very appreciable results), while being immersed again in a more fundamental experience would erase the memory of an immense disillusionment. No, we cannot allow ourselves to be distracted in this way from what is essential. For us, the task entails recognizing the true implication, explaining its meaning, and uncovering its practical and theoretical consequences.

This task is all the more imperative in that it is inscribed in the fact itself, insofar as an incapacity to proportion a coherent action with respect to the lived experience is revealed. At least that is my interpretation. What was *positively* experienced could only be expressed *negatively*. The experience was the capture of speech. What was stated was a contestation that, by calling the whole system into question, could only be betrayed by every existing organization, by every political procedure, or by every renewed institution. A massive movement from below escaped from preexisting structures and frameworks; but, by that very fact, every requisite program and idiom were lacking. In this society that it denounced, the movement could only be expressed marginally, whereas, nonetheless, it already constituted an experience for society. Its own "refusal" thus also betrayed reality since it merely marked off a barrier without stating what the inner landscape was—that is, the experience itself. For tactical reasons, the contestation also camouflaged the disparity of experiences in order to have them assembled under the flag of an identical counteroffensive. In fact, the capture of speech, a collective invention, could only create differences. The latter needed to be recognized if the former was to be analyzed.

Moreover, every negation is content with inverting the terms of the affirmation that it contradicts. It is its victim, at the very moment when it denounces it as authoritarian. Among many others, this sign still acknowledges a pedagogy or institutions that are incapable of furnishing other generations with the instruction that would allow them to recognize an experience other than that of their "cadres" or of their teachers. Clearly, then, violent encounters with power have outlandishly distorted this reciprocal incapacity; and since then, collaborations between students and teachers or between workers and "directors" have tended to overcome this alternative between contestation or the defense of the *same* terms. But the main problem today is posed by the disparity between a fundamental experience and the deficit of its language, between the "positivity" of something lived and the "negativity" of an expression that, in the form of a refusal, resembles more the symptom than the elaboration of the reality being designated.

This problem immediately has a political bearing. A refusal of "consumer society" calls into question the political regime by which it is supported or whatever might change the axioms on which it is grounded. From the very beginning, students saw this and said so. But they learned that this theoretical lucidity left entirely open the question of a mode of action, and that it was not directed at the forces at play and their availability for a modification of structures, that "student power" (an afterthought, moreover, that appeared once workers' power had been made manifest) drew its efficacity from a latent opposition to power, but would not succeed in constructing another. Challenging the organs of the country's real powers, the "movement" could only be used and "co-opted" by any one of them. Failure was inscribed in advance in the global and permanent contestation. The students did not have the right to consent to this failure, politically speaking, even if it were in the name of new relations to be established between laborers and university workers, or between society and the teaching corps. Lacking this, one would have to opt for an evanescent utopia or a conservative "realism"; the movement would be shattered into a thousand pieces in order to become the occasion for a few reforms, the theme of a literature, the source of a cynicism, and, at the borders of the nation, this anarchism of desperadoes whose process of disintegration Victor Serge not long ago described so lucidly.[1] These consecutive evasions from the inability to give practical and theoretical force to a profound experience would lead us to believe that the initial protestation had already been an alibi.

This political turf is not mine on which to play (except as a citizen). I merely want to underscore the gravity of the question and its urgency. It is not enough to assume a stance of retreat that, in the form of a mental resistance, would still amount to a denial. Without risking the ruin of that which we seek to defend, we cannot abide by this inner assurance that inspires, in the name of an experience that cannot be co-opted: "No longer will we be swayed by power. We no longer have respect. No longer are we bending to the authorities." If it is not organized, if it is not inscribed, even as a strategy, *within* the network of national forces in order to *effectively* change a system, this demand of conscience will be neither reformist nor revolutionary, but it will be extinguished in departures for other nations or in inner exiles, negating its request for participation in order to take refuge in a vagabond emigration or in an ideological and sterile resistance.

The same question reappears on the turf that the movement directly sought when it made its case for a cultural revolution. The taking of speech, first of all, left its impact in matters of culture. It also needs to be analyzed in these terms, for it questions the possibility and the conditions of a renewal, as well as the relation between a decisive experience and our conceptions of culture.

Theory and Innovation

Contestation bumps directly into an organization of culture. But will the theories that preceded the events find some way of curbing their meaning by "explaining" them? In areas where the consciousness that a society formulates for itself, will the experience of the past ever have a sequel? Will it bear an influence? Will it displace our common language? Or else, will it be reduced by the preceding ideas or co-opted by a past already thought, such as a hole in a system capable of immediately obliterating it and covering it with prefabricated slogans? Will it be "alienated" by "human sciences" that are developed enough to integrate nonconformism into conformity and strong enough to impose on the "discontents" of civilization the interpretation that this very civilization has precipitated?

At this level, which concerns the relation between culture and a new form of experience, there also exists a relationship of forces. Generally speaking, we can already observe the fact every time that an innovation seeks to be born within an established system. Current events, but also history, describe to us the detours by which a displacement or unforeseen resistance is shown and is concealed in common, cultural, and scientific language. Novelty remains opaque; it "cannot be taken" in the name of what it consciously represents; it too is "unsayable" (if a term can be borrowed from one used in the past with respect to an analogous crisis),[2] for it takes the shape of a subterranean slippage or an unexpected emergence. For want of being able to determine a new mentality, in order to express itself it can only *regress* to an older situation that defends it from the established order, or *be marginalized* in pushing contestation to the borders of society, in the form of a space of its own (the "essential" of experience becoming the outer surface of a culture) and under the disguise of ideas or of notions still being extracted from the contested system.

To innovate is, first of all, to betray oneself. We have seen it happen in this month of May — first, in the pre- or antitechnocratic references that the protests assigned to themselves by *returning* to a Trotskyist, Fourierist, existentialist, or "primitive" past (the latter thus appearing "retrograde" in respect to "progress"), and second, in the retreat that, in spite of itself, progressively led back to a fundamental experience in a ghetto (the Sorbonne, for example) in which it became enclosed and where it had at its disposal only, so to speak, notions torn from the culture or the sciences being rejected (in this regard, it appeared "marginal" in relation to public opinion).

The easiest thing that a sociologist or a psychologist can do today is to employ the well-known expression "I told you so," to recuperate the "heresies" in the apparatus of its technique, and to explain with all of the specialist's knowledge what, for a moment, eluded their grasp. We are in fact witnessing a vast operation that seeks to reintegrate the "aberration" (the event itself) into systems that are already in place. The operation benefits from the handicap from which "contestations" that are still lacking an intellectual mechanism of their own are suffering. The psychologist or the sociologist can thus easily "understand" what took place and interpret the events in their language since the experts specifically find in their opponents either the concepts that they themselves put into circulation or the positions that they feel they have superseded. What remains are only the many interested parties who do not see themselves fitting into these schemes; they refuse to explain themselves the way they are being explained.

From a cultural or scientific standpoint, this "recuperative" interpretation represents a reaction analogous to the recuperations enacted by the labor unions or the political parties. How could things happen otherwise? But, in terms more familiar to us, the same issue is posed time and again: *how to make manifest and recognize the newness* of an experience that is both the occasion and, perhaps, the predictive sign—but not yet the reality—of a cultural revolution? It is likely that today we are better armed, intellectually (and socially), to ponder systems in the rationality that belongs to our own type of civilization than to analyze the process of mutations (I mean: those not inscribed in a homogeneous "development"). It is a symptom—an alarming symptom—that calls for a diagnosis. But if we take current events seriously, we will be obliged to correct this penchant for tautology and a logic based on the tacit refusal of what is not the Same.

To the very extent that it happened upon us the way it did, the event has to teach us how to cast doubt on mental habits or social reflexes that would lead us to call it meaningless or to forget its significance. From an epistemological point of view, the event puts on the agenda of every discipline a new task, a task that cannot be dissociated from a pedagogical relation, that is, a relation with the other. The reintroduction of this *relation* into science is the same problem as that of the *event* in a reflection that is too imprisoned by the development of a system.

As far as this either too rigid or too vague thing we call "culture" is concerned, the task can be envisaged on the basis of two immediate data: on the one hand, the character of the *"demonstrations"* that were already produced; on the other, the *conceptual instruments* furnished by recent works. This double reference can allow us to launch an analysis that would be the exercise—or, if one prefers, the experimentation—of the very problem that will be taken up: our procedure will be proportioned if it permits us, simultaneously, to make interpretations as a function of the event and to inscribe the event into the register of our theoretical apparatus. Without this confrontation, the process of thinking, both scientific and practical, would never be deployed except according to its assumptions or its "evidence," taken up in justifying and in multiplying its own conditioning, and in eliminating all contestation by its own process of integration. Conversely, the originality would be diverted toward aberration in order to be reduced to nothing more than a cry, a peep, a resistance lacking a vocabulary, an irreducible silence. Once again, we cannot consent to it without some mental cowardice, but also, I believe, without renouncing what is most fundamental to faith, its most essential challenge that opts for a personal truth unveiled in communication and that builds its most absolute experience on the language of a society.

"Accident" or Principle?

We cannot be satisfied with this initial form that contestation takes when, first of all, it talks about itself. Like the event, it begins by being a narrative, and often an autobiographical, eyewitness account. But such an entry into language remains surreptitious. It is placed under the rubric of the *also*: whoever takes speech is *also* accepted, no doubt, because of the person's modesty, and because for that reason he or she can easily be tolerated by a society strong enough to swallow a foreign element and make use of it. Wealth always goes to the rich: a well-structured society takes advantage of a protest by the minority.

But the situation changes when, going beyond the fact that some people capture speech in a structure inoculated against this kind of poison, one begins to wonder if the act of taking speech is not or must not become the *constitutive principle* of a society: in short, when the exception assumes the weight of a rule; when the "accident" assumes universal proportions. At that point it becomes a subversive matter. The whole system is called into question. From the standpoint of a scientific theory of culture, it is thus crucial to know if the contested fact can either be "explained" or is revolutionary, if it requires a development in theory or if it turns it topsy-turvy.

To be sure, the alternative in both economics and politics never appears in such simple terms; but for all that it is no less real or pressing. In the face of this option, conformist thinking has the knee-jerk reflex of the first hypothesis, and it hopes — with the blindness of its duplicity or its naïveté — that the problem will be decided in a *quantitative* fashion, in order, then, to pass, if need be, to another conformism, of a new majority. This privilege granted to quantity consists in adhering to "opinion." As far as I know, the latter has never been married to a requirement of truth! Rather, an endless divorce separates them (even if we are all led to believe that we are thinking well when we think in conformity with others).

Another concern can collectively tie us to the event in that it requires a meaning *of its own*, in that it begins something and that an action, by being deployed, implies and appeals to a theoretical revolution. Those who inquire of it have to discern and elaborate this implication through a labor that aims less at "making" the revolution than in exhuming it right where *it is inaugurated*, but without yet being quantitatively imposed and thus without being anything other than a new *possibility*. This is where there operates, in a field of reflection, a labor necessarily coordinated with (and relative to) the action that questions political apparatuses or economic systems. Already the law of its thinking no longer has the function of protecting the laws of a society.

But the problem entails knowing *if* such an event is endowed with the value of a "principle"; in other words, analysis must show how a qualitative change is already made manifest, that is, revolutionary, although it still affects only a minority.

"Symbolic" Demonstrations

In this respect the only ultimate criterion is experience when it becomes both the irreducible element of existence and its wager. An event is not what can be seen or known about its happening, but what it becomes (and, above all, for us). This option is grasped only in risk, and not by observation. It is therefore clear that what happened last May has become for many an inaugural or revealing event. But this affirmation is not telling enough when it remains at the level of biography. "I was there, that's what it meant for me." An irrefutable, but personal, fact. Thus we have learned something more and different, which directly concerns theory. In a social system, a relationship of forces can *already* plot the course of its mutation. Paradoxically, this lesson was written into the most suspect aspect (and also the easiest to "explain") of current events: their symbolic character, that is, what prompts us to speak now, and unmistakably, of a failed revolution. A symbolic revolution, rather, as is proved by the nature of the gestures through which, first of all, it was expressed. But in order to understand this symbolism, we must, I believe, get beyond a description of the place in which it was anchored, beyond "exemplary actions."[3]

Movements can only make use of terms belonging to an established order, and yet already evince its overthrow. A displacement is effected, but it is illegible as such in its expression since it uses the vocabulary and even the syntax of a known idiom; but it "transposes" the idiom the way the organist changes the score by giving it a *different* tonality. Nothing betrays the organist's game, which remains faithful to the written notes, except for the register the organist has taken, the single visible indication of the transposition being made. The comparison is not entirely adequate, but at least it signals a phenomenon of an entirely different amplitude: a culture can be lived *in other ways* after a slippage whose sum of words and gestures is not yet the sign, but whose recognition is the coefficient affecting everyone. This coefficient unhinges all gestures from their normal use, conferring on each and every one a new status that is symbolic of an experience other than the one they organized. Today, this coefficient is the capture of speech.

Such a transposition is formidable because it is deceptive. It attracts and it offers what is needed to justify reductive interpretations. Innovation is folded into an old language that allows it to go unnoticed. It is deceptive because it makes blindness possible. It is presented as a known commodity. Thus the explanations are not erroneous in noting that the crisis has a "repetitive" or "staged" aspect; but, in my opinion, the symbolism would be badly situated if it were defined as a reedition, an imaginary opiate for action.

Quite possibly the historian will unearth in all of this a Petrograd, soviets, a commune of 1848, the workerist ideology, Fourierist utopia, or a Trotskyism of yesteryear; recognize how much the new fact mimes former events and tends to be reproduced (thus, drawn from revolutions that have since become legendary, the barricades reiterated a gesture that can no longer be spontaneous, and that will be repeated over and over again, since a university will fall into dishonor if it does not have its own barricades). The historian can rightly discern in what is taking place what already took place. That is true enough. But it is not true that the innovation can be explained through elements that have already been recognized but recombined in different ways ("Professors, you're giving us grey hair!" one poster proclaimed). This position would, moreover, be strange for sociological historians: in harboring the illusion of bringing the present to the new staging of older episodes, a double contradiction would result. On the one hand, these sociological historians would avow that contrary to what they claimed to be teaching, nothing ever happened since, in principle, all of history could be explained in the same way as current events: their understanding of the present would judge that of the past. On the other hand, by identifying the historical fragments with which they would like to piece together the puzzle of the present, they would not grasp the fact that the "staging" is the event itself, and that the new status accorded to older "figures" makes language accede to what did not conform to these figures, in short, to what they were unable to express.

Psychologists would also miss the mark of the events if they were only to see in them (which is, moreover, obvious) the theater of a frustration, a "Rogerian palaver,"[4] a collective psychoanalysis, ultimately, the broadly based "application" of phenomena that have been analyzed for years, given to therapeutic and scientific exploitation, and entirely familiar to students — in short, the monumental example of the "doctrine studied above." A theory that takes as its theme (and often for a taboo) "what is happening" would be precisely the means of eliminating what is happening here and now. It would be discreetly but surely and, once more, with all the trappings of a justification since the heterogeneous element has been a priori eliminated.

We thus are choosing a type of culture, of truth, and, quite simply, of profession; we are making a global choice that reveals our personal options as soon as we are led by the event, under more or less subtle and hidden forms, to abide by this proposition that in my opinion is contradictory: "We know what is happening." This knowledge denies in advance the possibility of the object that it claims to know, assuming that nothing can happen other than what we already think is happening.

So, here, then, is the event that turns what we know into something symbolic. It affects our conceptions of society in every one of its forms. Fundamentally, it concerns the pedagogical relation in that it touches on academic, but also familial, institutions and, in a broader sense, the relation between cadres and their adherents, executive officers and those administered, governing people and people governed, in other words, every situation in which the relation with *others* (students, children, etc.) is effected in the field of a *common* language, but inflected with a *particular* meaning by the participants who occupy a position of force. We must not only observe but also admit that our gestures and our history are likely to *return* to us with a meaning that takes us by surprise; that our own words can express an experience that is not contrary to (for that would be a form of the Same) but different from our own; that they become the instrument of a protestation, the vocabulary of others.

At the very least, it is *possible* that students, by mimicking the Commune or group dynamics, or that workers, by repeating 1936 as their union context and by demanding a raise in salary, are in reality *taking* this language in ways other than those for which it had been used until now, and already investing a new requirement in these actions or these traditional demands. I believe that this is what is at stake right now. It is only a personal interpretation, and who among us would not hesitate before the complexity of the facts? But there would be blindness in not inquiring into this *possibility* and in eliminating the hypothesis that it may have taken place.

The more a society coheres, the less it is susceptible to change. Formerly, modifications produced splintered movements that in a loose social webbing were expressed by new checks and balances. It cannot work the same way in the immense system of today, a system whose syntaxes, laws, and combinations have been analyzed by so many structuralisms, economic theories, and political analyses. Yet for all that, change has not been eliminated. Long delayed by censure and more powerful integrations, the entire framework is out of joint. By growing larger and larger, the system can only allow global contestations because it is repressing partial changes. The mode of totalitarian social systems is that of revolutions.

This first becomes perceptible in the slippage of the entire system, and the gap is expressed in the new coefficient that affects its totality. A social language thus becomes "symbolic" wherever it acquires a new status. It signifies a qualitative change that is not yet a quantitative change. Here the symbol does not refer to what we already know or what we have already defined, but by way of what we know, to that of which we are unaware: an advent that affects the whole. It means that our own knowledge has become the language of others and of another experience. That is exactly what happened in the "human sciences," the originary site of the crisis: a knowledge that organized relations according to the model and in the service of a consumer society found itself "taken" in a different way, "occupied" by those who today declare that they want to speak out on their own account, less "broken" than "liberated" by them, for their usage, of the meaning that we were ascribing to it. The system itself has become symbolic. It states in known terms an innovation that had remained unknown.

This revolution steals our knowledge from behind. It has what it needs to beguile us. Because it subsists, transposed, a scientific, historical, or cultural language offers us in advance all the means for a recuperation that will be a lure.

But, and this is more serious, this language also risks betraying those who speak it differently. What indication and, if I may say so, what proof do they have of being *different* (since, ultimately, their language is the same, and any professor or union leader can demonstrate it to them)? Only the fundamental experience that for some remains irreducible, and for many others confused, which is translated as the capture of speech. Will workers be led to believe that basically they want only a raise in wages, and students some pedagogical reforms? Will they be taken by ready-made words put before them, and thus be "trapped" by the logic of the system they are using to contest the general state of things? They risk being the pawns of the speech they thought they had liberated. In order to defend what they are, they have only the *new* use they make of these words they have *received* from others. This new, fragile truth that makes up their experience can be taken away by the constraint of a language of which they are not the authors. The expressions they have taken from the system they are contesting can be turned against them. They have no other guarantees that might assure them of not being lured into claiming an experience of their own. Their demonstration is symbolic. It is still not *their* language.

A task corresponds to this ambiguity. No response exists other than the risk taken in the name of a certainty. But in the midst of this risk, something irreducible has already jostled language, an affirmation whose insufficiency states—or claims to state—the necessary fact: life in the future can be lived only by alienating one's speech, just as existence will end when we begin to renounce the temptation to create.

Chapter 3
The Power of Speech

In Charlie Chaplin's *The Gold Rush* (1925), the swirling winds of a blizzard push the cabin in which the tramp is spending the night to the edge of a cliff. After waking up, he walks across the room to go out the door. With his footsteps, the cabin starts dangerously to lean, with the doorway opening onto thin air. If he opens the door, he will fall to an instant death. When he backs up, he brings the cabin back to rest, but he is enclosed in a desperate state of affairs. Now and again his feet go forward, then retreat, gingerly touching the floor that pivots on its invisible axis . . . The image of a space in which it is equally impossible to live and to leave is comparable to the situation that was endured last May. For the inhabitants of an entire society, is there nothing more than a doorway opening onto chaos and a security anchored in conformism? Many signs indicate that a change has taken place. Drawn by unexpected choices, a line hereafter demarcates, between order and speech, our cultural "floor." Although still intact, it has vacillated from the one to the other.

Two opposite movements, in May and June, show how the ground has been shifting. The events have shown that they originate from neither the left nor the right because their stakes conform to the same laws. Their two reactions recall, rather, the movement that led the tramp to the back of the cabin or that brought him toward the empty space outside. But today there are many more people who obey the law of a reaction that seeks equilibrium. Their number provisionally ensures the stability of the cabin, and they even have the power to throw out the door, as "adventurists," people who never wanted to be evicted. Others prefer exile, whether mental or physical, from this closed order.

Such a "stability" nonetheless remains illusory. It accepts the instability of the "event" created by displacing the entire system; it is satisfied with compensating for it and camouflaging it. In reality, a *global* problem can be discerned in the contrary reactions—a problem of the infrastructure. A society is no longer sure of its grounding. The *event* engages the *structure*. The whole order is at stake and, first of all, it seems to me, a system of representation, what grounds both knowledge and politics.

Language and Power: Representation

Representation always remains a convention (Rousseau already made the point), but a convention that has the triple character of making manifest a *totality*, in itself not graspable, of being susceptible to a form of *control*, and finally of having an *operative* function by exercising a certain power. Here I am using the notion in a very broad sense in that it is equally affected by a discrediting of *knowledge* and a *political* malaise. The recent crisis invites us to examine the homology. Their abrupt coalescence and, no less, the analogous doubts of which they are the object, reveal a relation essential to the organization of our society.

As for political representation, "a real figure that the public adopts for lack of being able to express itself directly," Julien Freund underscores that it "gives a concrete existence to what it represents; it embodies what it represents."[1] Between representation and what is represented, a particular type of relation emerges: those who are represented are not juxtaposed to representation, but representation makes them present to themselves as a totality, without, however, any of them being identified with that common language. In a few of these aspects (but with differences that need to be specified), knowledge also becomes a representation: a discourse expressing a totality that otherwise could not be grasped. It is offered and must be offered to a permanent scrutiny (that refers it to theoretical postulates and to originary situations); it is operative, but in a way that by developing them reveals the nature as well as the limits of what it represents.

The events of May and June 1968 now recall for us the need for a control exercised not only on the functioning, but also on the inner *coherence*, of a system of representation. They have also allowed us to grasp better how this always fundamental, yet always fragile, equilibrium gets *displaced*.

Even if it is taken from the admirable album of images that Charlie Chaplin devoted to *Modern Times* (1936), one parable does not suffice to account for the slippage that we have witnessed. One characteristic turns it into an event without a prior "model"; it is indicated by the (cultural) *place* and by the (symbolic) *form* of the "accident."

On the one hand, the region in question concerns culture and knowledge in the university. On cursory glance, a language was summoned, its representativeness was challenged, and it was opposed to the "capture of speech," a direct expression of what a mode of teaching or a culture was censuring. On the other hand, its form corresponded to the site of the contestation. The protests or demonstrations translated into this very language—which could only betray them—a new and different type of communication, still bereft of a politics or a theory suited to it; thus it remained "symbolic," meaning "something other" than what they succeeded neither in articulating nor in doing.

What seems to be involved here is the relation that a society maintains with its language, the power that society holds over it, or even the right that it has to "verify" its own law.

This right has created a divergence. As in "blurred" photographs, a margin appears on the borders of frames and institutions. It is the site of a doubt that withdraws what is represented from its representations and that opens the space of a pullback. Through a sort of contagion, all social mediations became involved. They were in their very principle. Labor union delegations, political delegations, and scholarly theories are affected to their very roots if we cast suspicion on what they "represent." Does a system of communication leave aside what becomes "essential" to it, and does it withdraw from that essence its power of expression? That is the question. A relation has become problematic, the evidence of which has until now assured the functioning of language. It based exchanges on the value of words, a solid currency. The gold standard of reality guaranteed the representativeness of structures, authorities, and a common culture. So now a devaluation has taken place. Just when the represented and the representation are connected, a fundamental vice is denounced. The rift is located right there, creating an invisible axis around which a society, once solidly based on the recognized values it postulated, has suddenly begun to tremble. The ensuing reaction following this event is not enough to fill the void that caused it.

It may be naive to require language to make itself perfectly clear, to make a knowledge do something other than what it says it will do, to make its delegates identify with a power other than what they have received, to make the law express something other than what it says. But that is precisely the question. It is general. Formerly, it was "normal" to distinguish marriage from love, and consequently to have the wife, no longer loved, accompanied by a mistress. Today, marriage is supposed to "express" love in a way that it becomes "normal" to divorce if a reciprocal fidelity is no longer represented. Formerly, an abusive or narrow authority was tolerated because a libertarian thinking was adjoined to it in the form of a mental minefield. Today, authority is required to state clearly the community it is supposed to represent, and if it fails to do so, it is denounced and brought to trial. An infinite number of examples could be marshaled from all kinds of origins — the state, the university, the church — and could recover a problem identical to what the crisis of last May made so apparent. The sickness (and it is a sickness!) to which such a profound evolution attests consists in *taking language seriously,* or in refusing to let it become a game, anybody's game.

Referring to what is being taken seriously are both the scrutiny that each group wants to exercise over its delegates or its representations and the common right to demonstrate the imperatives of their consciousness through public acts. If, in both Christian and other communities, the double requirement especially contests collective expressions (liturgy, common rules, authority, etc.), it is not in order to destroy the language, but to restore it through a reorientation toward real communication. More than a deterioration of language, what we are witnessing today is a *need for language.* As one student said: "We want to have a *human* relationship with our professors."[2]

We have to force ourselves to grasp the meaning of what happened in the event itself. We cannot give in to the lyricism of certain apologists of contestation, nor to the resentment accompanied by the will to bring an end to disorder. Both constitute legends; they are more than willing to assign "evil geniuses" to one group or another, a mythology that is indefinitely available and reversible. Moreover, they bring us back to the problem of representations foreign to reality. These are mystificatory and ideological representations, *required* readings that are superimposed on the facts and that do not let the latter speak for themselves. The legend is what, in any case, *is required reading.*

Every legend would like to consign history to oblivion, denying that something took place. To the contrary, we have to strive to recognize this history, as something that has come about and that belongs to us.

We have to begin again from the phenomenon. It must, I believe, call into question our entire system of representation. In my opinion, the "capture of speech" and a "return to order" that followed equally indicate what needs to be done. Both the accusation, in the way it is expressed, and the defense of institutions, in the fashion in which it has functioned, in fact present an identical symptom: the *dissociation between power and language* (a dissociation, from another angle, that is matched by the one that separates theory from practice). On the one hand, despite the project that it was making manifest and that it seeks to maintain, the movement of May has splintered into two elements: violence and song—the cobblestone and the poem—as it was furthermore divided between political action and the revision of institutional expressions. On the other hand, the defense of order has revealed, behind its instrumental institutions or doctrines, a force of repression apparently lacking any relation with them, and we have seen the most democratic language or the most liberal science serve something quite different from neutrality or relativism.

This dangerous division probably allows us to offer a diagnosis of the nature of the illness that was, initially, anchored in sites of knowledge and that soon spread to all modes of representation. It initially defines what makes fascism possible, that is, if by fascism we mean a power that has lost its representative function. Even if it attacks the very equilibrium of the system, a general displacement shows that it has both political and theoretical symptoms. A rapid overview of these two sectors would merely be a warning against a surgical operation that would gladly proceed to removing an organ, whereas the "illness" is global.

From the Capture of Speech to Speech "Recaptured"

May 13–June 16: one month separates the "liberation" of the Sorbonne from its "reoccupation." Up to the smallest detail, the second event repeats the first and inverts it, as if a parenthesis were imagined closed when the moment was brought back to a zero point. Tracks are covered. Cobblestones are paved over. That it could have happened this way is above all what remains problematic. How could the speech that was taken be so easily retaken?

The "contestants" were often reproached for expressing themselves with very limited intellectual means. "Two dozen words": consumer society, repression, contestation, the qualitative, capitalism, and so on. The fact is exact. It signifies a new experience that can only be expressed through the very language that it *reemploys*, with, moreover, these few global signs that designate another way of speaking the language and thus measure the space uncovered by the shifting of the entire whole. From this standpoint, the innovation that emerged in the "capture of speech" — a *different* use of a language *already used* — could easily be co-opted by the knowledge that it sought to place in the service of an autonomy. That is what happened. "Liberated" speech was "recaptured" by the social system. The movement was used by the political parties as a foil or a platform. It was explained away by the forms of knowledge already elaborated. Finally, it was reduced to its past, taken on its own terms (which were not its own), brought back to social and intellectual hierarchies that it contested (but without yet being able to change them). Did the affair "become history"? In reality, it was simply being turned around.

The rift has in fact been reopened. It will not be easily concealed. It brings certain people (or many?) to ponder the irreducible aftereffects. The current lull wafts over us but does not suppress a resistance that is folded within but concedes nothing, or that only continues to adhere to institutions in the name of self-interest, in order to take advantage of it with the cynicism that comes with disillusionment. On a broader scale, a disquiet is spreading over the stability of language. Especially, we shall remark, the trace of the event can be seen in the entire social organization, for the crisis has seeped into social *functioning*. A social body has its inner logic: the shock wave is felt in the institutions that, reacting to the accident as they do, reveal what they wish to remove. The malaise that an opposition no longer has the means to declare now surges up in the defense that takes it up through its response. The "disorder" first brutally announced by the crisis of May reorganizes the forces that are now pitted against it. The event *is rehearsed* in the orders seeking to consign it to oblivion.

But, before analyzing how the "restoration" presents symptoms of the very disorder that it claims to suppress, we have to linger over the passage that led from the capture of speech to speech being recaptured. Here current events offer us a phenomenon that enlightens the procedures of acculturation or of cultural change. They open intelligence to the possibility of new paths, such that an *interpretation* could still be the sign of *events*, at once their consequence and their entry into knowledge. Present history—the history we are living—teaches us how to comprehend past history, however it is written or taught, in *other ways*. *Knowledge* can change with *experience*. From the angle of this particular phenomenon—the taking of speech and speech being recaptured—we are, furthermore, brought back to a fundamental problem that quite possibly was obliterated by social stability and its accompanying systematizations: How can a change come about? How can the sun rise on a new day?

A beginning is always characterized by an uncertain moment. This time of "passage" is ambiguous enough to furnish many people with proof that it is still night. For others, words that skirt real issues, as well as a new nonchalance of the moment, are signs of something else. Clear-cut decisions are hard to make. Unlike the cosmic order, in history there exist days that do not dawn. In order to be seen, innovations are disguised, and often stifled under borrowed old clothing. This fragile moment is no less that of human decision, which will select among possible destinies. To this instant that allows for the glimpse of a mutation corresponds the memory of a few words that, when a whole system is ajar, announce the color of another culture, with a different kind of taking of speech.

Yesterday, for example, *negritude* was the indication of a mutation affecting the entire "received text" of Western culture, but without yet succeeding in reorganizing it or replacing it. A few "impoverished" words were already translating a fundamental change: life, communion, and so on. We know today that it was our Western knowledge that was impoverished when it proved incapable of discerning in these "vague" notions what they meant to us; when, victims of our own law, we were satisfied to "recuperate" or "recapture" words heralding an invention already (and solely) symbolized by the reuse of a syntax that remained unchanged. But this very reuse made all the more precarious a "capture of speech" under the banner of "negritude." Irreducible but disarmed, the latter had at its behest only the terms organized in a manner foreign to its purpose—our purpose. As a result, it was endlessly relegated to areas other than where it sought to be. "Retaken" by blacks in the name of their own experience, "liberated" by and for a use that was their own, we were constantly "retaking" their speech in the very name of knowledges and modes of logic inscribed in the language that they attempted to speak in their own name.

The Power of Speaking

During this time of inchoate innovation, the blacks could be recognized only in what Western knowledge *made* them express by "explaining" them according to its own reason. They were thus faced with the problem of their *identity*, as in every instance where language is no longer adequate to what it claims to state. Prisoners of the culture from which they were already escaping by virtue of an impregnable experience, of "a certain affective attitude with respect to the world,"[3] in order to explain their autonomy and to identify themselves, they only had access to a "regression" back to an ancestral tradition or to a "marginalization" and a retreat to the borders of modern society. This, up to the point where their identity is affirmed when they ascribe to themselves the conditions necessary for the constitution of a language of their own, that is, by taking unto themselves the *power* of organizing a *representation*. *Political* autonomy was the basis of a *cultural* identity. Many other examples show how: it is impossible to take speech and to retain it without a taking of power. To want *to be heard* means being committed to *making* history.

Every innovation begins as a transgression signaled by a few surprising vocables on the surface of an established society. The immediate response is repression. This is a normal "recuperation," by which every society is defended; it reintegrates into its system the speech that still used it as a means of escape. Therefore, it is not excluded that, from these few words issuing from elsewhere, only a stain remains on the surface and, in the depths, the waters fallen from a forever unstated experience. But, conversely, speech as something already other, still alienated in the poverty of its own vocabulary and in the coherent riches of the system in which it attempts to awaken, can become the indication of two complementary—but in reality, indissociable—requirements: that of *representation* and that of *power*. Insofar as people wish to run the risk, in this double form, of existing—insofar as they notice that in order to have speech its power must be assured—they will give to their *identity* the historical figure of a new *cultural and political unity*. Otherwise, they will be necessarily "recaptured" or exiled, reintegrated into the system or destined to be nothing more than fugitives, prisoners of a repression or alienated in a regression.

The events of last May recall for us this law of existence. Entire populations now run the risk of being the political *subjects* of a cultural organization, that is, of acquiring the power to speak; in this respect, the insignia of Cuba or of Vietnam on flags and in the mythology of the Paris Commune is not accidental, but it symbolizes only the question to which we must respond in terms of our own situation. By contrast, other peoples and other human beings have become the *objects* of ethnology; they have been captured in this equivocal region where the Western recuperation of the foreigner holds sway. Because they have neither known nor been able to defend their speech, they have seen the law of our own curiosity imposed on themselves. Reduced to being nothing more than border dwellers frozen in a return to their primitive history (a point that Alfred Métraux has made, for example, about Indian messianisms), they exist in communication only by dint of what we say about them.[4] Their marginalization (which eliminates them from our society, if only as objects of interest), on the one hand and, on the other, their integration in our knowledge (where *we* have given them a place) are the reciprocal forms of the same failure, that of their cultural and political autonomy.

Today, the victory of the established order risks having a double effect. On the one hand, will those who have attempted to speak be brought back to their past, but to a past that would make of last May the legend of a lost paradise and the mental primitivism arresting history on these barricades from which it would be as difficult for them to climb down as it would be, for others, to climb up and out of the trenches of Verdun? On the other hand, will they become the object of a literature, a profit for editors and a pabulum served up to the needs of a clientele of voyeurs? We have to wonder: Will we turn our fellow citizens into our own Indians in the hinterland for this sort of consumption that always begins by withdrawing speech from its objects? Will they themselves — and we with them — know how to draw from their real experience the political and cultural lesson written within? The moment of passage between the taking of speech and speech retaken is the site of a decision. Our society will be judged on the basis of the choice it is able to make.

A Rift between "Saying" and "Doing"

No matter what our decision, the crisis has affected the nation at large. The reactions it has prompted attest to this. The crisis accused nature itself — indeed, the possibility of representations that otherwise assure the coherence of social exchanges.

Such a dangerous question had almost immediate reverberations in the area that a democracy assumes to be the cornerstone and the sign of the relation between the nation and its representations: the government. But it vacillated. It collapsed in a few hours, or perhaps in a few days.[5] It is a fact so "incomprehensible" that, for a moment, no party dreamed of taking power.[6] It was probably because in this instant of silence that rejected the deputies because of their rhetoric, and the "represented" because of violence or terror, no one could grasp *why* the state was coming apart. But not to understand "why," and no longer to know one's position amid the forces in play, were indications of the same rift. A language was breaking up at the moment when the basic link between power and representation was coming untied. The wave that finally called this linkage into question, and that opposed to all delegates its basic speech, directly turned against the state. The power that gives itself credit for representativeness seemed, for a moment, blown away, slyly deprived of what had justified it through a contestation that came from everywhere and nowhere, and that revealed a solution of continuity among representatives and those represented.

Aiming at authority in the name of what constitutes its legitimacy, this interrogation was matched by the contestation extended to the generation of the parents through the revolt of their children. Here and there, the menace came from *within*. Pampered like opiates of happiness by which adults are "amused" through their labors, but also destined to prove through their ritual initiation of attacking the society that prepares them, the "children" of a culture, the privileged subjects of a system, were those who themselves rose up against the role (that was assigned to them) of being, through their indefinitely prolonged vacation, the security of those with property, the alibi of a present moment otherwise stripped of meaning and of the guarantee of a homogeneous development. That the students, "our" students, promised to the destiny of becoming (but of becoming only in the future) a well-integrated elite, should rise up in anger — that is what was intolerable! That is what took society by surprise — from within. Thus there was a *need* to assign a less dangerous and more comprehensible figure to this menace. Something normal, it had to come from without. A propaganda went on a rampage in sustaining it, and with the complicity of a totally disquieted public. It denounced foreigners, riffraff, "Katangese," and so on.[7] The blame had to be cast on an enemy that was not one of "us." It conformed to the old instinct that has always created witches for the purpose of hunting them down. Everything was worked out in terms of *groupuscules* that had victimized "our children."[8] Or else: everything came from China. Even the reflexes that in France have always played a role in the face of a menace were awakened: anti-Semitism, anti-German chauvinism, and so on.

To be sure, in this way incontrovertible facts were established. We are learning how better to recognize them. But how have they been able to be passed off as "explanations"? I fear—or rather I believe—that the nation needed these witches in order to eliminate, along with them, an otherwise serious threat that originated in its youth. In place of heirs who were denying the value of the promised inheritance and who challenged the right of a knowledge or a social language to "place" them by making an abstraction of their decision and their existence, adversaries and causes that were easy to fight were substituted. Established facts were amplified and assigned a new role. From then on, information had a latent function, which was no longer in the service of truth. It was used for unacknowledged ends. It had a different and hidden, but determining meaning, and very distantly connected to its explicit function. A knowledge was put in the service of something other than what it claimed. It did not function according to what it said it was doing. As a result, it confessed to what it was accused of doing. This particular case tended to prove already that the demonstration had been well intended (although in overly general terms) when it reproached sciences or representations for being merely a society's "instruments of repression." In the way the "representatives" of the country used information to stave off all criticism, they admitted that it was right.

The same can be said of the "redeployments" of which the crisis of May 1968 furnished myriad examples. At the moment when institutions and ideologies found themselves under the same suspicion, when, from every quarter, people or systems were challenged as being non-"representative" (an accusation that the CGT [Confédération Générale du Travail, the main labor union] addressed to student leaders, but also that the workers addressed to their shop stewards and employers, and the latter themselves to members of the government, etc.), a strange phenomenon became general and multiplied recourse to old references, but only in order to clothe them with a character different from what they had meant. Here, 1936 was being repeated, and a struggle between social "classes" prevailed; there, it was 1940 or 1944, when the vocabulary of the Resistance or its procedures were

taken up as signs of Liberation . . . But, in reality, these theoretical strat-
agems, whether verbal or institutional, were clearly inadequate to
the new situation, and underneath, they played a very different role.
The archaism of the formulas concealed a usage that had little relation with them. No longer at stake was the analysis or representation
of what was happening, or of proportioning to it new institutions or
theories. These redeployments of a regressive manner stressed the
gap between the explicit and the real function, between the revolutionary slogans of the political parties and their parliamentary games,
between the mystique of France and the leader's "jealousy of decid-
ing."[9] The equivocation spread throughout the entire system through
a play that gave a double meaning to a superannuated patriotism as
well as to postwar existentialism, to the mythology of the Liberation
as well as to the ideology of class struggle — all things having become
the legends of *another* history that was deemed effective, and that
Edgar Morin has called a revolution "without a face."[10]

The elections themselves seem to have inherited a new role from
the circumstances. In one way, they are as "inexplicable" as the events
of May and, I believe, for the same reasons. It would be simplistic
merely to see what in high places has been called a "reaction" or a
"defensive reflex," a wish to erase the evidence of what happened,
as if after having done something improper. But the legislative procedures were no less displaced, borne by the evidence that they constitute a *hapax legomenon* without precedent in the last Republics. This
time they have been the means of ensuring its function in a system
of representation thrown off balance. They used to allow for the designation of political options in the framework of a system that seemed
infallible. Today, however, little interest is generated for programs
(that, moreover, are quite similar), and votes were massively cast, on
occasion, for unknown candidates who were not going to be heard.
In other words, the *regime* was being helped. A social organization
had to be saved. The rift that had for a moment cracked it open had
to be filled. A guarantee had to be made against a fundamental insecurity.[11] Ideologies and parties counted for little with respect to the
"Defense of the Republic." These were elections of a very special kind:
their goal was to keep institutions functioning; they themselves were
their own goal. The nation no longer indicated its preferences. On
the faith of what it had learned, it voted for its own preservation. In
that way, recourse to elections, a procedure established for 120 years,
acquired a new meaning.

But since a society of adults thus tried, as a whole, to prove to itself that it still functioned and to guarantee the safety of its organization (since it was self-confirmed), must we conclude that the question had been eliminated? I do not believe so.

On the one hand, the pollsters had no right to speak, and they did not participate in this "defense" under the flag of participation. This situation makes them the *objects* of a concern or a fear; it eliminates their representation and, at the same time, their accusations against a system of representativeness. From a procedure that directly excludes the majority of the "protesters," can a result emerge that allows or tolerates an opposite policy? It is a thorny problem, since July brings students back to their initial "misery" in a society, without making it possible for them to forget the echo that the expression of this situation elicited throughout the nation. In the same way, how can a demand bearing on participation in power and a broader distribution of decision making be confirmed in the name of a massive movement that carried centralization to its highest point, diminished the chances for pluralism or political bipartisanism, and even eradicated this traditional remainder of a regionalism that was the difference between the North and the South, and thus gave power a *form* contrary to the *program* that it should have enacted? Unless the government sought in this support contrary to its real intentions . . .

On the other hand, even if the analyses of the elections up to that moment remain uncertain about what to make of them, an interpretation can nonetheless be tendered. I believe it is true even if it is incomplete. The institution charged with controlling or choosing *a* politics inherited as its new function the restoration of *the* political body. In the terms I used earlier, I would contend that on this occasion it seemed to restore the relation between power and representativeness. It was no longer the means, but the end. It was the very defense of a society entirely threatened in its own language. The preservation of the system replaced the prospective choices that are otherwise permissible. In a political function, it is no longer its object but its very functioning that has become the essential point.[12]

The Law of "Disorder"

But the institution thus plays a role other than the one it announces. Here too, it *does* something different from what it *states* that it will do. Henceforth, it is "symbolic" of the new service demanded of it.

Should we conclude by saying that the deck was stacked? No, because everyone knew more or less clearly the use to which the procedure was destined, but nothing was said about it. It concealed this displacement as something that was understood. In order to rescind the requirement evinced by the entire system of representation—that precisely it was "representative," that it gave speech to everyone, that it was true—the fundamental political institution has increasingly shown the deficit that motivated the process. It bears witness to the "disorder" that it sought to suppress—if "disorder" there is when an institution plays a role different from what it is explicitly supposed to play. From this point of view, there too the interrogation born of a gap between signs and what they ought to mean cannot be assailed. Far from being eliminated, it is intensified since it is again opened by the very answer said to address it.

There are no grounds for celebration here, especially if, in addition, at their different levels the political, union, and academic apparatuses also began to function in such a way as to defend their representativeness through force at the very moment when their "base" was *lacking*; conversely, in the same space of time, the power to valorize its representations was also *lacking* at the base, which was, moreover, uncertain about its goals as well as perplexed about its directors, and finally brought back to a strong degree—but by lassitude or self-interest—to its habitual cadres, who at least had the advantage of existing.

In turns, the contestation and the established order sought to *establish the law*. In reality, it happened that they had to *submit to a contrary law*: "liberated," speech found itself recaptured, retaken; "repressive," the institution avows the disorder that it must censure. What, therefore, is this ubiquitously recurrent law that underhandedly displaces explicit expression of willpower? That of a "disorder" that affects the very organization of a society.

Thus something was broken, which consigns to contradiction the two symbolic "sides" of language—each having as its secret (and its negation) the absence of the other. Between a social organization that uses representations as a front behind which are hidden the (necessary) defensive reflexes of a power that espouses a will to survive and, also, the powerlessness that the "demonstrations" avow in the name of a right to speech or a request for *meaning* and truth (equally necessary for communication); between the force of a system and the irreducibility of consciousness; between the buying power tied to public powers that guarantee it and the claims of a capture of speech held to be the condition of true social exchanges, is there an antinomy? Analysis always leads us back to this question.

Such a global questioning—of which I have only marked a few pertinent signs and perhaps in a partial way (but *how* can one ever speak impartially?)—could not be eliminated without causing a society to perish, a society that in fact has been displaced and challenged. The privilege given to the old order would create a national "ideology" without any relation to what happened underneath. Besides, order is found only in books and museums. These are not models for a culture, even if a certain mode of teaching has sometimes led us to believe so. The "solution" is hardly outside of the system, on the margin of order, in negation (which always immobilizes structures or divisions by inverting them). It is in union, but only if this union is based on the new structuring called forth by the event.

A different *organization* is required. It will allow for the rejection of the antinomy that would set truth in one or the other of the two stances that the tramp in *The Gold Rush* offers his viewers: to localize "order" (or "disorder") either *here* or *there* is in advance to legitimize the opposite thesis, which as a result will be no less superficial. It means denying a general displacement that is already legible in the institutions that seek its control, or in the "demonstrations" that are incapable of expressing it. It means opting for an ideology or a legend, whereas what we really need is a language. In practice as well as in theory, *what is different is never contrary.* In theory, we refuse to have to choose between history and structure; in practice, between the "movement" of May and the "order" of June. In reality, a different order is at stake.

Chapter 4
For a New Culture
(Paris, September 9, 1968)

The Return of Language

"May is selling well." So observed *L'Express* at the end of July 1968.[1] Since then, the phenomenon has reached even greater proportions. Soon books will have to be written on this tidal wave of books already published. The mass of commodities offered for consumption is stupendous. I count about sixty works, and I am omitting the special issues of journals (which are often better than the books themselves), foreign publications, pamphlets, satirical broadsheets, and records.[2] The flow of writing corresponds to the ebb of "speech." Private reading follows public assemblies. Bookish information comes after the immediate and brutal effect of radio broadcasts, emitted during and after the events. Television under surveillance or censure continues to frustrate a public that wants to know.

This silent literature that extends all about the event is in many ways quite revealing. It responds first of all to a rush of readers; it makes the latter manifest, all the while that editors are turning it into an object of speculation (with the excuse of a gap of two months in their sales). Everywhere there is an urgent need to understand what happened. It aims at overcoming the irrational element of the event; for some, to defend themselves from it; for others, to defend it; but probably for everyone, to work through and to mend the tear that it produced in the system of social relations.

In May, the "silence" of some people combined with the "capture of speech" by others. The relation was reversed in June. This was an almost physical sign of a division among fundamental options, often unsuspected until that moment but then suddenly revealed, which ripped asunder the very thickness of words and arranged an apparently identical vocabulary under meanings that in a flash became in-

communicable. The irruption of speech then created or uncovered irreducible differences that splintered the continuous network of sen-
tences and ideas. Writing seems to respond to the will to fill or to sur-
mount these gaps. It is a text, literally, a cloth, that weaves together,
that seems to fill—but only in the silence of reading—the needs of
solitude and leisure, the distance that the indissociable speech of a
face-to-face encounter had unveiled among people of the same political party or of identical convictions, between colleagues sharing similar "ideas" or the same disciplines. Writing is plied into these gaps.
It circulates in areas where speech is muffled for lack of being heard.
It passes before everyone's eyes and from one hand to the next. The
newspaper itself, which gave a place to a public reading during the
events, now turns into a piece of writing, the *object* of a gaze, a silent
language. Perhaps, after all, a function of writing is compensatory,
restorative of communication in a minor mode, recaptured in the silent
spaces of interrupted exchanges.

At the very least the problem was opened in the successive relation between the speech of protest and the "business" of writing. For
texts and their readings, we are still lacking the equivalent of Evelyne
Sullerot's remarkable research on radio broadcasts and how they were
heard during the month of May.[3]

In any event, it is unlikely that the 150,000 copies of *Le livre noir
des journées de mai* [The black book of the days of May] or *Le réveil de
la France* [The awakening of France] by Jean-Jacques Servan-Schreiber,
the 100,000 copies of *Pour préparer l'avenir* [Tackling the future] (by
Pierre Mendès-France), or the 75,000 copies of *Les murs ont la parole*
[The walls are speaking] sold at the end of last July were really *read*.
For many it was no doubt enough to have *paid* for them. This tax paid
to the nation and to history is a monetary language, in itself constitutive of an exchange, in which knowledge plays no role, whose only
vocabulary is one of consumer products. These book-objects that dec-
orate apartments do not really constitute sites of reading—often for
lack of time, or for lack of an interest that might exceed the symbolic
act of purchase, the sacrifice of reconciliation. But in that way, these
book-objects are the objective vocabulary of a culturally national activity. Money is a culturally impoverished idiom, but an idiom nonetheless. These books are prices, not readings, that represent the extreme case of a language in which meaning disappears in the physical
density of the goods being exchanged—a communication without

content succeeding meanings that heretofore were difficult or impossible to communicate. But analyses on this topic too are still needed.

The same does not hold for another capital aspect of this literature. *Information circulates.* It spreads out in time and in space. With a book in hand, anyone has time, at his or her behest, that submits to a personal rhythm. Everyone "has" time. A distance can be gained on facts that only days ago exploded rapidly and brutally, in each case differently from what the preceding facts led anyone to expect. Intelligence is taking its revenge on the surprise, the stupor, and sometimes the fear provoked by the unintelligible violence of the events that took place.

The diffusion of dossiers "offered to the public"; publications that restore, in the empyrean of books, the constellation of authorities for a moment faded and sapped of power; the possibility henceforth given to confront, to recoup, and to recompose a geography of the events with controllable bits; the means, finally, to possess in a continuous text what was happening in so many scattered and isolated places, whether in universities or factories, in Paris or in the provinces — all this information that turns the past into a universe subject to knowledge is a reconquest of space. It shapes yesterday into a world of fragments. It orders it into a knowledge. Like the turning of the tide in the elections, the book is a return to order; it grows when the newspaper diminishes, whose print run is the barometer of crises.

From Events to History

In such a massive production, the works are quite diverse. Not only because they belong to various literary genres and refer to often contrary intentions (combative writings, "objective" dossiers, chronicles, free interpretations, etc.) but because — and this is what I would like to emphasize — they also represent the very different modalities of the fundamental *relation between the event and the tools that make it possible to be understood.*

Even a dossier is always organized. It results from a sifting. It expresses a way of understanding, even if it is enlisted in the "politics" of a publisher who is only interested in profit, whatever its origins, whether pornographic or revolutionary. Each work therefore offers a more or less developed solution to the problem put before everyone: with what kind of intellectual grid, through what perspective can be grasped (or, which finally amounts to the same thing, causes to be grasped) that which resists both a mental order and a social order, namely, "the events"?

It has been claimed (something that is possible, after all, but, as Jean-Marie Domenach has noted, not so easily decided) that the revolution of May brought a coup de grâce to structuralism.[4] People wanted to feel that the event had won out over structure. Let's say, first of all, by way of whimsy, that the event had to be directed through the force of structures in order to make possible the expression of this thesis on the death of structuralism, a thesis, moreover, that is profitable to the defenders of traditional continuities more than to the witnesses of innovations, the sources of discontinuities. But let's be serious! The question rather involves knowing *if* and, in the affirmative, *how* the event resisted the (intellectual, political, etc.) systems that preceded it; in other words, if it modified them or if, to the contrary, it was explained and recuperated by previous types of knowledge, such that, after having momentarily suspended the process of thinking, it would disappear when taken up again.

From this point of view, the condemnation of structuralism can only be the repetition of an already entrenched conviction that would attribute to every circumstance and every surprise the value of a confirmation: whatever it may be, the future has in advance a place in this type of explanation. To be sure, the problem is put forward quite specifically in connection with structuralist analyses that leave a blank space and consider unthinkable the passage or commotion as the basis for the organization of a social coherence. But the problem must be located at a level other than that of a professor who declares to his intellectual adversaries: "I was right!" He or she refers to the fact attesting to the success of the book, that is, to the introduction of heterogeneity in the homogeneous order of a language.[5]

Pondering the relation of order to event is also the task of politics and theory. In the latter aspect, every work offers testimony to an experience and an option. The way it makes *intelligible* what has *come about* assumes the taking of a position in respect to what defied the rules of a (social, scientific, philosophical) reason, like its "incomprehensible" or unforeseen contestation. Seen as a piece of information, a justification, or a reflection, it presents a particular form of the relation between an intellectual order and the irruption or resistance of those facts. Let's say, in raising the debate to the level of the stratosphere of concepts, that every text implies a doctrinal position on this relation between *theory* and *innovation,* betweeen *language* and *violence.* The very function of history (of historiography) is probably to constitute — but with lucidity — a discourse that expresses a relation between reason and its "other," with events.

This relation, internal to the text, also defines its position with regard to what is external to it, namely, readers or the future. It is ultimately the very object or the material of the book when it narrates or explains. But it also betrays the attitude of the author before readers who will not necessarily be of his or her opinion and whose future disagreement might possibly — like the events of May 1968 — surprise the author. By virtue of the very fact that it "comprehends" the event, every interpretation thus characterizes what it tolerates and what it excludes. It is a closure of reason. Reason is *already* situated in relation to interlocutors to come. Here the publication of a knowledge, by ordering yesterday's "stupefying" facts, marks off in advance a place for possible contestations. In the form of a discourse that maintains a relation with a heterogeneous past, the book contains *in itself* the announcement of the relation that the author would like to have with what still remains external and partially unpredictable. For example, an imperative interpretation of the past is already intolerant of future listeners or events. Literature on May 1968 can be analyzed from this point of view, as the test of a knowledge or the testimony of a society about itself.

The same relation, I believe, always holds true. Erasing the past by mobilizing it in the service of the ideology that it is supposed to confirm also means negating the alterity of others or of the future. This defense by knowledge is all the more engaging when what is at stake is initially more troublesome or perplexing. A lucid view of the past is the way in which — often unbeknownst to itself, as if in a backward movement — the taking of a position can be formulated vis-à-vis the present or the future.

The Same and the Other in Knowledge

This is coupled with a problem that has been discussed over recent months concerning the human sciences. What is the connection between *knowledge* taught and the pedagogical *relation*? It is fundamental. The "expert" is already situated in front of his or her pupils (a first form that the event assumes in its professional work) by the type of interpretation that he or she gives to psychological, social, or historical facts—according to which, for example, he or she sees an operative process taken up in a network of relations or a closed system raised to the status of a required reference. Conversely, a protest by students, especially serious and far-reaching, reveals the theoretical relation on which was based a knowledge of man, society, or the past; by his or her reaction to the unexpected resistance, the teacher sheds light on what was being concealed in his or her analytical procedures, what they postulated, what, ultimately, he or she understood or tolerated as a "human" deed on the intellectual map.

This homology between the professor's scientific attitude toward the facts of which he or she speaks and his or her behavior in front of a class of pupils who are being lectured, this interference between the human as object and the human face-to-face, represents the grandeur—but also the danger—of so-called human disciplines. Finally, the "facts" themselves rise up before the science of the teacher when the students begin to take the responsibility of speech. In this respect, the pedagogical, face-to-face process judges knowledge. But it removes nothing—quite the contrary—from the need to theoretically formulate this relation, or to explain it in a "reason" (a scientific epistemology) that ensures their intelligibility and offers their rigorous language to the exchanges that constitute a society.

In the closed world of the university, what was and what remains in question is the incoherent, artificial, and "mendacious" combination of the relation with the human facts as expressed by a *discipline* and of the relation between students and teachers, or between workers and directors, as established by an *institution*. It is also, conversely, the theoretical justification, through the *content* of teaching, of a practical *mode* of social exchanges that is henceforth deemed unacceptable by them. Less than individuals, protest once again aims at a system. In this particular society, it rises up against a language that no longer expressed reality or that expressed an intolerable reality. It aims at a style of exchange defined in terms of production: commodities of thought, results of examinations, brains that might be put to work. Not that all that is either ill-founded or impossible! But this entire totality has to allow everyone to *exist*, to be different in his or her very relation with others, to be able to create (and to become other than oneself) in a collaboration defined as an inventive process.

Under this ambition a question was posed: is a language (and that holds for culture in general) made of objects thought or possessed—or rather, of words? No one will be surprised to learn that the question inspired in many teachers (when they themselves were not the first ones to beg the question) their passion for instruction and not only their desire to know. "After having spent so many years in teaching and having so often dreamed of leaving the profession, finally, all of a sudden, I discovered just how thrilling it was." For their part, the students, far from calling for the disappearance of professors or even of certain ones among them, asked that knowledge be defined on the basis of a mutual, entirely simple, interrogation, and furthermore having on so many occasions asked in offices, firms, or research committees: "And you, what do you think about it? And you, my friend, over there, what do you have to say?"

A Problem of Civilization?

This requirement is more formidable than it appears. It puts to the test a *knowledge* identified with a *power* that acts upon *objects*. The conception criticized in this way is perhaps originally tied to the development of all technical civilization, a question fundamental not only to science but also to the "Western" type of society that it creates. First appearing on the borders or in the "academies" of classical Europe, this postulate slowly submitted to its rule the civilization for which it fostered prodigious growth. In this progress, the Other—the resistance of the Other—was for a long time set apart, in a spiritual region that concerned ethics and private conduct. That is no longer possible. Productive knowledge, the principle of a growing formalization, can no longer tolerate what it had so long allowed to dwell along its borders. Beyond a threshold in the success of a discovery, by virtue of its own development, it compromises the triumph it makes possible. And now an "other" reappears in the heart of science as an idiom that contests it. For some this idiom is puerile; for others it is decisive. I believe that it can *become* one or the other, depending on how the question it poses is perceived, depending on the response that is given to it.

A system becomes problematic, and it does not suffice to believe it either changed or justified merely by words: it is a system of quantitative exchanges between objects *created* by a discipline (a knowledge, or ultimately, a production) or *possessed* by virtue of it (a social status, commodities, or finally, a consumption). It transforms human relations into relations of power, into exchanges of commodities, the creative reciprocity of subjects.

It is striking to see the most indiscreet question surging forth—
"How to create *oneself*?" —where reigned the imperious urgency that
asked, "Create *what* and how?" It is alarming to observe that the question from now on might appear *outside* of the system created by this
urgency, and thus in the form of a violence; that the combination of
production and consumption constitutes a social rationale whose rai-
son d'être seems to be lost; that, as a result, the order is no longer
lived as a value; that, in other words, the conditions of life are detached
from reasons for living; finally, that economic rationalization, imperative *logic* of products and needs relegates to the margins what it ought
to express, the *act* of self-creation becoming either the contestatory
speech that it eliminates or the revolutionary rupture that overturns it.

This is not the place to evoke the problem opened by a question
on the *meaning* that cannot yet be formulated in our language, and
still less the future of a civilization that for the first time is not religious—as Malraux prophesied—and is driven to find in itself (but
how?) the values on which it is based.

Even if this crisis bearing on the "meaning of history" that was
monopolized by Marxism, and calling for a less "dated" recourse,
seems to have cured a French intelligentsia of its guilt with regard to
the party, we merely need to recall the task that was made manifest
in Marx's attitude in 1848. He was then "among the small number
of those who were not impressed by the universal euphoria." He refused to "play at revolution," because he wanted it to be genuine.
"At the moment when true revolutionaries had to teach workers how
to use firearms, Marx was delivering lectures on political economy,
and was doing his best to calm passions and transform workers into
doctrinaires!"[6]

But thinking is also a task to be done.

Chapter 5
The Publishers' Harvest:
May Seen in September

A General Presentation

The best-informed and most solid book is clearly the one that, among the very first, was presented by Philippe Labro, the former collaborator of the television program, "Caméra 3," and the cosigner of the motion by television journalists against the "scandalous inadequacy" of the ORTF [French Radio and Television Service] on May 11.[1] The various points on the horizon are illuminated in turn in this excellent panorama that extends from the beginnings up to mid-June: Nanterre, the red nights of Paris, the police, the information, the labor unions, the government, the university. This circular track is marked by a certain number of interviews or points of view, from Daniel Cohn-Bendit to Maurice Grimaud, from Alain Touraine to André Malraux, and so on. A short historical reminder accompanying each interview provides a deeper context and allows the reader to grasp each one as a story that opens up onto the crossroads of the events of May.

Two aspects of the crisis stand out in this dossier. One is noted by Alain Touraine with respect to the students: "It is *a base* that acted, not an elite that thought" (40); various witnesses look at (an unbelievable or normal fact for them) these demonstrations without leaders — a sort of birth or popular creativity that sifts through the slogans, that is characterized by the joy of being able to invent that gives the "leaders" the role of being "loudspeakers" rather than of "leading." The other, which Touraine also points out in speaking of Cohn-Bendit, is the *restorative role that speech plays for communication* and as a victory (ephemeral? symbolic? effective?) on social compartmentalization. "What deeply touches me about a man like Cohn-Bendit is this almost mystical but profoundly political belief in Athenian democracy,

49

in speech. I believe that he is a man who is horrified by violence, and who wishes to weave back together the fabric of democratic life beyond silence, beyond whatever stifles, and so forth" (42). A strange crisis. It seemed to send people back to their own institutions and to this fundamental public institution of language. "Everything turned on language" (235). Hence the importance of one of the best analyses of the events to appear thus far, Evelyne Sullerot's "transistors and barricades" and the "phenomenon of the 'rumor mill'" (124–42). For the demonstrators, the transistor was information carried on one's person. It furnished the power to "dominate the movement" instead of being lost in it. It also became confused with the event since it allowed it to be *done* at the same time that it was *saying* so. Finally, it turned the actors into heroes at the very instant when it offered to each person the means for controlling information on the spot and choosing one's course of action.

From the volume also emerges the investigation of the police (otherwise not treated enough), or the brilliant and amusing notes by Pierre Marcabru on the Odéon, this "revolution in fabric." By contrast, the dossier on the workers is thin,[2] and even thinner, as elsewhere, are the pages on the movement of the secondary-school students (the CAL, or Comités d'Action Lycéens), far less known, and perhaps the most important for the future, and often much less ideological and more "realistic" than the student Commune.[3]

Chroniclers

Alongside this volume is a whole array of supplements. Mention must be made of that of Andro and his friends that follows the chronology quite closely, a kind of diary that also speaks of soccer players and hotel porters: it concerns "everyday life" in the streets of Paris during the month of May.[4] More autobiographical, but always astonished and vigilant, is *Le Piéton de mai* [May's pedestrian], a collection of news flashes — illuminations and glances — published from day to day by this uniquely "awakened dreamer" in *Combat*.[5] More "telling" of the event but endowed with this British humor that knows how both to *see* without *saying* and to suggest without denouncing is the work by Patrick Seale and Maureen McConville, which teaches us how better to look at the event through the fog of memory than merely to reflect on it.[6]

Sounds, Images, Quotables

Here, we are between munchies and documents; between editorial speculation that abuses the public for its own profit and brilliance, diamonds created or carried in the flow of poetic imagination; between a literature intended for "voyeurs" and the accounts of an unexpected spring. Must reading includes *Les murs ont la parole* (Paris: Tchou, 1968 [75,000 copies were sold by the end of July!]), an epic fashioned from graffiti, a rousing song sung over the cobblestones, confessions and anonymous cries in which bad jokes strike the chord of fundamental issues. A city began to talk, and what remains are these texts extracted from a time that is already dead, like the frescoes cut out of the thickness of the walls of Mari. Thus too, *Les Poèmes de la révolution. Mai 1968,* a protest against "absent poetry" (an island that brings together words far from the streets) and for "un monde pas nouveau / mais si Dieu / veut / différent" [a world not new but if God wishes different].[7] Songs of war and songs of hope. "The sun shines in our hands":

> Croire enfin
> Lorsque toute raison de croire n'est plus
> Donner
> Puisque nous voilà déshérités.

> [Finally believe / When all reason to believe is gone / Give / Since there we are the disinherited.]

From there we fall into the journalistic anthology, with Alain Ayache's collection, which is pretty thin, or with *La Chienlit de Papa* [Daddy's masquerade], which is more polemical and funnier.[8]

Among the photo albums, the ninety-four items presented in *Paris, Mai-Juin 1968* furnish in a few remarkable images the fog pocked by nocturnal silhouettes (see photos 20–21) and especially the irruption of these unknown faces suddenly filling the streets of Paris—a sudden visibility of students and workers.[9] Walter Lewino has made a selection that arranges the photos of Jo Schnapp in three identifiable stages in the style of revolutionary inscriptions and imagery, at first quite abstract in the density of expression, then lyrical, and finally rhetorical.[10] In my opinion, it is the most intelligent analysis of the mural language that emerged from the events. Philippe Labro's photographic report is more commonplace, but not without interest.[11] The iconography of the revolution has to a degree abused these nights illuminated by fire and these days darkened by smoke and gas.

The same is true for the record *Mai 68*, an underwhelming register of noise to which are added a few statements by Jacques Sauvageot and Alain Geismar and a few extracts of official speeches.[12] This is a memoir for those who might not have heard of the event, a replacement for the memory of those who were not there.

Humor and Drawings

The verve of caricaturists carries a more faithful memory. It reconstitutes a style: the sleazy and oddball side of student "transgression," by Joseph Henz, or, incisive and violent, his combative aspect with Siné, to whom *L'Enragé* had offered a free space to bury once again its old nightmares.[13] Cabu was more classical, opening in his spirited drawings of the Sorbonne the "balloons" of speech, items heard in passing that make the viewer's smile become something like the distance that the observer gains on the event.[14] Less subtle, Hubert Tonka created a sort of filmed comic strip that is somewhere between a hoax and a commercial enterprise, an ironic and pseudo-"popular" register of a satire against the revolutionary jargon of an intelligentsia.[15] In spite of everything, it is a limit of the literature on the topic.

Three Dossiers

Since *Le Livre noir des journées de mai* [The black book of the days of May], which commands our interest for being the first and most useless of all the dossiers,[16] scores have followed. Three are impressive by virtue of their quality. First, a "critical and documentary collection," a first work in a new collection in small paperback format, edited by Marc Kravetz, former secretary-general of the UNEF [National Union of Students of France], whose several remarkable articles published in 1964 and 1965 allow us to understand the current crisis by finding in it a confirmation that comes after the fact.[17] It covers only twelve days and is restricted to events in Paris (because of "this impermeability between Paris and the provinces illustrated by the permanent insufficiency of information published by the national, that is, Parisian, press"). In this field, defined by the period of the student insurrection and arranged in chronological order, the book furnishes the most effective documentation that we have (leaflets, testimonials, etc.) on the facts as they were lived. The counterpoint of a commentary that is both sarcastic and militant turns these pieces of a dossier into a projectile: the summation is also a cobblestone.

La Révolte étudiante contains interviews sliced through with Daniel Cohn-Bendit's picturesque, brutal, and realistic statements on his anarchist and ultimately "apolitical" conception of the revolution: "The important thing is not to develop a reform of capitalist society, but to thrust ahead with a complete break from this society, an experiment that will not last but that allows us to glimpse a possibility. We notice something transitorily, and then it's gone."[18] In his preface, Hervé Bourges notes that the May events "signify the failure of a certain form of civilization and call for a total rebirth" (9). The texts gathered by the CRIU [Center for the Regrouping of Information from the University] refer to this requirement for a new culture.[19] Deprived of any context, they nonetheless offer the interest of coming from these distant lands that are the French provinces and of opening a corridor in communication for the work accomplished inside the high schools (90–98). Leaflets by the Action Committee are also included: "We Are Moving Ahead" (142–221), in particular its founding charter, "Amnesty of Eyes Bashed Out" (144–50), a declaration dated May 13 that was displayed for a long time in the halls of the Sorbonne and of which several versions existed (we should like to compare the variants to the "received text" that was imposed on us: the critical apparatus of the Manifesto supposedly signaled its history and better situated its publisher). That is an important series. Once again we owe much to the effort that the Seuil publishing house did to inform the public at large. It still needs to publish the enormous dossier assembled by Alain Schnapp and Pierre Vidal-Naquet.[20]

Eyewitness Accounts

Added to these three most important works are the items assembled by Sylvain Zegel; by giving us an echo of the event in each professional sector, these polls allow us to measure the sociocultural distances set in place.[21] Also revealing, in the photographic sense of the term, are either Jacques Durandeaux's "dialogues" with a few students (between June 1 and June 10) or the texts edited by students in science that were presented on May 9, in taking an exam in mathematics, and to whom A. Deledicq proposed, in its place, a free essay on the crisis of the university.[22] Among the latter, along with the desire to open a real dialogue between teachers and students, was the will to have "an innovated faculty, in which the personality of each person can bloom before our eyes" (100); what is sought is not another "discipline," nor the suppression of teachers, but an initiation into creativity, a method for "learning how to learn," that is, how to think (104). More conscious of the political and cultural complexity of the problem, Durandeaux's interlocutors analyze further the labyrinth of "academic" itineraries. In his eyes alone, the review of their studies is already a bill of indictment against official plans that have successively displaced the programs and their university structures.

Along with the witnesses whom Durandeaux is not satisfied to simply allow to speak or to be heard, but whom he engages, as a Christian, a priest, and a philosopher, mention must be made of the collaborators of the volume *Les Chrétiens et la Révolution de mai*, who are eager to document past and present indications of a "revolutionary" faith and tradition.[23] Despite everything, the justifications remain less convincing than the option, that was then quite evident among many believers, without there being a need for a precedent or a confirming theology.[24] One problem remains intact, that of the relation between this option, which divided communities of believers like other groups, and the expressions (dogmatic, liturgical, and so on) that represented the religious *unity* of these communities.

The ORTF (French Radio and Television Service)

Two books. A lively chronicle stuffed to the gills with details, the first book—despite its more general title—provides only the story of the strike led by ninety-seven of the 125 collaborators of the TV news (only one of 173 professional categories represented at the ORTF, that is, thirteen thousand workers), not, as it has sometimes been reported, against the government (many Gaullists figured among the strikers), but with a view toward "depoliticizing television."[25] Anyone who watches television should have this little book, which is as engrossing as a novel. For a "good use" of his or her TV set, the viewer will discover between the covers some useful information: the reality of censorship (120–26); the role of the SLII (service for intergovernmental linkages of information, 23–24); and also, an appeal to a political consciousness-raising, an evocation of the control that the nation, rather than the state, might exercise over the ORTF (130–34).

Personally, it was difficult for me (my naïveté, perhaps, but a naïveté born of the bizarre friendship resulting from an almost daily frequenting) to read what was being suggested to me in somewhat overly muffled allusions about Léon Zitrone, while "the number one thinker of the team" (114), Emmanuel de La Taille, was being raised up as a star among the stars. But that's only a minor story!

Much sketchier, Manel and Planel's work locates this debate on the broader horizon of "the house."[26] The style is not as flashy, but the information provided is more broadly based. Despite all this, no book yet is commensurate with the importance of the problem. We are still waiting for the dossier prepared by the Interunion team with the collaboration of Roger Errera, who has already written interesting studies on the topic.[27] But cannot the deficit of publications be attributed to a lack of interest on the part of those who watch television? Would we thus be the "couch potatoes"?[28]

The March 22d Movement

Even if they suggest that a struggle needs to be prolonged, the few analyses placed under the flag of the Movement hold our interest for having already presented a theory. I especially note the chapter that specifies the nature of "exemplary action": an intervention can be effective precisely because it is "symbolic"; insolent or brutal, it is situated at the point where a threshold can be passed, where something appears *possible* that throws topsy-turvy the organization of the impossible and of interdictions.[29] Whether students sit in the chairs reserved for professors in their conference rooms, or whether, by the mere fact of *constructing* barricades, they have an *active* behavior, they cross the threshold of fear or of passivity. This movement is crucial; it is "symbolic" because it opens (but does not yet achieve) new possibilities; in that very way, it "posits a situation that will go beyond itself and then be exceeded" (69); at the same time that it unveils the adversary's fragility, it triggers a process. The tactic consists in locating or in creating, at a given moment, the threshold that will be crossed (or not), and beyond which a "normal" type of relation (between humans, between powers, between workers and students, etc.) can be modified.

One style of action that is described here is much more detailed than the programs (which are quite gassy). It seems that by ascribing to itself this deft method, the Movement nonetheless feels the need—

but also the difficulty—to develop a strategy. From a historical point of view, through examples that are provided, the reader notes the tension between the inner necessity for a structuring (that accompanies a critique of "spontaneity": *Ce n'est qu'un début*, 92–93, 129, etc.) and the rejection of the Leninist concept of the Communist Party as the vanguard of the masses (ibid., 136–40).[30] In the melting pot of a *groupuscule*, the oppositions that divide or distinguish the revolutionary movements reappear.

The March 22d Movement is narrated as much as it is explained. But the narrator, Patrick Ravignant, when he speaks of the Odéon, reiterates the problems that the Cohn-Bendit brothers—Daniel of Nanterre and Gabriel of Nantes—had already discussed at length.[31] The result of a long-standing collaboration, published simultaneously in Hamburg and Paris, *Le Gauchisme remède à la maladie sénile du communisme* is henceforth the "theoretical" document of left-wing anarchism.[32] Set under the sign of the Paris Commune of 1871, the book is long ("concision and precision require a good deal of time" [7]) and was well subsidized: "the editors gave us a handsome sum (a down payment of fifty thousand German Marks to Danny Cohn-Bendit before a single line was written), although they (the capitalists) know that this money will be used to assemble Molotov cocktails, and because they believe that the revolution is impossible" (11). To a discerning reader: welcome! If the positions taken here repeat those seen everywhere in interviews and manifestos, the analysis of the plight of students (21–56) incessantly refers to these two fundamental points that a politics does not fail to contain or to overlook, that is, an atomization of individuals under the apparatus and the desire to replace it with an open-ended *communication* that could create a language and be created by action. Moreover, it takes up a crucial text, written prior to May, *De la misère en milieu étudiant*, published in Strasbourg in December 1966, in my opinion still by far the most lucid treatment of what in everyday jargon are called the "causes of the malaise."

After having furnished numerous details on the events of Paris (the UNEF emerges with a few bruises), the Cohn-Bendits' work extends into a vast critique of bolshevism and the Communist Party, with the goal of specifying a program based on self-management and on workers' councils. But the real program, the one that makes or breaks all the others, concerns *expression*, the characteristic trait of the Movement: "Every group must have its own form of expression, of information, integrating the outside into the life of the group and thus allowing a generalized form of expression to be nothing more than the coordinated sum of the autonomy of active collectivities" (270).

Political Commentaries

The "Contestation" collection that was born of the events (its title refers to them) has already inspired several essays. Jean Bloch-Michel draws a map of governmental stupidity and anachronism, but his generous adhesion to a "living revolution" does not give a precise definition to a program whose association with the name of Pierre Mendès-France remains, for him, sufficient.[33] Marc Paillet, one of the thinkers behind the FGDS [Federation of the Democratic and Socialist Left] assembles (and reconstitutes) in the May situation an ordering of political consciousness; he thus turns May into a program more than an event.[34] But this interpretation establishes a meeting point between facts to be recognized and a doctrine to be maintained, between a "utopia" to be mobilized and a "realism" to be respected. It is a "case" of political intelligence whose study will be more instructive than reading the book in which Jean-Jacques Servan-Schreiber assembles his hastily written articles for *L'Express* by exploiting the worthy success of his *Défi américain*.[35]

For its part, with the serenity of one who possesses a vast capital of information and experience, the Jean Moulin Club has put in the service of the revolution the results of its reflections. It proposes six priorities for action.[36] Through this small, dense, and well-conceived book, it claims to compensate for the deficit of the left ("which needs to adapt its thinking and its outlook to the concerns of our time" [13]) and that of the movement of May (which "has not found its language" [11]). It betrays a liberal and technocratic inspiration in each of six sectors (economy, enterprise, ORTF, university, etc.), through the untiring return to two principles: pluralism and concurrence.

The anthology of earlier writings published by the "Society" collection seems to me ultimately more suggestively rich, although it does not originate from such serene altitudes.[37]

To Explain or to Understand?

Beyond the facts, the perorations, and the pleas J. Jousselin uses to paint a great picture with all of his experience with youth;[38] after all the historians, collectors, and brokers who store the documents in freezers that readers remove and thaw for their needs; after the militants who fight with writings once their speech has been taken away, or who reconstitute a politics with the crumbs from the May table, now come those who "explain." The intellectual superstars. Those for whom we have been waiting with bated breath, such as Sirius [the pseudonym of Hubert Beuve-Méry, director of Le Monde until 1969], now tell us what we need to know if we want to "understand" what it was all about.

Four teachers, four seducers: the "polemologist" or artisan of war, a triumvirate of sociologists, an eminence of political sociology, a psychologist. Four important books, therefore. But now we've got to choose, since they don't agree! Or else we can read them all (they aren't long) and decide for ourselves.

André Glucksmann wants his thinking to serve as "a guide for action."[39] In an ironic and precise style, he shows how the ghost of the revolution has returned to haunt us, and how it gets embodied. A meticulous account, written in the style of Henry James. In order to prolong his image, it might be said that the ghost had a voice without a face: speech was the instrument of an egalitarian politics and a moral renewal. The second chapter analyzes the "depoliticization of society by the state" (the converse of a centralization that always leads the state to say: "I am the sole philosopher") and the nature of a movement that "gets right to repoliticization and de-statification." In unveiling what was latent—a power struggle—the crisis also reveals the contradictions, implied by their policies, between the theory and practice of the government or of the Communist Party: an "adaptation" has led each of them, according to Glucksmann, to practice the opposite of what they continue to preach in their programs. The end of the book flags (when the author has to define not a tactic, but a program of action), as if Glucksmann were packing his bags before going on summer vacation. Probably the most astute analysis of the events ends in a constellation of uncertain ideas. But that too is the sign of an action in search of a theory.

Of the trio of sociologists who are united under a label that alludes to one of Cohn-Bendit's slogans ("open the breach"),[40] the first is well known: Edgar Morin reedits the two series of articles he had published in Le Monde, of which the second (63–87) sketches the "dual character, both traditional and vanguardist," of the May revolution. That means going beyond the historical reminders on which the first series insisted ("The Student Commune"). It means starting a sequel that characterizes as original this combination of an archaism and a futurism, a crisis that is probably characteristic of a "society with a weak community" (86). Claude Lefort points to the "new space" created by the movement, this "nowhere" out of which emerge those who would challenge a society that tends to put everyone in his or her place: a formidable "nonplace" that is at once that of "irresponsibles" and of nonconformists. Jean-Marc Coudray offers a more constructive perspective; he seeks a "qualitative" change that will not be exiled from a quantitative organization; he does not accept that "rationality and imagination" are mutually exclusive (102).

The same publisher has issued a book in which Raymond Aron speaks of the "Trotskyists or anarchists such as Morin, Lefort, or Coudray."[41] The author spells it out clearly: it is first of all a "visceral" reaction against disorder, against the capitulation of the professors, against "the airhead aesthetes facing an ardent youth." A princely anger—a prince who has the stylishness to enumerate the antipathies from which he "profits," those of the left as well as those of General de Gaulle. That said (because Raymond Aron says so himself), he has written a great work, as impassioned as it is passionate. For, as his analysis progresses in its response to the questions posed by Alain Duhamel, the resistance of the event provokes him, it sharpens the prodigiously effective instrument that he has at his behest, it makes him hesitate and then move ahead again. This revolution is a psychodrama, a "collective delirium," a "comedy"; it is futile to talk with young people who are inebriated by their exploits; "we have to redo everything that went before, and then move on to something else." Such are the initial hypotheses. But he is led to take up the history of France, and discovers in it a reciprocity between "lightness" and centralization, between the ideology of brains and the rigidity of institutions. He extracts a doctrine—how necessary and yet how absent—of intermediary bodies. Moving further ahead, he declares, "One of the lessons that I draw from the events is that modern societies are more fragile than we thought" (44). Can he still conclude that the "accident" is merely a comedy? He stops there. However, violence erupts everywhere (46). The electoral success of Gaullism "has not unified France. France remains divided" (105). There is a "general crisis of authority and of obedience" (109). "We know from now on that behind the facade of order hides a potential for insurrection whose power even the most skeptical observer cannot misunderstand" (131).

And then he turns away, unable to forget it, from the crisis of civilization evoked by Malraux. His clear and vigorous sentence is extinguished with dark forebodings (152–53), after lengthily circling a disquiet that he must — and wants to — reject. Thus an order, a stabilization, seem as "impossible to find" as the revolution! But Raymond Aron prefers not to realize it. He refuses something other than a political surface. He holds on to a raft that, he knows well, has no mooring.

Épistémon, for his part, is more optimistic and serene.[42] He is the sage who lives in Berserk City, a professor on the faculty at Nanterre. He knows that in "understanding change means to be changed" (12). "I'll only speak," he admits, "of things that I have lived in flesh and blood." He will thus confine himself to the student riots with which he felt solidarity without losing his critical judgment and his own point of view. Thus he had to wonder, "With what concepts can they be thought?" (66). He interprets the event as a psychosociologist, as an immense group dynamic; speech plays a central role in it because, ultimately, the problem being posed is that of a *relation*. As his title indicates, he also sees in the riots the consequence ("the incubation") of ideas that have been professed in France for a decade, and, with a professor's nervous tic, the victory of certain professors over others — the victory of Rogers over Lacan, of Sartre over the structuralists, in short the confirmation of his own teaching. He avows, however, that "we cannot know what the human being is nor what he will become" (110). Victory cannot be taken for granted, after all! But, far from being terrified by a crisis caused by the discrediting of a knowledge that no longer guarantees power, he discerns a promise and a task, that of a new culture. Placed under the sign of Erasmus and Rabelais, going by the pseudonym of Épistémon (an accomplice of Pantagruel's ambitions), this honest, deft, and astute book opens up the perspective of a "second Renaissance."

From this standpoint, *statements* leave open the question of *power*. True for the *speech* of the past, is it no less true for the *writing* of today? What, after all, are we to *do* with all of this literature, whether written or still to be written?

Chapter 6
A Literature of Disquiet:
A Year Later

A society that has become incapable of reflecting on itself—that is what, above all, the writing inspired by the events of May 1968 has opened in the continuity of time, in a language of prosperity, in the social sciences, and in politics itself. Since the school year began in October, more than seventy books have accumulated—and the list is not complete—that diversify and transpose the same doubt (at least that is a personal way of reading them). The immensity of the information spread out before us (and which is still being written), and the rich variety of so much lucidity (which still wavers, but with a few exceptions), form the moving, agitated, but also indefinite surface of a more pervasive interrogation imposed on the nation at large. It comes with the decisive, although ephemeral, experience of its fragility, along with the fatality, the desire, or the risk of having to change things, accompanied by the urgency and the fear of another style of communication.

There is something momentous in this confrontation with one-self, in the fever of the body infected by such a splinter. To be sure, every normally constituted person will ultimately be irritated by the endless repetition of the same titles, the same pictures, the same posters, and the same headlines, in short, by the tautology of this rhetoric broadcast once and for all (the originality of each publisher lies merely in the slogan on the red paper label on every new book). We also need to take account of what is meant by the hypocritical attention drawn to an "event" for which a "souvenir" needs to be made so that, in the mirages of information or erudite knowledge, it will rejoin other centenaries, other pasts commemorated with the certainty that it is a question of dead heroes, and other legends that make apple pie of the past and leave us in the satisfaction of inaction. All that being said, there remains the question that each of these books takes up in its own way, mulls over, and leaves aside in order to take up again, but that cannot be avoided. Perhaps in this way May 1968 *is becoming* an event: in what we are required to *make* less of it. For the works on May 1968 that emerge from or are preceded by so many studies, seminars, and colloquiums, reveal a fundamental "disquiet" far more than they overcome it.[1]

This disquiet must not be confused with a psychological pathos. It is of the order of a fact. In itself it is neither bad nor "dramatic." It refers merely to a *change of arena* (but which? opinions differ), from which follows a gap between the available instruments in relation to the situation to which they are applied. Between the operative procedures (public institutions, social sciences, and the like) and a "reality" that escapes them, a dangerous, indeterminate rift opens up an area of play in the mechanism, and the resulting transmission becomes unsure. Thus appears the psychosocial "disquiet"; thus, to the fear of disorder (with its entire decor of collective phantasms) responds a violent need for security.

The books on May 1968 are riveted to this connection; they look for the missing or ill-fitting piece. Everyone opens the hood and bends over the engine. Everyone presses around. Everyone has his or her opinion and indicates the cause of the breakdown. From one angle, all these discourses start to resemble a comedy. From another, they touch on the essential and are a manifest sign of it. In this respect, the true literature about May 1968 is already less (and will soon cease to be) the one that talks about it. After a first span of time, that of the chroniclers and of defensive or apologetic reactions, after a second span of time of analyses centered on the event, comes a third one of self-reflection for each human science and each institution. They all attempt to elucidate the questions that have been asked, through interpretative deficiencies or failures in action, their difficulty in accommodating, in thinking about the present and changing it, in avoiding the alternative between a pragmatism endowed with *useful* myths and a production of *utopian* theories. A surfeit of strategies, methodologies, and epistemologies picks up where the last episodes of the "May 68" soap opera left off. They are no longer attracted to the historical object but to the instruments of thought and of action that it brought forth. They already indicate, by way of the books written on the event, their intent and their method.

Understood in this way, despite the diversity of their origins, the seventy books sketch out a limited number of problematic "places." Like a pile of maps of different scales and proportions that are laid one on the other, they recoup each other. Here and there, in red or in green, along contours and relief, corresponding forms can be discerned. Putting them together is a first way of classifying a mass in which the topography of the questions is less heterogeneous than the explanations or the proposed itineraries. Here we can retain only a few points that catch the reflection.

Reflective Points

The authority crisis. It not only affected families, employers, leading organizations, and the state, but also power (held to be illegitimate), knowledge (an accomplice of power under the appearance of neutrality), culture (accused of being repressive), patriotism (seen as a relic of the past), party ideologies (contrary to the interests they in fact serve), and so on. Everything that "seemed to have authority" has been marked by the same suspicion: what motives are hidden behind it?

How can this crisis be explained? Responses get juxtaposed, but they never meet or touch one other. A political interpretation calls into question the present obsolescence of public powers, which reinforces the traditional rigidity of French society: on occasion, and by way of compensation, the body breaks its corset, but thereby only submits further to its constraints, after a few reforms caused by these "revolutions" (Raymond Aron). A socioeconomic interpretation refers to the disparate shifts of business enterprises (some being "meso-modern," others "neomodern") and to the ultimately explosive gamut of mixed developments in which the university, representing an extremely archaic position, is seen as constituting a new, marginal and revolutionary, proletariat (Alain Touraine). Still another, of sociocultural designation, opposes the minority of the "hard-core radicals" to the enormity of their influence, and chalks up all the noise to the mass media, deceivers and the deceived (Raymond Boudon at the Sorbonne, or Sadoun at the IFOP [French Institute of Public Opinion], etc.). The upsurge of youth is an equally valid explanation: generational conflict has been quickly aggravated by values, responsibilities, and autonomy that make young people, represented by students and flattered or supported by an intelligentsia, into the Anabaptists of consumer society (Henri Lefebvre, etc.). Finally, prophetic-type intuitions discern in the challenging of authority a "crisis of civilization" (André Malraux) or a "metaphysical crisis" (Jacques Maritain).

The relation between the past and the present. Here is another site of questioning: is the event a repetition or an inauguration? Is it a resurgence of something archaic, a resistance to evolution, or is it rather "a beginning," the premises of a revolution? Is it 1848 in relation to 1789, or 1905 in relation to 1917? From the first days of May 1968, Edgar Morin raised the issue and wondered how archaism and futurism were being articulated.

The equally opposed responses constrain researchers to wonder what criteria we have at our disposal to decide what is an *event* and what is not. Either constituted "reasons" (psychosociologies, philosophies of history, political theories, party programs) easily digest the facts, the exploding mass of which provide enough grist to nourish every thesis, or else the event is turned into a principle allowing every explanation to be contested and displaced. In any case, the interpretation takes no distance in relation to the current events it addresses; it is relative to an option that it develops but does not justify. Is it therefore impossible to analyze what changes in the present time?[2] Are social sciences destined to be blind to the new and know only what is homogeneous?

The fantastic. For a long time the imaginary, introduced into culture through science fiction, television, and the stereotypes of the news item, seems to have acquired a determining role in national life.[3] The events of May 1968 allegedly made manifest to what point a society functions today as a "fiduciary" system; all operations within it are carried out in terms of "representations" that postulate but never display the real, which is as absent as gold and silver are in credit. Hence the impact of the protests that call "confidence" into question, oblige power and knowledge to acknowledge themselves as "metaphorical" (Merle), and, moreover, replace a mythology of order and well-being with that of a society without conflict and of a paradisiacal democracy.

This reenchantment of the country is betrayed by the "magic" sign that affects an entire grounding vocabulary and that turns the terms being used (contestation, revolution, apparatus, order, fascism, etc.) into imaginary categories, into keys to the universe, into diabolical or salvational symbols. This is the case in particular for those drawn from Marxism (class, bourgeois, capitalism, etc.) or Freudianism (Oedipus, the death of the father, desire, projection, etc.). Divided between the good and the bad, constructed according to the schema of a fable ("me and chaos," "the system or freedom"), pulling every proposition in the direction of either the "revolutionaries" or the "fascists," the language of a society would be organized like that of a comic strip. The phenomenon is understood by some as something superficial, by others as a new and decisive element. In order to decide, everyone would have to take reality for granted and find a ground for such judgments, which float like rafts on an endless ocean.

A reality in shreds. Enigmatic *passages* from one "time" to another in the course of the month of May (from the student rebellion to the labor strikes, from the latter to the political crisis) also show how problematic are the conditions of every science and the relations among disciplines. "Serious" time (which will decide what meaning to give to the remainder) is in fact determined according to a personal investment and a professional competence. The cracks in the real refer to the divisions among knowledges and the tightness of the lids screwed on national sectors. The breakage that came with May 1968 has shattered in every direction. Thus sociologists will wonder if their interpretations are not resulting from an insufficient clarification of their relations with the powers that be, from a lack of effective relations with them, and from the partition that separates them from psychologists, historians, and politicians. From the connections that need to be established among facts, the question goes all the way back to the flow of communication that must be restored among different methods.

Interdisciplinarity. This constant of all technical literature on the topic is an indication of the pressure that evocation of "totality" (as Lucien Goldmann tirelessly repeats the term) exerts on the social sciences. It is translated by the appeals, winks, or flights by every discipline when it wanders outside of its own field. It often responds to the need to fill the gaps, in each interpretation, of what it leaves unexplained. Thus, having to admit that they cannot account for everything, sociologists or politicians find themselves facing a "remainder." They will relegate this leftover of their analysis to psychoanalysis or they will baptize it in the name of something "spiritual." The unconscious and the spiritual thus represent an irreducible element that is so in-

definite that anything that defies understanding can easily be attributed to them. Thus strange hybrids are born, aberrant combinations
of psychology and psychoanalysis, recourses of explanation unwar-
ranted for a spirituality that is generally pigeonholed in the name of
sorcery.[4] Borrowed from another science or from religion, a "scientific" explanation only retains what it needs to plug up its holes.

᾿ Similar syncretisms express no less the necessity for exchange
among disciplines, with a view to inaugurating a global set of problems. Every serious book bumps into a totality but is incapable of
grasping it. Among other things, the designation of this horizon has
blown the "cultural" all out of proportion. "Culture" has become a
conceptual putty that can be squeezed and shaped for any purpose,
at once necessary (because of the problem treated) and deceptive (because it no longer states anything precise). Thus, the conjugation (or
the succession) of the crisis and of structures, of mobility and of continuity, remains the latent problem in all these texts, the stimulus to
thinking, just as it is, in the lectures of specialists invited to confer-
ences on the topic of May 1968, the center of conversation.

The intellectual in society. Behind the leftover, a last question concerns
the authors themselves. For if intellectuals are so ill equipped to furnish a nation with its instruments of thought, then what place do they
have? What can they *do*? A dizziness sweeps them off their feet. After having formed a substantial group in the beginnings of the rebellion, are intellectuals now those most victimized by it? Or are they
witnessing a situation in which they are the first to be affected? Many
works take up the topic, even apart from May 1968.

The reform of the university, its role in the nation, the relations
of researchers with industry or public administration, the insertion of
university faculty into regional areas, the relations to establish among
students and workers (this last point representing the students' most
recent demand)—all these objects being studied and debated re-
volve around one of the initial questions of May that has since been
endlessly repeated, that of *the intellectual and politics.*[5] Far away on
the horizon is the wonderfully naive conviction of Épistémon, per-
suaded that the professor is producing "thoughts that will turn France
topsy-turvy." And obsolete, too, the intellect à la Sartre, who certainly has the courage to bet on audacity, but who, with words, throws
gasoline on the fire and uses his authority as a writer to bless and
sign copies (and the student responds with a "Thank you, daddy").

But to a great man who ages so badly (it is sad to say), who varnishes a somewhat senile sympathy over everything said to be young and "revolutionary," to other gurus who play, dazzle, seduce, escape, but who never dig into things, correspond, in the case of others, the scorn for theory, the utopias that lose sight of necessary causes, "spontaneity," and "prophecy"; which are the victims of their old slogans — a sign that the rigor of reflection is the indispensable counterpart of a true praxis.

If, as Alain Touraine believes and as facts demonstrate, university faculties are losing their importance (not quantitative, but qualitative) in the totality of higher education, and if they are being proletarianized and suffer on account of the events, all the while the elite schools have profited by their demise, strengthening their own social and scientific advantages, it is because of the recruitment of university teachers (more massive and more modest), their type of training (less narrowly defined), the careers offered (less and less guaranteed by diploma and the "old guard"), and so on. But I believe that the prosperity of more technical courses, which are better inserted into professional training, is compensated for through their limitation and that, perhaps, the "lowering" of the faculties is *also* relative to a more pervasive insufficiency of an independent form of thinking, critical and "global" in quality, that, for example, refers economics back to its historical assumptions and to the philosophy of man invested in an economic or urban model.[6] Bound by a similar "misery" (even if the one appears to be the opposite of the other), the professor and the student show the nation its own incapacity to reflect on itself. Equally stripped of their national prestige, they are accused, one of incapacity, the other for petit bourgeois banditry, but in the name of an unjust group reaction that accuses its most visible witnesses of evil, which leads a party or a church to exclude its intellectuals for not having to think, which rejects academics as witches and attests, with this very gesture, to the imagination and the fears (and perhaps, tomorrow, the terrors) with which their absence is dearly paid. Their deficiency too. That so many journals that used to be so incisive and so committed are today emptied of content, and that an intelligentsia takes refuge in esoteric salons, is the other side of the same fact, the very object of refusal and of protests since the beginning of May 1968.

No one wins with the separation of (rigorous) intelligence and (true) politics. Wherever it is serious, the literature on May 1968 is a meaningful reflection at once centered on and torn by a violent event that observation fragments into multiple images ("the events") and that political unity reconstitutes from a national commotion. It is its interest in being a laboratory, even if the questions are progressively detached from the fact that posited them, even if they are henceforth elaborated merely for themselves.

An Annotated Bibliography

The books below have been classified according to their subject and their nature, with only a few remarks that might orient choices and readings. Reflective works have been placed at the head of the list since, from now on — Alain Schnapp and Pierre Vidal-Naquet's dossier excepted — they represent qualitatively the most important part of this literature. If only two books could be kept out of all of them, they would be, it can be said directly, the works of Alain Touraine and Schnapp and Vidal-Naquet.

A. Political Analyses

1. General Studies and Essays

Jean Ferniot, *Mort d'une Révolution. La Gauche de mai* (Paris: Denoël, "Réflexions," 1968), 238 pp. Analysis of a fundamental problem: the collapse of the left and the disintegration of the opposition. Easy to read and must be thought through.

Jérôme Ferrand, *La Jeunesse, nouveau Tiers-État* (Paris: Robert Laffont, "Contestation," 1968), 108 pp. More general than informative.

André Fontaine, *La Guerre civile froide* (Paris: Fayard, "Les grandes études contemporaines," 1969), 194 pp. A journalist for *Le Monde,* the author knows how to speak of Sirius. Somewhat academic but objective, his analysis is no less remarkable, one of those that best situates the "revolution" of May in the international context.

François Fonvieille-Alquier, *Les Illusionnaires* (Paris: Robert Laffont, "Contestation," 1968), 196 pp. An open letter: daddy writes a friendly letter to youth and encourages a realistic point of view.

Max Gallo, *Gauchisme, Réformisme et Révolution* (Paris: Robert Laffont, "Contestation," 1968), 190 pp. An important historical study (65–103) provides its precedents on the grounds that the "left" breaks away from "leftism." How can the "good" revolution be distinguished from the "bad"? The way that the question is formulated becomes the focus of this impassioned and passionate essay.

Gilles Martinet, *La Conquête de pouvoirs* (Paris: Seuil, "L'histoire immédiate," 1968), 192 pp. A history in the past conditional — what should have been done — accompanies a severe, lucid, but also rather narrow-minded criticism of the tactics adopted by the instigators of the May riots. The marriage that the author celebrates between socialism and productivity is probably more "reasonable."

André Philip, *Mai 68 et la Foi démocratique* (Paris: Aubier, "Histoire du travail et de la vie économique," 1968), 144 pp. A noble thought, tied to the event, and that refuses to dissociate from "spiritual engagement" a detailed observation.

Also worthy of note: Général Beaufre, *L'Enjeu du désordre, De la contagion révolutionnaire à la guerre atomique* (Paris: Grasset, 1969), 188 pp. The specialist of polemology embraces, through a fascinating inventory, the international context in which war and revolution are combined. A "calm man," lucid and impressive for all of his honesty, faces up to the universe in peril and the question "What can be done?" For May, see pp. 122–31.

2. Communist Options

Annie Kriegel, *Les Communistes français* (Paris: Seuil, "Politique," 1968), 320 pp. The author, who left the party, presents in her conclusion (231–56), in a remarkable picture, the problems facing the Communists during May and the logic of their reactions. Clearly it is not an "orthodox" analysis.

Claude Prévost, *Les Étudiants et le Gauchisme* (Paris: Éditions Sociales, "Notre Temps," 1969), 190 pp. Published in March 1969 and dated "summer 1968" (why the delay?), the book is polemical, as could be expected, but has a first part that is well informed and very helpful on "the ideological themes of leftism" (17–83).[7]

Waldeck Rochet, *Les Enseignements de mai-juin 1968* (Paris: Éditions Sociales, "Notre Temps," 1968), 96 pp. A program, not an analysis, but for that reason an important work. Also, *Qu'est-ce qu'un révolutionnaire dans la France de notre temps?* (Paris: Éditions Sociales, "Notre Temps," 1968), which, in my opinion, is more exact and more interesting.

Laurent Salini, *Mai des prolétaires* (Paris: Éditions Sociales, "Notre Temps," 1968), 176 pp. The book adds nothing to what could have been stated beforehand.

3. "Leftist" Views

André Barjonet, *La Révolution trahie de 1968* (Paris: John Didier, 1968), 45 pp. The book was already reviewed in the preceding chapter (note 37), but to it must be added *La CGT* (Paris: Seuil, "Politique," 1968), 192 pp., which provides the author's choices with a union backdrop and positive content.

Daniel Bensaïd and Henri Weber, *Mai 1968: Une répétition générale* (Paris: Maspero, "Cahiers libres," 1968), 160 pp. Explaining with a great deal of clarity the views of the Revolutionary Communist Youth (JCR), this notebook is probably the first book that needs to be read, and perhaps the only book, for an understanding of a position that is too often hidden in action and slogans.[8]

Action Committee for Health and Medicine, *Ce texte n'est qu'un début* (Paris: Maspero, "Cahiers libres," 1968). A statement of principles that has been superseded by more detailed studies.

Gilbert Mury, *La Société de répression* (Paris: Éditions Universitaires, "Citoyens," 1969), 334 pp. At once a chronicle, a program, a synthesis, and a partial epic of the century for a defense and illustration of Maoism. The reader is made dizzy by this voice that knows so much and says the same thing over and over again. It has to be heard. Taking up Marcusian theses on the society of repression, it makes inadaptation the cause of the problems and also their goal.[9] Especially noteworthy is an interesting study of "spontaneity" (123–32).

4. The Government's Side

Edgar Faure, *L'Éducation nationale et la participation* (Paris: Plon, "Tribune libre," 1968), 124 pp. The speech of July 24, 1968, is reprinted with a new appendix — in short, a summary of the Faure bill.[10] A "liberal" opens up culture and closes the door on politics.

Raymond Marcellin, *L'Ordre public et les Groupes révolutionnaires* (Paris: Plon, "Tribune libre," 1968), 128 pp. Some hypotheses that have not changed and that are worth mulling over.

Two more books that ought to be placed in the space that separates the two preceding titles:

Maurice Druon, *L'Avenir en désarroi* (Paris: Plon, 1968), 120 pp. Some rather disengaged yet disquieting thoughts: are the ill winds of the time blowing over the perch of Zeus? The reader is informed but not convinced.

Alain Griotteray, *Des Barricades ou des réformes?* (Paris: Fayard, 1969), 70 pp. Starting from an examination of the issues put before the administration, a program — decentralization — and a simple hypothesis: if it doesn't work, it's the fault of the Communists.

B. The University Crisis

There is a whole literature by professors on the university. It alone would be worth an extensive study. It offers several formulas: either it is restricted to the space inside of the wall of the academic institution, caught in the moat and thrown to the lions or jubilant on a Canary Island, or it reads into the university crisis the signs of a crisis affecting French society as a whole, or it prefers to analyze the evolution of the student milieu toward becoming a new proletariat and the possible links between wage earners and students.

Above all else, the following exceptional books need to be read:

Antoine Prost, *L'Enseignement en France, 1800–1967* (Paris: Armand Colin, "U," 1968), 524 pp. A clear and precise presentation detached from a history that has shaped French culture. Accompanied by documents that are indispensable tools of research, this book tells of the politics, and also the crusade, of a teaching "body" that remained a defrocked clergy, with an orthodoxy as intransigent as it is apostolic.

Bernard Andrey and Louis Millet, *La Révolution universitaire. L'expérience de l'Institut de psychologie de Grenoble* (Paris: Bordas, 1968), 76 pp. Finally, a concrete experience that is studied with a lot of acuity. Essential reading because it is short but informative.

Jean Chardonnet, *L'Université en question* (Paris: France-Empire, 1968), 176 pp. Quite polemical in their criticism of the illness of "reformity" and hardly liberal, the author's hypotheses are based on a rich exposure to facts and bring into view ample data on the conditions of student life in higher education (105–38).

Jacques Drèze and Jean Debelle, *Conceptions de l'Université* (Paris: Éditions Universitaires, "Citoyens," 1969), 200 pp., with a preface by Paul Ricoeur. Long known for his studies on the role of the university in many countries (for example, at UNESCO), Drèze provides, with Debelle, a clear summary of his thoughts on very diverse situations. He broadens and clarifies the question. The book will be read as one by a wise citizen of the world, even if his tendency to separate problems of *intellect* from those of *power* gives pause.

Guy Michaud, *Révolution dans l'Université* (Paris: Classiques Hachette, 1968), 144 pp. A little too much of a chronicle to offer anything new.

Jacques Perret, *Inquiète Sorbonne* (Paris: Classiques Hachette, 1968), 128 pp. The book of an informed person who was attentive and present at the events but unable to "understand" them. There is something pathetic about this meditation. It should be read as the autobiography of hundreds of other professors who were trained for a world that is now disappearing. Refined Latin scholar that he is, Perret, in order perhaps to bring more hope to what he chronicles, ought to add to his moving eyewitness account a commentary on Saint Augustine's thoughts after the fall of Rome. There is no proportion between the two events, but surely there is between liberties.

André Piettre, *La Culture en question. Sens et non-sens d'une révolte* (Paris: Desclée de Brouwer, 1969), 228 pp. "Humanism" is here the stronghold opposed to protest, to subversive philosophies, and to a new "betrayal by priests." The author believes that he clearly knows what the "meaning" is in whose name he battles against the hydra of meaninglessness. The security of the position taken would today make many people envious.

Jacqueline de Romilly, *Nous autres professeurs. Ces maîtres que l'on conteste* (Paris: Fayard, 1969), 122 pp. This formula "the rest of us" says a lot about the work, but quite often its provocative character is deceptive, for it covers a keen analysis on this métier (this artisanal activity) of teaching Greek. "Protest" causes the professor to confess what she had kept secret or buried in her work.

Jules Vuillemin, *Rebâtir l'Université* (Paris: Fayard, "Le Monde sans frontières," 1968), 84 pp. This plan for reform, formerly audacious and based on extensive experience, is a good working paper and meditation. Especially noteworthy are the pages dedicated to a subject too infrequently studied: the *grandes écoles* (71–79), the "elite" formation so dear to the author.

Works that are products of teachers must be distinguished from analyses published by professional sociologists:

Paul-Henry Chombart de Lauwe, *Pour l'Université. Avant, pendant et après mai 1968* (Paris: Payot, 1969), 176 pp. The debate over the university is referred to history (since the notorious Langevin-Wallon plan) and to the totality of national life. This dossier thus addresses the relation that teaching holds with the city (67–78), human sciences with the established powers (97–112), or interdisciplinarities (113–42).

Jean-Jacques Robert, *Un plan pour l'Université, du primaire au supérieur* (Paris: Plon, "Tribune libre," 1968), 170 pp. An earlier text (1967) that the flow of events has brought back to the bookstores. Already a document, it is also a little too "coherent" to avoid the utopian style, but for that reason it remains useful. Reform cannot be implemented without a history of its preparations.

C. Sociologies of the Crisis

In this sector we find the big books. They envision either the new "dispatching" of groups and their tensions in an unevenly industrialized society (see Alain Touraine), or the unforeseen relations that introduce into the "society of abundance" the claims of a different youth, a new force that all the while is alienated by what it protests (see Edgar Morin, Touraine, etc.).

Alain Touraine, *Le Mouvement de Mai ou le Communisme utopique* (Paris: Seuil, 1968), 304 pp. Even if the edges are slightly blurred, it is still the most remarkable of all studies on the topic. The concept of an "antisociety" becomes a useful and exact concept that studies the depth of economic, demographic, and sociological data and allows them to be taken into account. In many other fields of research, Touraine's "model" will be useful. Whoever is more or less interested in social sciences should read this book.

Henri Lefebvre, *L'Irruption de Nanterre au sommet* (Paris: Anthropos, 1968), 178 pp. To this study that is placed under the flag of "Sociology and Revolution" must be added *Introduction à la Modernité* (Paris: Minuit, 1962) — which became the bible of so many "situationists" — and *Le Droit à la ville*, rev. ed. (Paris: Seuil, "Points," 1974). Some dazzling but fugacious intuitions envelop lightning bolts and long nights of reflection always fixed on the relationship between ideologies and institutions. The book must be read in segments, but also as fragments that are everywhere scintillating and that predict a political sociology of change. In this respect, Henri Lefebvre is unique.

D. "Cultural" Essays

Maurice Clavel, *Combat de franc-tireur pour une libération* (Paris: Pauvert, 1968), 208 pp. A reedition of articles that first appeared in the *Le Nouvel Observateur* and *Combat*, the book in inhabited by a voice. It is also an inner debate between an irreducible element of conscience and a loving spite with respect to Gaullism.

Manuel de Diéguez, *De l'idolâtrie. Discours aux clercs et aux derviches* (Paris: Gallimard, "Les Essais," 1969), 300 pp. In a comic tone, but a comedy affected by the events of May and veiled with an incredible nostalgia, a mobile, inquisitive, suggestive discourse on the political role of ideology and the intellectuals. This "priest" still spits fire.

A. Jelokhovtsev, *La Révolution culturelle vue par un Soviétique*. Paris: Robert Laffont, "Contestation," 1968), 240 pp. China "seen by a Soviet": the publisher is prudent. Nonetheless, a gold mine of information.

Jacques-Arnaud Penent, *Un Printemps rouge et noir* (Paris: Robert Laffont, "Contestations," 1968), 184 pp. Included here because of the picturesque and "sly" chapter (123–69) in which the reporter for *Combat* studies expression, the press, and writers.

E. Documents

The pile is enormous. It is the biggest of all categories. The fundamental work, the "annotated dossier of the May movement," needs to be put at the head of the list:

Alain Schnapp and Pierre Vidal-Naquet, *Journal de la Commune étudiante. Textes et documents. Novembre 1967–juin 1968* (Paris: Seuil, "La Cité prochaine," 1969), 880 pp. (second, enlarged edition in the collection "L'univers historique," 1988). The Introduction alone, by Pierre Vidal-Naquet, is worth an entire book, offering at once data and their interpretation. Then 362 documents are dated, explained, and situated before being followed, in accord with the strictest norms of academic research, bibliographies and very complete "indexes." In this work by historians, almost everything will be found on both "myths" and tactics. It is a pyrotechnic display at the end of an immense labor undertaken by the Seuil publishing house in this domain and, from now on, *the* basic book on the subject.

In addition to the latter, some productions of varying density and content:

1. Student Struggles throughout the World

Combats étudiants dans le monde—Berkeley, Berlin, Rome, Madrid, Tokyo, Ankara, Belgrade, Prague, Rio, Varsovie, Mexico (Paris: Seuil, 1968), 320 pp. With many documents and exact chronologies, this impressive inventory nevertheless exerts pressure on the texts in the name of ideology that assembles or isolates them, thus, from their context.

L'Hypothèse révolutionnaire. Documents sur les luttes étudiantes à Trente, Turin, Naples, Pise, Milan et Rome (Paris: Mercure de France, 1968), 270 pp. By M. Thurlotte, the same translator as for the *Lettre à une maîtresse d'école par les enfants de Barbiana* (Paris: Mercure de France, 1968), the dossier is for Italy the equivalent of Schnapp-Vidal-Naquet's, but much less complete. The relation of Italian students with a political tradition, quite different from what happened in France, seems much more rich and, at least with academic institutions, more concrete (perhaps because on every occasion the "struggle" is more specific in relation to a regional university).

2. Students and the French University

Jean Bertolino, *Les "Trublions"* (Paris: Stock, 1969), 420 pp. Written by a talented journalist, this is a series of portraits and comic, perspicacious news flashes restricted to the first days of May. Two well-documented chapters are devoted to *groupuscules* (83–154) and to Nanterre (223–382).

High School Action Committees, *Les Lycées gardent la parole* (Paris: Seuil, "Politique," 1968), 156 pp. The future is being made in these laboratories, which are quite different from the mercurial and anonymous "masses" of students. The works presented here are almost entirely dedicated, it will be noted, to structures of secondary education, to the disciplines taught in them, and to the social postulates of culture. An impassioned, stimulating, and comforting reading.

P. Feuerstein, *Printemps de révolte à Strasbourg. Mai-juin 1968* (Strasbourg: Saisons d'Alsace, 1968), 116 pp. A history that has been overlooked (especially important, however, because of the "situationist" movements that preceded the May crisis), as is always the case whenever it is a question of the French provinces.

Michelle Perrot, Madeleine Rebérioux, and Jean Maitron, *La Sorbonne par elle-même. Mai-juin 68,* in *Le Mouvement social,* no. 64 (1968), 416 pp. The collection, the most exact and complete on the Sorbonne, is a major part of the dossier. (Jean Maitron is in charge of bringing together the archives of the student movement at the Institute for the History of the Labor Movement at the Sorbonne.)

Pierre Peuchmaurd, *Plus vivants que jamais* (Paris: Robert Laffont, "Contestation," 1968), 176 pp. Diary of a summer that burns with the memories of a student who moves and laughs in his writing.

La Remise en cause de l'Université, in *Les Sciences de l'éducation* (July 1968), 288 pp. Includes many documents, especially on the provincial universities and the preparatory schools, but "in disorder."

UNEF-SNESup, *Ils accusent* (Paris: Seuil, "Combats," 1968), 288 pp. Dossier that is aimed against "repression." But (is it a shameful amnesia or the consequence of an excess in the pleas?) too many real deaths have since dulled these invectives, there now being too many current problems that prevail over the past recounted here.

3. "Situationists"

Éliane Brau, *Le Situationnisme ou la Nouvelle Internationale* (Paris: Nouvelles Éditions Debresse, "Révolte," 1968), 192 pp. Whether one likes it or not, the best analyses of the student situation come to us through the current that Élaine Brau presents here, with a strong bibliography (172–85). They have, furthermore, the rare quality of being as amusing as they are lucid. It is in addition quite strange here to see an orthodoxy searching for its identity, something that is both necessary and contradictory.

R. Viénet, *Enragés et Situationnistes dans le mouvement des occupations* (Paris: Gallimard, "Témoins," 1968), 320 pp. Well documented on the relations between situationist students and workers.

4. Workers and Labor Unions

Philippe Bauchard and M. Buzeck, *Le Syndicalisme à l'épreuve* (Paris: Robert Laffont, "Le Monde qui se fait," 1968), 368 pp. A review of meetings, rich in facts and reactions, the book needs to be set next to those of Barjonet (see chapter 5, note 37).

Juliette Minces, *Un ouvrier parle* (Paris: Seuil, "Combats," 1969), 96 pp. A voice finally comes out of a silence that contrasts with the student clamor — the voice of a militant. A text of the first order that should be read before most of the others.

5. The Churches

In addition to the work presented by Robert Davezies, and in addition to a chapter by André Philip (*Mai 68 et la Foi démocratique*, 78–86, mentioned in section A1), see the following:

M.-J. Le Guillou, Olivier Clément, and Jean Bosc, *Évangile et Révolution au cœur de notre crise spirituelle* (Paris: Centurion, 1969), 128 pp. How can one not turn a revolution into a new politics drawn from Scripture and, from the adaptation, a trivialization of what is irreducible? Confronting this two-pronged question is a book with a violent title but a sagacious answer.

Jean Marny, *L'Église contestée. Jeunes chrétiens révolutionnaires* (Paris: Centurion, 1968), 254 pp. On Catholic Action, especially its students, recent information indicates the end of the movements whose ups and downs played an important role.

Robert Serrou, *Dieu n'est pas conservateur* (Paris: Robert Laffont, "Contestations," 1968), 272 pp. Placed under a word of Monsignor Marty (at that time the archibishop of Paris), many things that the journalist for *Paris-Match* saw and that, as usual, he "nails down" with art and conviction.

Un Geste risqué: L'Euchariste de Pentecôte 1968, in *Christianisme social*, nos. 7–10, 385–592. Important "reflections" are added to the documents (493–588) on the foundation of a unified expression and its relationship to religious divisions or political dissent.

6. Chronicles

Christian Charrière, *Le Printemps des Enragés* (Paris: Fayard, 1968), 428 pp. *Paris-Soir*, but in book form.

Roger Gascon, *La Nuit du Pouvoir ou le 24 mai manqué* (Paris: Nouvelles Éditions Debresse, 1968), 124 pp. A broad and much-debated topic: was power vacant? In response, a rather colorful, but also sordid, testimony by a former "student bouncer." Edifying information on preparations for the elections.

L. Rioux and R. Backmann, *11 mai 68. L'Explosion de mai* (Paris: Robert Laffont, "Ce jour-là," 1968), 616 pp. A very circumstantial account, the best of its kind.

J.-R. Tournoux, *Le Mois de mai du Général* (Paris: Plon, 1969), 512 pp. Hale and hearty, right on the nose, in short, a marvelous historian who also knows the fine lines and keeps hidden the secrets that are not to be revealed. (See also Philippe Alexandre, *L'Élysée en péril* [Paris: Fayard, 1968], 336 pp.)

Pâquerette Villeneuve, *Une Canadienne dans les rues de Paris pendant la révolte étudiante, mai 1968* (Montreal: Éditions du Jour, "Cahiers de la Cité libre," 1968). No, not Zazie, but if I may be permitted, Bécassine in Paris. Touching, irritating, and really quite funny.

7. ORTF, Films, Posters

Roger Louis, *L'ORTF: Un combat* (Paris: Seuil, "Combats," 1968), 192 pp. A study of French national television that supplements those published before October and that only whetted our appetite: an important testimonial and a harsh judgment on the syndicated labor unions.

Christian Bouyer, *Odéon est ouvert* (Paris: Nouvelles Éditions Debresse, 1968), 124 pp. Provides a filmography. But, for the most part, it deals with private documentaries available only in inner circles. Godard is going to produce his own, *Un Film comme les autres*, in which a voice, a prisoner of a small and faceless group, is the sole actor. Other films are being awaited (see Yvette Romi, "Que sont devenus les films de mai?" *Le Nouvel Observateur* [April 14–20, 1969]).

L'Atelier populaire présenté par lui-même, 87 affiches de mai-juin 1968 (Paris: Usine, Université, Union, "Bibliothèque de mai," 1968), 96 pp. One of the rare serious collections.

In exiting the library of this immense literature, the reader is overwhelmed, without having been able to find its secret. But the key is at the bottom of the country, as if at the bottom of a well.

Part II

The Americas:
A Political Awakening

Chapter 7
Violent Mystics and Nonviolent Strategies

Violence or nonviolence: a number of Christians have delineated ideological positions according to this opposition. They probably still have practical implications but are built less and less on the efficacity of struggles or debates. The declarations of principles (for example: "Christianity condemns violence") obtain their force from political, ecclesiastical, and other groups that sustain them and in which they play a motivating role. That is how it works (and has worked) in countries where the coherence of the ecclesial institution held the capacity to organize the credibility of a struggle (for example, for order) and even furnished its protesters from within (those who announced the need for "violent" action) the point of support from which their opposition would have a political effect. But in most Latin American countries—although the case does not hold for Argentina or Bolivia—this situation changes with the shrinking of the powers that ecclesiastical institutions had at their disposal, with the divisions that national differences were introducing at an increasing rate, the rifts between classes and political divergences, or with the slow drift of original European religious groups (Catholics, Protestants, etc.) toward nationalist movements such as the Umbanda in Brazil,[1] corresponding to what Robert Bellah rightly called "civil religions."[2] On the fissured and moving ground of the churches, doctrinal declarations have much less impact or interest.

The same holds for political formations on the left when, crushed by an autocratic and/or military power, they have to move from "shot" to "shot." Their theories and programs for action in which Christian convictions have long played a decisive role, turn into symbolic memorials;[3] deprived of public or organic support, they disband and scatter in the polluted air of the mass media or withdraw into the secrecy of private conversations. The theory of the *foco* (focism), which dates from 1965, is already past.

Periodic interventions are kept at a distance from a common discourse. Too scattered to be controlled by the powers that be (the repression of one case does not affect all the others), they constitute an infinite number of socioeconomic laboratories in which people of very diverse origins are much less determined through their role as "delegates" of parties (and thus too as the representatives of the break between a militant vanguard and the masses) than through local collaborations in search of new formulas. A swarming at grassroots level, this proliferating activity probably removes much of their relevance to discussions of past years about violence or nonviolence. Thus one should rather analyze what directions this multiple writing takes in the opaque complexity of different areas, wedded to their falling back, moving, almost illegible. It is also a revolutionary murmur, across the indefinite plurality of "contracts of action" among laborers, peasants, prominent people, or intellectuals. A few indications suffice to evoke it.

The Guerrilla Martyr

Following the deaths of Father Camilo Torres, a Colombian priest killed on February 15, 1966, by the national army, Father Ildefonsa, killed in Uruguay, and Father Domingo Lain, shot on March 22, 1974, during a protest against government troops, a tradition developed that Michael McKale labels a "mystic guerrilla."[4] The tradition honors militant clerics. From their deaths an entire literature has taken shape consisting of stories, songs, and images. The blood of dead heroes has defined a site of meaning in which is symbolically sealed the alliance between Christian faith and revolution, and in which is recounted, at the same time, the ebb of guerrilla movements decimated by repression. These political Christs produce a *sign* that cannot be dissociated from their failure and that thus acquires a "spiritual" — much more than exemplary or strategic — value. This "evangelical" literature does not teach methods or tactics. It is, rather, the equivalent — in itself also a vehicle for mobilization — of the *lists of martyrs* that formerly inhabited Christian communities. It articulates a faith — its revolutionary violence — in a political arena. It constitutes a new Christian discourse.

"It matters little if they accuse me of being a guerrilla or a communist because, in a world in which three-quarters of the inhabitants are dying of hunger, what's the difference if they kill a simple person like myself?" This message, sent from Teoponte (Bolivia) by the Father José Prats in 1970, crystallizes many of the effects of this discourse.[5] Here, the misery of the people marries Christians to these two excommunicated figures of earlier times, the guerrilla and the "communist." A hagiography brings value to these two banned figures. Heroes do not die in vain. Through them another ideology—another Christian symbolic pattern—has been signed and legitimized. On their subject, a Brazilian journalist spoke of a "second Good Friday."[6]

Monks and Christian martyrs continue to go into guerrilla struggles in the mountains, just as they used to take refuge in the deserts of Egypt. Thus, Father Domingo Lain took part in the "National Liberation Army" and was the "head" of the Colombian guerrilla movement beginning in 1970.[7] He declared in that year: "Now begins my true priestly consecration, which requires total self-sacrifice so that people will be able to live." Also in Colombia were Fathers Laurentino Rueda, Pedro Duarte, and José Esguerra, not to mention the priests accused of using mailboxes to aid the guerrillas;[8] and in Bolivia, the Argentine Nestor Paz; in Panama, Gallegos, a Colombian priest. The list goes on.

These "delinquent" priests have provoked a public debate that prompted the following to be written to Javier Dario Restrepo, in the very official *El Tiempo* of Bogotá: "The case of guerrilla priests such as Camilo Torres or Domingo Lain in Colombia has helped to put the entire continent on guard against those who accuse the church of being subversive. It is a fact that the Latin American priests have reached the conclusion that the only viable solution for the radical change that the continent requires is armed struggle."[9] Even if, in most countries, it has become impossible or increasingly less likely; even if, in the clerical world, the great reformist views of Medellín (1968), like those of the Vatican II in Europe, are now receding, appearing utopian, but that are no less "subversive," this guerrilla poetics (orchestrated, moreover, through reactionary literature that underscores its dangers) has caused the *mystical* element to turn in the direction of revolution and to create a Christian symbolic process.[10] It remains inhabited by the mythic figure of "Che" Guevara. It has sent many Latin American priests toward risky social tasks that are for them laden with meaning, and it has turned them away from the individual happiness and professional security that in Western Europe so often serve as exits from the disillusionment engendered by an outdated ideology of "vocation." More important, the spirituality ushered in by these deaths has created a space for hope; it has given credence to the revolution that was fading away; it has mystical force at the very moment when it is losing its immediately political influence.

"Impasses" and New Inroads of Popular Religion[11]

Combined with a conception of Christian faith, the political failure of the *foco* also had as a practical effect a massive orientation of the pastoral letter, of pedagogy, or of the catechesis toward "popular religions."[12] The revision is distressing. Prior to 1970, the militant vanguard criticized, with a strong degree of violence, the "folkloric" religiosities, the social alibis, the causes for political inertia (and, as a matter of fact, the great spiritualist popular religious movements were often supported from the inside or outside by the United States, for example, as means of closing the door on revolution by opening another onto salvation). The collapse of democratic political organizations leads to the vast, ostensibly immobile, regions of popular religious expression. It has been observed in Brazil since the coup d'état at the end of 1968. The fact has been even more spectacular in Chile since the military junta took power in September 1973. Nonetheless, in this current some very diverse elements have to be discerned and, at the very least, put forward.

1. An increasing importance is given to the *economic* analysis of intolerable situations that, stemming from a system impervious to change (the revolution will not come tomorrow!), call for *operations* of a cooperative nature, of professional training, or collective enterprise. There needs to be introduced, *locally*, in current organization, another *social* experiment of cooperative management and modest *technical* means made available to everyone.[13] Insofar as this promotional activity seeks to work through the adherence and participation of peasants or workers, it encounters their "mentality" as a sum of fundamental experiences. Even if "resistances" to innovation are at stake, they carry weight and meaning. The search for technical means that are better adjusted to an action must be associated with long fraternal advances of understanding and thus also with another

intelligence about what is said in *religious* languages that are, moreover, often mixed, stratified, and complex.

2. Also invested in the study of popular religions is a very old Latin American nostalgia for an "inner country," a hinterland, a "place of its own" dominated and eclipsed by networks of multinational socioeconomic and political structures. Popular religion is told through fables, the memory of a people. Its history is concealed in these metaphors in which a will is maintained. Through folklore can be glimpsed this black sun that never rises. Henceforth, the return takes a much more *anthropological* and *nationalist* form. It is aided by more technical labors: scientific activity in anthropology, ethnology, or semiotics often pushes to the margin or makes impossible involvement in political activities.[14] But in each country is also born a reserve that is more suspicious with regard to protests belonging to other Latin American nations, a fortiori with regard to generalities on the division between the elite and the masses. A nationalism is sought — and in fact appears — in a religious form that announces to everyone what still has a political efficacity for no one.

3. The falling back of ecclesiastical cadres on popular religion is in their case linked to a failure that has the two-sided form of a betrayal and a humiliation. It is of course brazen to speak of it in that way. Nonetheless, on the one hand, priests in Brazil, Chile, and elsewhere have, as a majority, abandoned — at the moment of decision, danger, and conflict — the militants whom they initially encouraged. On the other hand, their alignment (which is also "prudent") with the established order did not bring them any additional power. On the contrary, it resulted in a marginalization and a dependency in relation to the real forms of power (economic, military, and technocratic). It was a betrayal of priests and a humiliation of the churches. The silent work that brings them toward the people seems to be driven at once by the desire to serve on the modest scale of local units (that of parish priests and grassroots militants) and by the need to recover, in a sort of half-common "poverty," adherences and alliances that have since become illusory in the political places where people have to be content with exploiting, on behalf of the regime, a religious dependability that is, moreover, less and less needed.

Within this whole, a growing disparity is produced between the two terms that were initially associated with each other: *popular* and *religion*. The interests of the militants move from the latter to the former. The religious element is not, in their eyes, an *object* of conservative or museographical operations intended to collect valuable *remains,* nor is it a *means* of recovering in popular culture the proximities that compensate for or express the marginalization of the churches. Rather, it refers to two components that are combined within it. The one has to do with the possibility of a class identity; the other, with the *rural* or popular base of necessary socioeconomic transformations. The one and the other designate what must find a revolutionary form rooted in a living tradition.

To this twofold relevance of popular religions in militant practices must be added everything that, designated as syncretism, in fact refers to a transit or a *cultural passage,* and everything that, in a religious form, indicates the relation of a *dominated culture* with a language that has long been dominant, that is, with an imposed language that is used as a mask. This last aspect especially needs to be stressed. So-called popular culture surreptitiously reappropriates dominant culture in the same way that it uses it. It is the ruse of expressing oneself in the language of the *other*—a way of doing and undoing the power that is imposed, and of acceding to a subject-position without (yet) having one. The religious field is a privileged site for these strategies of language that, with an invisible violence, is characterized by a redeployment or a practice of the received language right where no autonomous expression has yet been legitimated.

The rural and even subproletarian populations of the *sertão* or the vicinity of Recife thus assign a particular role to "messianic" protests.[15] A kind of cultural bilingualism develops within them. A first discourse *takes account of* an organization of powers connoted by their fatality (the reason of might makes right), by their mendacity (the rich are always hoodwinking and stealing), and by the silence that they create ("everybody knows but they cannot say anything about it"). It does not accord the slightest religious justification to this ill-conceived world that can only be dealt with through deceit. Next to it, religious practices and representations constitute another, symbolic, space in which a hope can be evinced. This second discourse utters a *nonetheless.* It avails itself of a poetics that for the most part was imported by the European colonizer. But the native *exploits it* in order to construct the objective picture of misery on the poem (that is still atopical and without grounding) of a different, egalitarian society in which the poor finally make good and the bodies of the sick are cured. Here what *cannot be observed* is stated as *possible,* extraordinary, and miraculous. This religious language, inhabited by the ex-

perience of sorrow, increases as the effectiveness of democratic institutions decreases; the former is weakened when the latter is strength-
ened. It is the figure of what cannot yet be articulated in any sociopolitical form.

A "revolutionary" protest inverting the order of forces is kept in
a "sacred" space, in absence, and in the anticipation of the coming of
the means necessary for its realization. It simmers under the social
metaphor of religious movements. Furthermore, everything often happens as if it were becoming the symptom of a strategy that has no
place of its own (a party, a force, a representation), but that diffuses
into the dominant organization. It already signifies the murmur and
the silent force of an erosion that, without yet being named, makes
manifest the demand of the dominated in the very language of the
dominator. All the while the repressive order is (or seems to be) accepted, for lack of any power opposing it, a thousand tactics begin to
infiltrate, in the camouflage of adhesion, the possibility for another
ambition to reappropriate it. A subversion is insinuated through the
order of participation. It is resistance compatible with weakness. A
patience arms these compromises.

It is not forbidden to think that today, removed from their weakened and splintered ideological pretensions, churches practice comparable compromises with respect to the established powers. They
are not identified with what they accept. Their weakness is not a renunciation, even if it is not glorious. They thus may be compared to
popular practices. In this regard, the rare official ecclesiastical interventions that mark an opposition (such as that of Monsignor Camus
in Chile),[16] and whose influence the authorities seek to attenuate, take
the allure of "noise" relative to ecclesial glory of years past, and are already secondary in relation to the resistances concealed under a hu-
miliating docility of being "poor."

Laboratories That Take Charge

It is striking, moreover, that the bishops favor nonviolent methods in
their conflicts with the ruling powers. Thus, Monsignor L. E. Proaño in
Riobamba (Ecuador), Monsignor A. Fragoso in Crateus (Ceara, Brazil),
and Monsignor P. Casaldaliga in São Felix (Mato Grosso, Brazil).[17] The
same tendency holds true in social struggles, as in the Perus cement
factory in São Paulo (a twelve-year strike and then a trial from 1962
to 1974).[18]

One symptom is the movement that coordinates the actions of "nonviolent liberation." Since the first Latin American meeting of 1971 in Alajuela, Costa Rica, a general bureau was created in Buenos Aires; regular continental meetings have been organized (Medellín, February 1974; Brazil, February 1976); and seminars (Buenos Aires, March 1975; São Paulo, October 1975, etc.).[19] *Rural* actions play a growing role, which directs them toward a peasant revolution. It is a matter above all of interventions that are not marked by specific ideological references (whether political or religious) and that prefer the analysis of techniques of action, and all the while nothing is stated about "nonviolence."

At a time when (Monsignor Fragoso made the point in Medellín in February 1974) "the forces of repression are increasingly developed,"[20] strategies thus elaborated in the collectives (and also in the movements defending the rights of man, political prisoners, etc.)[21] offer aspects from which some decisive directions can be taken in the near future.[22] By retaining a few of them, we can sketch out the issues and questions at stake at the present moment.

1. By leaving ideologies aside (indistinguishable from the militant elite that produces them), the intent is to promote actions that the locally concerned group can *control*. Thus the actions aim neither at objectives that escape the group nor at forces that go beyond it. The goal is to avoid a division of labor between theorists and those who put theory into practice, or the annihilation that follows irresponsible orders for which the base population always pays dearly. Conflicts must be proportional to the means of the group through the apprenticeship of a collective management of the relationship of forces. They thus constitute a "self-managed struggle," a positive, present experience of power, and in that way a "permanent anticipation" of the future.[23] This collective practice is nonetheless circumscribed in micropolitics and, as had already been observed in Buenos Aires, only with difficulty does it articulate actions distributed over a global project. But is it really possible?

2. Consciousness-raising thus defined assumes the form of *techniques of action* and furnishes instruments for the analysis of reality. Here knowledge is an action and is born of action. It creates—much more slowly, to be sure—something irreversible: the acquisition of social practices.

3. A characteristic of this experimental science is to bring *thresholds* into view. In the social participation of customs, it delineates new

impossibilities. Within "normal" behavior is drawn the cutting edge of a *non possumus*. Noncooperation is the initial, instigating rupture. Peasants refuse to pay a municipal tax (Panama); Guarani Indians no longer attend the schools mandated for them (Paraguay); the peasants of La Vega stop selling their beans at the fixed price (Dominican Republic); the bishop of Crateus (Brazil) or of Riobamba (Ecuador) refuses to take part in governmental ceremonies, and so on. A tactic of *no*, which corresponds to the first form of a new consciousness, mobilizes the social group and displaces the geography of legality by replacing it with a more fundamental reference.

4. In that way a *distinction between "authority" and power* is introduced. Whatever is credible has "authority"; whatever is imposed has power. Powers that today are increasingly strong but less and less credible are thus struck at their weak point when their authority is called into question, since they cannot function without general support. Through action that denies their authority while recognizing the fact of their power, they lose all "verisimilitude," which is the necessary decor for the violence of those who govern. They are deprived of an internal resilience when the brutality concealed behind authority is revealed. This action demobilizes and demoralizes functionaries deceived by what power leads them to believe; for the police and the military themselves need to *believe*, or at least to believe that they believe, in the *meaning* (order, nation, etc.) of the repression that they exercise on behalf of a power. By striking at this sensitive point, nonviolent strategies can thus also become — and this is even more important — laboratories where experiments are carried out that test the means a group can use to control the systems of power. On a small scale, it is tantamount to taking charge, in the name of a collective conscience, of the problem confronting the scientific and technocratic powers: a political apprenticeship of what is normal, credible, or just. There can be no doubt that religious experience, which has long "specialized" in *believing*, has a new and important role to play in this fallow field of political life.

Part III

The Everyday Nature of Communication

(with Luce Giard)

Chapter 8
A Necessary Music

Communication is the central myth of our societies split between the development of circulation and atomization. On the one hand, emphasis is placed on everything that circulates (people, things, and ideas), on travels, on modes of transport, and on schools and the media, these two great interchanges of ideas and images. On the other hand, our social organization endlessly scatters and fragments groups, individuals, and traditions; it collapses the inner logic that used to structure former ways of thinking, a use of relations, a language of everyday life, and the memory that used to inhabit gestures and speech. As the information that is distributed throughout social space increases, the relations among the practitioners of this space tend to decrease. Communication thus becomes the paradox and the system of the juncture of what informs and what relays: distribution of communication increases, but its reality diminishes. At the core of these tensions is located the place and that which pertains to locality.

To inform means, first of all, to overcome the resistances of a place and the opacities that belong to it for the sake of producing a system of transparence. It means leaving the local and the particular for whatever is less familiar, for what lies beyond the borders of place. To the contrary, relation means the singularity of a place specified as an intersection of individual paths that is transformed into a meeting point. Hence the subtle balances between these different levels and a fundamental contradiction among their objectives. Hence too the possibility of different policies, one of a technological nature, the other of a social nature. The former seeks to materialize through technical means the transverse paths of information; the latter is attached to creating, to restoring, or to protecting spaces of relation.

We do not have to choose between these two systems (which constitute two historical figures of society) any more than we must let ourselves be taken by the nostalgias of an illusory utopia decorated with all the charms of social conviviality and threatened by the dark clouds of technology. The question, rather, entails explaining the political and theoretical stakes that subtend a totality of proposed measures and of specifying how compensatory measures can be proportioned to the needs at hand, even though certain individuals seek salvation in the progress of technology and others recommend recourse to new technologies as one more drug circulating in society.[1] If these technologies cannot alone renew social relations, as one often wants to believe or have others believe, their combined effects raise—in increasingly menacing terms—the question of social relations, whose poor present state bears the visible symptoms of the success of psychoanalysis and the budding growth of therapy.

Levels and Registers

We ought to posit a few necessary distinctions in order, first, to evoke the complexity of levels and the skeins of problems in question and, second, to avoid mistaking for "communication" in general what is merely one of its simple aspects. We can initially recognize in it a *myth*, equivalent to what "salvation" was for the Middle Ages, or "education" during the Enlightenment. In this way, playing at once the role of an a priori, a paradigm, and a narrative, communication puts forward the principle of a link between the multiplication of economic exchanges and that of social relations. In that way it legitimates the extension of a technological apparatus of medias and invests in them the power that a society would have to reproduce itself. This part of communication has assigned itself a place (which is also a nonplace), the city, and this place has grown with communication. The language of this myth is the urbanization of territory.

But communication can also be a *politics*. Cast in this light, the valorization of communication is hardly innocent; for its prerequisite and its logic have thus been, since the eighteenth century, a policy of transparency aiming at controlling local centers by extending and refining the means of circulation that depend on a central power. In France, the ideology of communication has thus been tied to the growth of the state, to a management of circulation through public infrastructures (the postal system and telecommunications, the national railroad, the department of bridges and roads, television, town planning, not to mention National Education or culture). Wherever this type of communication appears, the presence of a state apparatus is visible.

Relative to a system increasingly distinguished from the latter and often opposed to it, or serving as a check and a balance, communication also participates in a *commercial economy* of supply and demand that tends to multiply exchanges and impose on them translatable and legible signs of a universal language: money. It brings together the immense labor of analysis and extension of relations applied to this general signifier. It transforms "social commerce" into "commercial commerce." The extensive network of these transformations ultimately puts outside of the marketplace, as worthless, negligible, discarded, or useless, exchanges that cannot be reduced to its own law (such as barter, hospitality, the exchange of services that cannot be remunerated, etc.), all these elements of a *subterranean economy,* whose role is nonetheless decisive for the survival of groups or of individuals.[2]

Because of these long-awaited political and economic reasons, in times of crisis, communication is often identified with *technocratic apparatuses* created to manage and extend its ramifications. From then on, it is seen as subject to the laws of the big multinational corporate powers, such as information processing. Common interests meld this international market with the administration of the state. Under the pretext of social promotion or of a transformation of social relations, the implantation of cable networks, along with the creation of new electronic gadgetries, serves these interests in ways that are no less elitist than those of the past.

A study crafted in sociological, and especially anthropological, terms would do well to sober up a public inebriated with these commercial crusades distilled from refined technologies. This type of analysis would underscore how communication is merely a strategy in a totality of social practices. No less important are the various techniques of retreat, of defense, and of the protection of intimate and private areas;[3] at stake too is their role in more or less secret spaces that pertain to the family, to the network of kinship, to the relations of neighborhood or of associative life. In these areas intervenes the difference between the encounter on a neutral turf (in the street, on the doorstep, or in front of the apartment building), and welcoming into one's household (the fact of consenting to "receive"), and so on.[4] Thus, communication is overtaken by its opposite: ruptures and subtractions vis-à-vis the practice of communication, the establishment of insurmountable barriers outside of the respect for certain conditions and for certain codes of social exchange, and the like. Furthermore, it refers to different figures of relation according to tacit choices, the nature of which defines types of social groups and styles of cultural practices. In this way it is constituted by a complex and subtle network of *exchanges and withdrawals, of openings and closings,* of silences and explanations, and is seen as a combinatory possibility, with multiple variants, of qualitatively mixed types of "communication" that are diversely stratified and mutually compensatory. It is in relation to this double equilibrium that the primary and secondary consequences of the introduction of voluntarist technologies and the weight of centralizing policies must be evaluated.

It would be impossible to neglect the psychosociological inquiry into the very nature of communication, associated with a *basic equivocation,* that is, with the existence of a type of exchange in which subjects find a meeting space for their differences and a mode of negotiation that can juxtapose fundamentally antagonistic strategies of action and desires for exchange. Seen from this angle, communication is the real means for allowing the social body to believe in working to build a consensus in this "public sphere" — if the vocabulary Habermas uses to describe bourgeois society can be invoked — that is more fictive than real, in which the virtualities of civil society unfold.[5] Communication is thus not measured by the quantity of equivocal messages that can be transmitted, but by the capacity of playing with pragmatic and semantic differences with a view to establishing contractual transactions among partners.

On very different terrains, from ways of looking at television to conversational practices, numerous analyses have shown us that communication cannot be defined by the identity of a content being transmitted or by the system of the medium of transmission;[6] rather, it depends on the *use* being made of the one and the other. Works of psychosociology, sociolinguistics, or psychoanalysis all demonstrate that by restoring a plurality of divergent or conflicting interests, usage reconciles them, in the way of practical, ever-unstable compromises, and that its semantic effect involves the production of equivocation vital for the continued life and mobility of social interactions. There can be no communication without ambiguity, that is, without the mark of a social plurality in the functioning of signs.[7] To specify the complexity of these problems would require a detailed review of research carried out over the past twenty years: on the nature of communication (with Bateson, Watzlawick, Labov, Goffman, etc.),[8] in American ethnomethodology, in the sociology of communities, with the "ethnography of speaking," with the pragmatics of language and other currents of ideas.[9] Space does not allow for discussion here. Reference to this swarm of research has to withdraw all likelihood of a simple, if not simplistic, solution offered by a technocratic panacea: the extension of the media will not in and of itself produce a miracle of communication. The role of a cultural politics entails underwriting experiments that favor social uses of space innervated by the networks of great technologies.

Options

Technological development is a fact and is here for good. It already is building the landscapes of contemporary civilization. Matters that can be chosen are of another order, concerning an appropriation or a social reappropriation of this technical apparatus by its users. Hence the privilege that this relation will accord to three types of elements: social networks, practices or the use made of transformative appropriation, and finally, the intermediairies or mediators who play an active role in the organization of these networks and these practices.

Constituting the initial condition of communication, *social networks* ensure its dynamism and its management. Wherever they break up, the social ties are undone and communication withers. The programs that have attempted to supplant and/or produce them artificially through the massive imposition of technologies (television, cabled networks, etc.) have been failures. Thus, after 1970, the experiment that was made in Quebec by establishing local circuits through cable, which was for a time the model for the French future,[10] proved disappointing. The technical gridding failed to transform the established social structures, and actually exaggerated them in reinforced hierarchies, that of notable local centers because of the diffused contents, and that of multinationals because of financing and advertising. The development of communication above all passes through the networks of its users, that is, through social movements. It cannot flow from the installation and rigidifying effects of technological networks (both commercial and political) that distribute information.

Rather than the inertia of a sociocultural system, the *historicity* of the latter is what needs to be underscored. "History" takes place when groups or some of their members appear as social actors, that is, as subjects of productive operations. Indissociable from an appropriation or from a reappropriation of information in circulation, the procedures of communication are practices of assimilation and of transformation, which are themselves connected with everything at stake in social relations. The life of a community, for example, is made from the harvest of minuscule observations, a sum of microinformation being compared, verified, and exchanged in daily conversations among the inhabitants who refer both to the past and to the future of this space. As an old lady who lives in the center of Paris leads her life:

> Every afternoon she goes out for a walk that ends at sunset and that never goes beyond the boundaries of her universe: the Seine to the south, the stock market to the west, the Place de la République to the east.... She knows everything about the cafés on the boulevard, the comparative prices, the age of the clients and the time that they spend there, the lives of the waiters, the rhythm and style of people circulating and meeting each other. She knows the price and the quality of the restaurants in which she will never lift a fork.[11]

The daily murmur of this secret creativity furnishes her necessary foundation and is her only chance of success in any state intervention. But the existence of such an activity of users can only be the assumption of a politics of stimulation and not its effect, however desired the latter might be. Hence the importance of locating this creativity and of recognizing its places and its role.

The *intermediaries* play a central role among all the social actors. Historical research has emphasized their importance in many different past configurations, including itinerant booksellers, preachers, schoolteachers, administrators of local academies, organizers of reading rooms, and so on.[12] But where, today, are these liaison agents, these relayers of communication and crucial mediators? It depends on the milieus and the situations. Among them can be found, as the case may be, booksellers and newspaper vendors, the pharmacist or doormen in large buildings in the suburbs, social or medical workers (for example, in a protection center, a halfway house for mothers and children),[13] and elsewhere people who, through personal experience or activism know how to mobilize an administrative competence, and also individuals contributing energies to neighborhood associations, workers who are members of business committees, and so on.

Every network has its *shifters*, specified not by a power of decision but, as Pierre Clastres noted in the case of "chiefdoms," through the capacity to put goods and discourses into circulation[14]—put into parallel circulation, for they are not aligned with administrative, political, or union organizations and do not refer to their orthodoxies; pragmatic, they always "connect" knowledge, new models of behavior, to practical needs. Through this dual characteristic of belonging to the group in question and built on vital necessities, these shifters are inner channels of communication par excellence. They select, diffuse, and dynamize information; they make it desirable and assimilable, and are the active agents of its appropriation and its transformation.

These options aim at locating within the functions of communication the elements relative to its social dynamics, whether they are points of braking or paralysis or points of stimulation or articulation. In that way it ought to be possible to identify the strategic sites in order to specify where and how to remedy, through political measures, the observed deficits and to support existing forces. A policy will have to shun the ambition of centralization and the totalizing ideology that haunts administrations in order to direct attention toward *compensatory and transitive interventions* proportioned to given situations. Its task involves maintaining or correcting the conditions required for an equilibrium that in itself is always escaping, and not of defining this equilibrium as such. The partial character, tactical in a certain sense, of the analyses and measures that are put forward here refers to the schema of a democratic society in which the state itself plays only a partial role, without for all that believing itself to be weakened or dispossessed of its legitimate powers.[15]

Needs

The most obvious trait of communication is its extreme necessity: it alone makes possible the life of an individual, that is, the apprenticeship of human nature and the insertion of the living being in these multiple systems of interaction that give to groups, as well as to the totality of the social body, a means of acquiring form and identity. In relation to this primary trait, the modes and means of communication are secondary inasmuch as the human voice, the relation with others, and the variety of situations of interlocution play a role in this communication. An *a contrario* proof of this necessity is the terrible weight of solitary confinement, the horror of the status of being incommunicado that the jails in Spain under Franco made famous or, conversely, the torture through the imposition of a continuous aural flow of words of indoctrination, and the immemorial presence of graffiti on the prison walls. Another mark of the force of this need, whatever the foundation and the context, includes the growth of messages circulated in the local experiments in telematics;[16] or the desire to create in factories advisory counsels in which workers can openly express their feelings about their work, although this freedom of speech is frowned upon.[17] For good reason. To speak means to come forward and to locate oneself in one's sphere of existence; it means to claim a modest quantum of agency. Circulation of speech carries the seed of the overthrow of the established powers, hence the interest that authoritarian regimes have in controlling the exchange of words, information, and ideas, and also their endless efforts to assure themselves total control over all modes of communication.

In the misery of situations of shortage, the everyday nature of communication can profit from the presence of the media. Thus the case of a former delinquent, describing what, after seventeen years of prison, it meant for him to have the right, finally granted in 1974, to have a radio in his cell and to choose his stations. With gratitude and emotion, he said that France-Culture became his favorite station because goods that could not be obtained in prison were not advertised, and because its broadcasts were rich in content and seemed to be "a window onto another universe."[18] Thus too the case of a child who was locked up for seven years in a closet and who resisted going crazy or falling into idiocy because of a few fragments of communication that were fleetingly whispered, at different intervals, through the keyhole or thanks to his younger brother who occasionally opened the door to be able secretly to watch television with him.[19] Like a window opened onto other places of human society, images of bodies and the murmur of words, information, and other stimuli were vital nourishment that kept a person's spirit alive.

No less indispensable for geographies endlessly reinvented through daily use are the intermediary sites of speech, the buzz of scattered messages exchanged in haste, at bus stops, in lines in front of administration windows, before the array of goods at market stands, on the stoops of apartment buildings or in front of the grid of their mailboxes, at the exits of schools or in front of the photocopier in the post office, at the laundromat or in the café, in all of these familiar and public places that are neither yours nor mine, that are made for passing through, to serve everyone, to exchange words and goods, to beckon others (somewhat, but not too much), to get information without getting aggravated, to mix without being lost, to comment and to discuss, at bottom, to verify and reactivate one's belonging to a neighborhood or work community. For the most timid persons, for those whose entry into society is uncertain, man's best friend comes to the rescue: "When I take my dog for a walk, people talk to me." They themselves talk to their dog, the attentive partner in infinite monologues. A strange modesty of the city inhabited by speech and silence, a city built of proximities and solitudes.

Chapter 9
Priorities

In the complex functionings of communication, not in what is deemed most valuable in cultural representations or in political economy, but rather, in what sustains and organizes it, three priorities are key: whatever is oral, operative, and ordinary. All three return to us by way of the detour from a supposedly foreign stage, *popular culture,* that has been the subject of a growing number of studies on oral traditions, practical creativity, and the acts of daily life. One more step is needed to break the fictive barrier and to recognize that in truth our very culture is also at stake, even if unbeknownst to us. For the social sciences have analyzed in terms of "popular culture" the functionings that are fundamental to our urban and modern culture, but that are held to be illegitimate or negligible in the official discourses of modernity. Just as sexuality repressed by bourgeois morality returned in the dreams of Freud's patients, these functions giving structure to human sociality, denied by the stubborn ideology of writing, of production, and of specialized technologies, are returning in our social and cultural space (which they never left in the first place) under the cover of "popular culture."

By progressively ensuring their autonomy (the condition of their rationalization and their development), industry and the technology of communication have been detached from these three sectors in order to make them the very object of their conquests. Oral culture has become the target that writing was supposed to educate or inform; practitioners have been transformed into ostensibly passive consumers; ordinary life has been mapped out as a vast territory open to colonization by the media. Nonetheless, as any analysis that goes beyond stereotypes will demonstrate, the elements that were considered eliminated have continued to determine social exchanges and organize the way messages are "received," that is, to transform the media messages and to make use of them.

Orality

To refer to orality means taking up linguistic modes of behavior as situations and relations of interlocution. These are studied in different ways in Chomsky's linguistics, in pragmatics, and in linguistic ethnomethodology. This aspect of interlocution leads to greater emphasis placed on expression or enunciation than on content or statement. We are thus led back to rhetoric, a central discipline in classical culture that has too often been reduced to an impoverished theory of figures of style. A priority is thus given to illocution, to the person of the locutor, to the circumstances of place and time, to the "sonorous materiality" of words exchanged, and to contextual interpretation. Slipping into the context is the entire diversity of plays of language, their inventiveness and multiform creativity, an entire staging of conflicts and of divergent interests that are understood without having to be spelled out: ruses, semantic derivations, quid pro quos, sound effects, neologisms, deformed words, proliferating dialogues. The manufacturers of messages in advertising are well aware of all these linguistic procedures, which they put to profitable use in making up their jingles and wordplays. They succeed when the transfer of credibility serves the glory of the products, the merits of which their slogans and posters herald with pride.

Ignored or scorned, rhetoric does not in the least fail to use its very old procedures to organize the use of television or newsprint, the formulation of sellers' lines or political choices, and the banality of everyday exchanges. An entire function of orality needs to be analyzed by updating the categories of classical rhetoric, by recognizing the legitimate and driving role of orality in the constitution of the social body, even for a society of writing or electronic communication, whether at the administrative and political level (public information) or in locales of daily life. The city ought to tend to the sites of speech in multiple places (as post offices have begun to do). Oral contests, poetry festivals, and so on, would have to be arranged to encourage the individual practice of recording and taping by creating small workshops for apprenticeship and demonstration of available apparatuses (what the FNAC [a major bookstore and media sales center in France] has done in its own way with its "photo, video, and sound theaters"), assist in the private circulation of cassettes with adapted packaging and a reduced postal rate (as in the case of books and printed matter). In school, homework submitted on cassette should be accepted on the same scale as written papers. In administration, oral consultations should be facilitated without resorting to the distribution of these printed forms written in a language that remains incomprehensible for most of us, and the production of useless and depressing paperwork should be limited everywhere.

A perfect image of our common difficulty is this old Algerian émigré displaying his wallet stuffed with paper of every kind (pay-stubs, working papers, Social Security receipts, etc.):

> My whole life is there. It's heaped up in there; it sums up my blood, sweat, and tears.... Fortunately I've taken precautions; since reaching manhood, I've always held on to my papers.... Without them I'd be lost. My France would have been reduced to nothing, I wouldn't have gained a thing.... You've got to hold on to all of these papers, trash or otherwise; you never know since you can't tell which one you've got to keep, you just keep them all.... That piece of paper you toss into the wastebasket today is the one you might just need tomorrow![1]

Operativeness

Culture is judged according to operations, not the possession of products. In the same way, with respect to communication, we would have to go from products back to the practices that gave birth to them or made them possible. Communication is not information, but a treatment of the latter through a series of operations seen as a function of objectives and relations with others, in a context of action that is at once aesthetic (adapt for one's ends the given material by using it differently), political (appropriate information in order to command knowledge, even if only a tiny parcel), and ethical (restore a space of freedom, defend the autonomy of something of its own kind).

If use produces communication, we have to be concerned about this plurality other than the masses consuming and repeating imposed models, and analyze in this plurality the types of operations at play, their registers and their possibilities of combination. The *types of operation* pertain to different formalities that belong to ordinary practices; they are still quite foreign to us because our analytical apparatus for the creation of models and formulas has been constructed for other objects, built for different purposes. Ordinary practices, the least known for now, are still in the realm of "ways of speaking," thanks to the research of Paul Zumthor, William Labov, George Lakoff, and so on, in the study of the supple logic of natural languages, of probabilities, or of modes of speech. Here the model furnished by the figures of rhetoric could be put to good use, indications coming from the logic of time or action.[2]

The *registers* of these ordinary practices might fall under the purview of anthropological distinctions: what pertains to the body and the use of the senses, what relates to spatial practices, what refers to time (the instant of chance, the patience of memory, etc.). But the economic field is also relevant: exchanges, practices of self-production, handiwork, helpers, loans and hospitality, gift giving, potlatch activities, and so on. In the same way one could take into account, first of all, the variables of place: inside/outside, private/public, as well as the weight of the rule or rules: a play at the borders of two otherwise distinct codes, practices of the double bind, and so on. Whatever the list of types of operation may be, and whatever registers are preferred, the essential claim of the analysis ought to bear on their subtle combination that actualizes and stages a *making use of, here and now,* that is, a singular act tied to situation and to circumstances, to the presence of particular actors. In this sense, ordinary culture is above all a *practical science of the singular.*

There exist true areas of knowledge that lose their validity if detached from the singular, but that gain it back as soon as they are used to interpret singular situations: a lesson that a number of texts, from feminine magazines (for example, for health problems) to American works for the circulation of scientific knowledge (whether dealing with mathematics, astronomy, or biology), have already managed to put to profitable use. Here, one must at once seek to overcome the deficit of theoretical analysis and encourage textual production and didactic materials (videotapes, cassettes, do-it-yourself things, etc.) that rely on the processes most closely related to the ordinary practices.

A Logic to Be Sought

The oral, the operative, and the ordinary do not constitute three separate or antagonistic elements. They are of the same order, or rather, they mutually reinforce each other, for they exercise the same type of competence, refer to the same use of implicit and circumstantial material, and appeal to the same modes of transmission and communication. They compose a culture with its own logic, that is neither irrational nor primitive, but that is hidden in the shadow of the autonomization of writing and the rhetoric of numbers, a logic still unknown by a rationality enclosed in its own "limits," lacking a clear awareness of them.[3] But a politics of communication cannot be based on forgetfulness or scorn for one of the two halves of culture: that of writing, legitimated production, and the scientific discourse of knowledge, and that of orality, ordinary practices, and everyday savoir faire. Both need to be developed, assisted, and encouraged, for each depends on the other, and each enriches the other through its rigor and invention.

Chapter 10
Networks

The idea of communication immediately calls up that of the network, with all of the ambiguity attached to that word. Does it mean networks materialized through an infrastructure allowing for the circulations of goods, furnishings, or persons? Or networks plotting the implantation of an administrative apparatus, the agents of a profession, the faithful of a belief or of an ideology? In the first case, it does not seem difficult to study the extension and the traits of the network in question; knots of interconnections, disfavored zones, and so on, could be noted. A cartography could be made of administrative networks. By comparing them, one could show the principles that have ruled their establishment in France since the eighteenth century (and without having the Revolution mark such a fundamental break as we might be led to imagine). As Yves Stourdzé has shown for the telegraph and the telephone, the advent of new technologies is often traced to earlier networks of public service. The distribution of professional networks is more complex, but it is not independent of the material and administrative networks that have already been mentioned either. Such would be the case for physicians with the adjunction of a few supplementary variables, for example, the localization of town spas or that of certain kinds of climate assumed to be favorable for the treatment of specific ailments.

More mobile, but less studied because they are delegitimized and lacking administrative ways of being stabilized, informal networks are nonetheless determining factors for the analysis of social facts: ethnic networks of immigrant laborers, networks of regional origin of "countries" that move into cities (the Auvergnats and Bretons living in Paris), networks of family or relatives (more or less active according to milieus and generations), "feudal" networks (alumni of the state preparatory schools, members of state bodies), and so on. Added to these, finally, are the networks by which people are bound by passion or shared convictions: amateur practitioners of astronomy, computer hacking, or music, nature lovers, adherents of alternative medicine, devotees of sects, political activists, athletes, and so on. A whole confusion of superimposed lines cuts across the social body that it seems at once to irrigate and enchain. Among the multiple possibilities of the circulation of goods, people, information, images, and sounds, we will confine ourselves to a brief analysis of what we believe to be three strategic points—the local, the ethnic, and the familial—and finally what pertains to labor, because their three domains seem to us to bring into perspective an imponderable (space, biology, the relation to a job), although they bear a specific weight in matters of culture and communication.[1]

The Local

In the archaeology of communication, the local has long been considered the enemy. Thus, in the eighteenth century, the network of roads organized space starting from Paris, the extension of administrations such as secondary education and the diffusion of its representations aimed at breaking the resistance of provincial places.[2] The new respect for minority and regional cultures and the administrative reform undertaken to regionalize management and powers put this question on agenda.[3] For some, the place and local power were no more than a "rhetorical object," a prop for administrative or technological discourse, the finery of a centralized power, or a fiction dissimulating the competition between state agencies.[4] For others, it was the site of a "peripheral power" necessary for balancing the dangerous hypertrophy of centralized power and distributed according to a complex mechanism between networks of public figures and other networks of clients.[5] For still others, the place was becoming the hallowed haven, a point of renewed solidarity in a culture itself, wrongly scorned by the centralizing state.

None of these points of view suffices to grasp the truth of the place, which is much more than a rhetorical statement (proven by the force of the new functionaries, the originary privileges needed to obtain the voters' mandate), than a counterweight to centralized power, or than the last bastion of a cultural ghetto. As Henri Giordan has underscored, minority cultures are not all territorial.[6] In obstinately wishing to remain or become so again, they ran the risk of being buried by setting down roots in a local area either too small or closed on itself. In order to make itself meaningful in its place, it would in fact have to seek a way to *think space* despite, in this respect, the failure of the Territorial Development, and thus would succeed in redefining locality, the site of residence and of activity that is particularized as "a small homeland," whether as the center of the city, the suburbs, or the mixed zones of "rurbanization."[7] Today, no matter where it is, the local site feels itself less as the overly neglected dependency of a national center than as the end point—with dimensions too small to influence the course of things, decisions, or disappointments relative to an international economy. With the new sense of consciousness that binds local space to the world beyond national boundaries, the new circulation of information and images furnished by the media is not strange. Thus the local enters into a new phase of modernity in which the importance of language (gestures, images, and words) supplants that of tradition, in which each is seen in the heroes of a remote soap opera and tries to mix the styles that come from afar into the specific features of its own history.

To understand what is happening to the local, we might refer to the model proposed by specialists in the ethnography of communication. They characterize the social group in its place through its way of dealing with its environment, through its fundamental strategies of communication, and through the systems that decode choices offered in matters of communication.[8] Created in the context of American society with its mosaic of ethnic and cultural heritages and its penchant for mobility, this model possesses the principal merit of being founded neither on the uniqueness of place nor the uniqueness of language, which means that it pertains rather well to a time of rapid and profound transformations in the economic and cultural spheres. According to this model, culture and communication are placed in relation with the manipulation of "codes" that define as many inventive and changing "dialects." The essence thus resides in the *styles of translation* that concern language as much as the occupation of space or economic activities. The group is therefore reduced neither to a grammar nor to a site (two forms of the same ideological conception).

This model could be extremely valuable for the treatment of the problem of minority or regional cultures. From this perspective, the real "place" would no longer be only that of the extended territory of a language and of its cultural heritage, but would include practical and recognizable totalities in ways whereby each could be dealt with: it would be valid for the Breton population, even those who do not speak Breton, as well as for immigrants, whether they belong to the first or the second generation. Another advantage of this way of looking at things includes how it is possible to get over the old political prejudice that, founded on the past, envisages in localities and their habitual occupants (the body, the family, nature) the enemy of the French Republic and supporters of the right, whereas the national level, Jacobinism, and centralism, good servants of the Republic, would depend on the left, for the nation would assign itself the function of uniting *language and place*.[9]

In fact, the development of the media and telecommunications allows localities to be seen as something other than the terminal point of reception of an influx originating from and carefully developed by a center. The adventure of free radio stations is already explicit: they have given new form and expression to the fragmentation of local territories, to a differentiation of publics, to the diversity of uses and "dialects." The success of Lorraine Cœur d'Acier comes from the emphasis it places on local affairs; the station offers a meeting place (the broadcasting studio itself) that is visible, open to everyone, and a means of expression for local social life, whether for the solidarity of struggling interest groups at work or the expression of a still-unknown artistic creativity.[10] A local radio station can thus reunite, for a time, a population that is learning how to use the media and find its own way of gaining a voice by obtaining these instruments of communication. The limited broadcasting range of a local radio station (and, for others, the short duration of their life of operation) does not appear as a defect; both qualities allow them to avoid the temptation to "expand" by producing broadcasts for a general public and, by the force of things, copied at low cost and with less polish than national stations.

In the same way, experiences with the "Web" and "E-mail" show that message exchanging and interactivity make it possible to break up the stodginess of local networks and to establish relations with new partners for given projects of common interest, in rural zones where the inhabitants are often too dispersed to meet in person, as well as in the suburbs and new cities where residents are too recent to have common meeting places or routines that bring them together. In this area, associations could become the favored site that would "capture" local life through new technological channels; helping them to create small experimental groups of this nature would provide access to innovation and to a sort of power of local consciousness-raising for younger generations (whose limited material means and still uncertain status would otherwise hold them in the networks of their superiors). The associative movement would thus serve as a research laboratory in communication and be adapted to local situations and to the needs of a diverse public and, from this angle, of a local center of animation, as long as it is necessary at once to create action groups of participants of such and such leisure activity and to help to organize local groups that can take interest in conserving a *broadened patrimony* for the environment and different traces of human activities, as, for example, the movements of industrial archaeology in Great Britain or permanent education in Scandinavia.[11]

The Ethnic and the Familial

The relation with the biological link has become impossible to contemplate in our systems of interpretation that favor the socioeconomic ties between "classes" and in our thought, which, proclaiming equality of rights for all individuals, dreaded to attribute their importance to inequalities of fact and racial prejudice. Thus the analysis of society in ethnic or familial terms has been repressed outside of our developed nations toward the field of "primitives" and outside of our rationality in the direction of the suspect field of the unconscious. Another probable motive of this conspiracy of silence is the need to think of giving the biological link its theoretical status in sexual differentiation. One indication among others is the proposition advanced by the Godelier research mission particularly to promote work on the family and feminist studies.[12] An additional indication, this time drawn from practice: the increasingly marked taste of amateurs for genealogies founded on research in archives (births, marriages, and deaths, various ministries, notarial minutes, etc.).

Now, familial networks appear to rank among the most solid of all; matrilineal or patrilineal circulations and matrimonial alliances among distant cousins seem frequent but are dissimulated in the webbing of socioeconomic stratification or neighborly relations. These familial networks are either reinforced or replaced by networks of ethnicity in immigrant populations. For lack of ethnic ties, people locate themselves by towns of origin; they sustain each other, they mutually inform each other; the first arrivals teach the novices: work, lodging, and leisure are thus overdetermined.[13] Here the ethnic ties do not replace economic relations, but they allow them to be developed. In the same way, they do not suppress the importance of the locality, but reinforce it, with ethnic groups seeking to find a common space by living together in the same neighborhood or along the same axis of trade or public transportation, whether in the city or in the suburbs, depending on the possibilities offered. Neighborhoods in the center see their old buildings handed over to immigrants, while a given corner of a suburb will be called the "Portuguese section" or the "Maghrebian zone."

These networks, whether familial or ethnic, and often both, are at once solid, supple, and efficient. They allow women to become slowly adapted to modern urban society and to learn new ways of daily living. They allow innovation to circulate in assimilable doses for those in the network. Innovation is furnished to them through intermediaries who are implicitly assigned to the task. They control or try to control the assimilation of these innovations by seeking, to the best of their abilities, ways to reconcile it with original traditions, or a part of these traditions. Moreover, these types of questions mark the limits of the power of the network, which in turn reaches its point of rupture under the pressure of the conflicts between parents and children of the "second generation," who are said still to be "French," because they were born or educated there. By virtue of its size, vitality, impatience, appetites, and needs, this second generation causes the old modes of control of the ethnic and familial networks to explode. It rejects their habits and their authority, without succeeding in replacing it with the solidarity of other affiliated or professional networks and without being able to be accepted in the networks established by the native French.

The children of immigrants reject the image and the destiny that their parents offer them; they want neither their inferior status, nor their employment in hard physical labor, nor their humiliation, nor their austere and frugal means of existence. They seek ways to move up on the social ladder, which, quite often, their failure in school disallows them, and a self-image that valorizes them. They want to go straight into modern life and taste its model of material consumption without their specificity of their origins being denied. These are fragile and uncertain borderline inhabitants, divided between two languages and two cultures, attracted by the production of images and sounds and their machinery. In this area, informational and audiovisual technologies could play a positive role. These adolescents are fascinated by these sophisticated machineries, a symbol of modernity and power. They dream of glorious careers in film, in the press, and in the computer industry,[14] professions that bring renown and status, precisely everything that their parents never had. To offer them a chance to get "hands-on" experience with this "hardware" would allow them access into the mainstream of our society of advanced technical culture and would give them access to types of activity where they would be able to get around the difficulty of placement examinations by the culture of writing: written language, with its imposition of norms of correction and its canons of classic expression, puts them at a disadvantage. Learning how to take part in another means of circulation and network of information with these apparatuses, they would quite naturally slip into the labor of the selection of information, coding, and translation. Their situation as borderline types living at the edge of two worlds, two languages, and two cultures has already trained them for these uncharted voyages between opposing codes and dialects, for multiple operations of translation.

The Bonds of Labor

Communication is also rooted in practices, whether public or private, with or without pay, that are tied to labor; it borrows the networks that these practices determine. There is surely a circulation of ideas, of information, of tools, or of material when practical needs have to be met and uses are brought forward to manufacture, to repair, to improve, and to compare. These situations lead to the application of practices and manual dexterities, and thereby provide the opportunity to control or create new effects, to invent diversions of common usage, tools or other materials in the place of what is commonly employed, and improved models. These practices also often lead to the production of useless objects that are taken as aesthetic, inspired by the love of a technique or a material. Many tales refer to the process: for example, these musical instruments that are put together out of rubbish collected from local factories (here the conceiver was a musical animator and the players apprentices in neighboring factories);[15] or this immense Don Quixote, installed at the entrance of the studio of Lorraine Cœur d'Acier and put together at Usinor with leftover shreds of metal.[16] From these practices, the painting, at the request of a patron of the arts, of four Parisian taxis by well-known artists, which transformed the common vehicles into ambulant art objects (while retaining their initial function), is ultimately nothing more than a public staging of hypertrophy;[17] the artist took control of a technical object that symbolizes a way of life and transformed it into a pure symbol of his or her activity of imagination, like workers who do their own work in the factory by changing material and tools imposed on them—a symbol of their submission to the law of labor—in order to produce, thanks to them, the symbolic object of their freedom of creation.[18]

Whether they belong to the sphere of public activity or that of satisfying domestic needs, the practices of production and transformation create strong networks of information; in them circulate elements of knowledge and know-how, information about economics, geography, or technology. These are the real networks of communication and pedagogy, even though an elitist and abstract conception of culture esteems them to be negligible. Their interest is to be the sites where operations and a confrontation/juxtaposition of ways of doing things meet head-on. Here is invented and practiced a way of refashioning the sociocultural environment, of appropriating its materials, and of making use of them for different goals, at the end of a series of transactions/translations/operations of transit and of transference.

A recent report proposed extending the notion of patrimony to the sum of all signs of human activity. In its own way, that was the project of Diderot's *Encyclopedia*. Until now the project has been almost impossible to complete: how can the treasures of the ingenuity of a know-how made of manual dexterity, circumstantial invention, and adaptations crafted for the needs of the moment be capitalized and memorized? The production, without great means in apparatuses or in technical competence, of videotapes and their free circulation, allow the difficulty to be overcome; now present gestures can be recorded and hence can be memorized and analyzed. By putting videotapes and cameras in the hands of users who are their anonymous heroes, by collecting their critical remarks and their explanatory comments, we can learn how to use the intelligence of these know-hows just as certain users are already using them, while dreaming of composing this "visual anthropology" of forms of knowledge without written notation or noble theorizing.[19] Such works will teach us more about the modes of acquisition and transmission of knowledge than every didactic project stuffed to the gills with good intentions and prisoner of its theoretical presuppositions. By ceasing to scorn ordinary practices and by seeking to grasp the theory of practices and the modes of circulation of theoretical and practical knowledges, we might someday succeed in making manifest the "culture of labor," "help it to identify with itself," and contribute to bringing nearer the cultural offer of the mainline equipment of real cultural practices and real communication.[20]

Chapter 11
Operators

If communication has its grounding elements in what is oral, operative, and ordinary, and if it composes and maintains its invisible networks, it only functions by means of operators of circulation, each inseparable from the other. The convenience of the analysis will lead us to distinguish intermediaries and mediators, original sources (the media), and practices of circulation and transmission. The quality of social communication, its successes, and its failures depend directly on the number of all these operative agents, their efficacy, and their dynamism. These are the three levels of elaboration and transit of information that a cultural politics must seek to assist and stimulate, with deftness and discernment, in order to respect their diversity and their autonomy.

Intermediaries

By borrowing our vocabulary from Roman Jakobson's linguistics, we should like to associate these mediator/intermediaries with *shifters* who can identify information that can be memorized in its general form, who retain it, and then retransmit it in a particularized translation that is set into a specific situation according to the requirements of the interlocutor, the circumstances, and the context of the transmission. In this sense, these cultural intermediaries are first of all *translators* who decode and recode fragments of knowledge, link them, transform them by generalization, convey them from one case to another through analogy or extrapolation, treat every conjuncture of events by comparison with a preceding experience, and, in accord with their own style, shape a juridical logic of the general and the particular, of norms, and of qualities of action and time.

These amateur mediators do not present themselves as leaders of communities, nor are they guides to opinion invested with a charisma that might give them a status of knowledge, power, and right to judge or decide about others. They are in fact linking agents, who have become that through an obscure co-optation, itself dependent on professional luck, history, or temperament. Alert and lucid members of a local community whose dilemmas they can perceive and whose necessities they understand, they distinguish themselves by the very particular interest and razor-sharp attention that they bring to the slightest issues of life, to the myriad incidents that punctuate everyday life and labor. They are probably driven by a secret dream of autonomy and utopia, but a utopia without constraint or violence. They are probably, in their own confused and illegitimate way, the laborers of a sociality who, like Saul Alinsky's organizers of an earlier time, wish to "create power in order to allow others to use it," in their case power produced by the communication of information that its receiver can digest and put to use.[1]

What do they do? They capitalize on the shards of knowledge that await their application—here an explanation, there a piece of administrative advice, and there the reminder of a rule or a legal obligation, or even the translation into clear language of the muddled and confused wording of a legal document. They carry information. Sometimes it might be a tip: an address that will provide an object someone needs, a name or place that can make a repair, a hand in completing a project, a good word that will help someone get out of a bind. Mobile, diverse, always changing, lacking official status or professional recognition for these information and mediation operations, these "go-betweens" are endowed with an aura of limited influence; their area of competence is no less limited, as is also the credibility they implicitly have at their disposal. Here there is no universal mediator in the way we might speak of a "universal language," but translators from one dialect to another, inserted in a given network of speech, whether ethnic or familial, based on the ties of work or of neighborhood, and recognized as the intermediaries in a given field of knowledge, of problems to be solved, or of administrative management. They are, in a certain way, specialized amateurs, anonymous heroes of communication, modest officials for the best interests of a micromilieu, people who inspire minuscule tactics aimed at making a social space congenial, not in its entire expanse but along the edge of a neighborhood or an apartment building.

Neither functionaries of official administration or of communication (but sometimes they can be recruited among them), nor elected politicians based on constituent clients, they play the unknown role of *directors for transverse communication* by giving a particular character to the anonymous space of social exchanges, in their own way creating a site of sociality, in the here and now, and always for an uncertain length of time. The group that refers to one of them, and on whom the latter depends as far as its credit of confidence and its elective function are concerned, itself has its own criteria of choice, its rules of functioning, its requirements and procedures, and, ultimately, its needs. It often is suspicious of professional channels of information and functionaries of institutions, either because the latter speak only in the clichés of official parlance, or because the group endows them, rightly or wrongly, with a dangerously discretionary power: it is better that these official agents not be too well informed, better not to hand oneself over to them in subservient ways (through ignorance of one's rights, duties, or a proper way of doing things). People will thus first of all obtain information from a mediator of their choice, whom they will thank in one fashion or another, but without getting involved in a relation of dependency or fearing the prospect of submitting to his or her authority.

For the mediator that the group has chosen can be challenged at a moment's notice, disqualified at will or because, if circumstances are changing, his or her information has become devalued. Worthy of confidence, but of a confidence blended with distrust and watchful so as not to be "ripped off," the mediator is recruited by the group by means of affinity, and is tied to the group that has co-opted him or her through a bond of friendship more than of allegiance. That is why the mediator is not dangerous—unlike the functionary who has a position in an institution. Neither the mediators nor the sustaining groups are, moreover, interchangeable (contrary to what happens to functionaries of the same rank in an administration); here too it is a question of *a generalized practice of singularity*, hence the essential weight of circumstantial elements, of the variable of time and context. We discover ourselves within a framework of oral exchange, in which the rhetorical situation of interlocution defines and rules the transaction, hence our difficulty in stabilizing the description of this type of communication, in explaining or formalizing the laws that determine its function, in specifying an optimum of exchange or the best possible path for the intermediary in question.

It must be stressed that the action of these mediators is possible only because one or several networks lead to them, because those who inquire of them have faith in what they say, because practices of circulation ensure the maintenance of their channels of transmission by keeping information flowing. Are these intermediaries the conductor or the lead soloist in a local harmony? They are akin to both, sometimes one more than the other, but their music can only be born of the simultaneous presence, in accord with its intentions and desires, of the group of other musicians and music-loving clients. In this sense, the person who demands creates the mediator, not the other way around. The mediator stimulates the intensity of the exchanges, increases their productivity, but wants neither to control nor to regulate them, nor, even less, to create them. Moreover, in all this activity of translation and mediation, there are many different degrees of involvement and distinct levels of action, running from the child, who has no social power but who is a vector in the circulation of things new (new purchases, new desires, new behaviors), to the amateur proselyte who leads a campaign to increase the audience of his or her favorite shows, an efficient means of exchange that, for lack of a better term, might be called "word-of-mouth advertising."[2]

In the culture of communication, intermediaries have their historical figures, editors of old books and hand-sold almanacs that mixed fragments of high culture with popular wisdom, and that thus made the former assimilable to the latter by inserting it into the frame of old wives' tales, including all those praise books and urban newspapers of the nineteenth century that expanded their audience at minimal cost, or even the teachers in rural communities under the Third Republic.[3] Currently, this mediator is perhaps a nurse who makes daily rounds to homes in the neighborhood, a well-informed mother who leads a parent-teacher association, a resourceful neighbor who reads women's magazines, who cuts out or copies their practical pieces of advice and various recipes, who experiments, corrects, and then recirculates them in her entourage. It might be an immigrant worker who has more experience and is more reflective than others, an esteemed and engaging merchant, a superintendent of a building who, because he or she has spoken to many of its residents, has become a font of administrative information, or it might be this sly retiree who has gone through different jobs, continents, and adventures.

The intermediary is basically this *mixed being* who stirs together old and new knowledges, who particularizes and relativizes, who combines the certain, the probable, and the plausible. Intermediaries are also persons of movement, or rather people who succeed in changing things in small doses, for, in the restrained areas of their known competence, they know how to catalyze the transformation of the groups that sustain them. The weaknesses and the limits of their ways of doing things are the same as in any situation of interlocution in which the transmission of knowledge is based on orality:[4] the fruits of this transmission are minimal because of the difficulty in accumulating knowledge beyond a given quantity and ordering it in a systematic way; there is also a dependency with respect to the circumstantial and the particular that often makes the information garnered the sum total of the dust of specific cases, without the informant being able to grasp its own logic, and hence to theorize its general laws, and so forth.[5]

What role does the state have to play vis-à-vis these intermediary mediators? If it does not have to ensure their selection and training, nor, furthermore, to legitimize their action, it also need not take umbrage at their existence or in principle be suspicious of their influence, which would lead it more or less overtly to thwart their activities, as is already the case here and there for certain social workers, who are jealous of preserving both their role and their clientele. The state has a clear interest in allowing these invisible informants and their networks to exist; they work for the best ends, according to the laws of barter and exchange from one individual to another, thus without incurring official costs and without salary, and as such they relieve municipal or national functionaries. The mediators maintain a certain elasticity in the social webbing through their privileged position as amateurs, which makes them "likable" and credible in the eyes of those who use their networks.

Therefore the action of the state must maintain rules to facilitate the "work" of the mediators, not to supplant them, to help in developing new intermediaries that are inventive, provisional, supple, and mobile, not to rigidify, organize, or hierarchize, and even less to professionalize. Implicitly recognizing their existence and their usefulness, the state ought to furnish them with *instruments* adapted to their operations of informing and translating: *information banks* with easy access for individuals, without any need for official justification of competence, without having to bump up against a prior censure by an institutional functionary, and offering simple possibilities of interactivity; *folders and brochures of administrative information* edited with clarity, without excessive technical terminology, but detailing how specific problems can be solved, and if possible presented in an attractive form, with contemporary graphics and — why not? — in the widespread and prized style of the comic strip; *relay sites of consultation and documentation,* endowed with a specific base of small dossiers and other sources of easy handling, allowing personal itineraries of self-documentation, such as the BPI (Public Library of Information) at Beaubourg in one sense and, in another, the CDS (Centers of Social Documentation) whose creation the Commission on Books and Reading had recently recommended in order to lead a new public of users to the reading of the written document and whose experimentation on a small scale seems to have yielded some rather encouraging results;[6] finally, *information campaigns* on specific topics, conducted in the language and forms of everyday culture, that is, by resorting to the techniques of *advertising*: posters in cities, television and radio spots with a brief, clear, exact content of the kind recently seen in the economic information campaign titled "Les yeux ouverts" [with eyes opened].[7]

Media Shifters

As for the media, it might be necessary to reorder its hierarchies or the image that we have of it. The central role of television is not exactly the one that is often ascribed to it. Television sets are usually left on, like a landscape in the inner space of a dwelling, a light that moves, the flame of a fireplace, a voice that offers a melodic accompaniment to everyday chores without being listened to and without the meaning of the words issuing from it being grasped, an envelopment of sounds whose volume is turned up in order to muffle the noise of the neighbors, cover up annoying messages, and reestablish *a contrario* the equivalent of an inner silence. Television brings into the home a magical encyclopedia that can be consulted without any problems of accessibility; everything is supposed to be given, shown, hence there is nothing that needs to be "learned"; it is a sacrament of totality in the dissemination of places and information, and in their atomization. But at the same time it furnishes a common symbolic form, that is, an equivocal discourse about which each person can have an interpretation and, as a result, it allows communication to take place, just as legends or fables in the past. It is not by chance that the most assiduous TV viewers are sought among children and older people, that is, in the two social groups that in the past used to listen to, repeat, crave, and transmit the treasures of legends and stories.

We have already alluded to radio, whose richness, flexibility, and interest as a means of expression for different types of publics have been underscored with the growth of free radio stations and local programming. They escape the influence of the state and the yoke of national cultural models as well as the commercial appetite of the radios on the outskirts of cities.[8] These new programs constitute a free tool for experimentation, whereby groups that until now have been silent or without means can reappropriate for themselves the space of public speech, or at least a parcel of this space. If adolescents and young adults, as well as immigrants, are so interested in these free radio stations, it is because of their common situation of living on borderlines, at a point between two ages in life, two styles of behavior, two cultures.

A third type of media also seems to play a central role in social communication: women's magazines and various practical or scientific encyclopedias, published in richly illustrated weeklies. Women's magazines are often accused of being stupid, but some of them are, at their own level, marvelous instruments of information about practical living, health, and food; they centralize countless new pieces of information on materials (fabrics, commodities), electric appliances for the home (ovens, freezers, washing and sewing machines), styles (home furnishing, decoration, clothing). One week they talk about dyslexic children, the next about various allergic symptoms, and the third the work of thermal insulation for houses. In each case, they inform in a simplified and fragmentary way, to be sure, but they are accessible and point out the existence of a problem and the importance of an area of activity. They are heuristic, without intimidating their readers. They furnish what we might easily call *firsthand information* that then allows greater circulation in social space, whether it is a question of reading product labels, distinguishing between different things needed for daily life, or choosing among different items for purchase. They have brought a fundamental contribution to the modernization of behavior and styles of consumption, both in the city and in the country; in the urban space, they serve as a reading prerequisite to the collection of information through window-shopping, visiting department stores, or questioning coworkers and family members; in the countryside, they are supplemented by the attentive reading of mail-order catalogs, with information gathered among the members of an agricultural cooperative or a rural labor union, and so on.

These magazines have the virtue of being lavishly illustrated and printed in several colors. Thus they contribute to visual education by proposing combinations of colors and forms and inviting a reading of their styles and proportions. They invite their readers to become active, by applying the many recipes they regularly provide, whether in cooking, refurbishing old armchairs, or knitting a sumptuous landscape into a handmade sweater. Some of the magazines even urge their readers to broaden their field of action or observation by proposing that they try out certain products, by taking part in the labor of a vast collective jury that examines books or films. They thus have a multiple role in exchanging information, educating one's judgment, and inspiring innovation, which is especially valuable for women who might be timid, inexperienced, poorly educated, or from traditional backgrounds; they allow them to acquire, without shame or difficulty, a minimal vocabulary in the language (of ideas, words, images) of modernity.

This very role of media shifters has a place in other areas of knowledge and know-how, especially in encyclopedias that present science, technology, and practice in everyday terms. "Practical science" is the name usually attributed to them, but we prefer to conceive them as modest *instruments for the circulation of knowledge*. To be sure, the knowledge that these periodicals put into circulation is neither exhaustive nor transmitted in the pure language of theory, nor is it accompanied by all the precautions and specifications for scientific use, but these are the very qualities that allow their public to assimilate it. Presented in small doses, in units divided up into weekly or monthly notebooks depending on their publication schedule, explained in simple language and with a broad use of diagrams and descriptive legends, sometimes sumptuously illustrated and accompanied by a few bibliographical supplements, these texts deal with scientific material (astronomy, physics, biology, nature), technology (mechanics, electronics, home construction), or practical matters (sewing, cooking, health, etc.). These texts often reveal a real wealth of expression; they instruct or inform without being boring, they make their readers want to translate into real activity the information they receive, they inspire progress, perhaps because they do not draw a borderline between theoretical knowledge and practical know-how. Like women's magazines, they have a dual function that in our view is essential: on the one hand, they offer a tool that is well adapted to those who need more schooling and to the silence of the institution that neglects the life of the body and the sphere of daily activities, whereas more precise or more complete didactic content—more clearly demarcated between theory and practice—had either tired out or exhausted the readers' interest and curiosity; on the other hand, they constitute an excellent auxiliary for mobility, whether in intellectual areas through self-education or in social areas through cultural enrichment.

Here, a cultural policy could encourage the analysis and reconsideration of this kind of publication so that these models of writing might be used profitably in other sectors and so that private publishers might produce small works of practical information from different areas of knowledge as well as from daily life. Through works of this kind, scientific and technical knowledge, even the most refined and elaborate material, can become rooted in ordinary culture and fragments of it can be made to circulate in the common language of speech and practice. The difficulties that the Centers of Social Documentation (mentioned earlier) have encountered in setting up a small documentary base, both accessible and responding to the needs of a broad public (often self-taught or with little formal schooling—but of great manual dexterity), shows the degree to which this kind of publication is still lacking in France, in contrast to other industrialized nations (notably the United States, Germany, and Scandinavia), where, it is true, the official educational model is less focused on the hierarchy of theoretical knowledge and the supreme values of abstraction.[9]

Practices of Circulation

Information, knowledge, and know-how would only be cheap commodities if they were not built on real practices of circulation, translation, and utilization. Already, the relation to some of the media is determined by traditional practices and customs, whether in older modes of communication for which an entire archaeology of gestures and ways of doing things is available, or of the media of recent creation, onto which the old habits are rapidly transferred by analogy and imitation. Thus, the reading of the daily newspaper, when it is a question of regular reading, begins with the columns devoted to births and obituaries, although these features have been dropped from national dailies, replaced by the sports page, or the results at the racetrack, the weather report, or crossword puzzles. The mode of entry changes, but the practice of an entry located on the margins of current events in politics or the economy, the main matter of the daily, is maintained, as if the important thing was to have an anodyne path to repeat regularly before entering into serious matters and dealing with "news shock." For the more recent media, rules are similarly based on a body of habits: listening to a local radio station in the morning in the bathroom or during breakfast, but in the evening watching the news on a given television channel before switching to another for a movie or a debate on current events. It appears that the multiplicity of available media has been integrated into the composition of a familiar landscape in which everyone defines his or her preferred itineraries and repeats them on a daily basis, the repetition assuring by its stability this fixed frame in which the flux of events of a world with extended limits and ever-changing dimensions can be seen. Everything happens as if each individual invented his or her technique to tame the technological tools of communication by skillfully making a montage scarcely changed from earlier practices, going back to a time prior to these tools, similar to what happened at the beginning of the twentieth century when the son of the village blacksmith often was the first to become the local car mechanic.

All these forms of material exchange play a strong role in the practices of circulation: hospitality, exchanges of homemade items (jams and jellies, sweaters, small furniture, decorative objects) and also exchanges of services (home repairs, from electronic appliances to the automobile; work to maintain or improve living arrangements). Repairs and do-it-yourself work concern tasks of greater and greater importance: the storehouse of tools that a few people maintain has grown over the last few years because of general prosperity and the sale of semiprofessional equipment; the economic crisis has not diminished the volume of these purchases of tools, either because the effort has been continued to avoid the cost of labor, or because it offers an opportunity for "undeclared" work as a source of supplementary income. Other practices concern activities whose sole purpose is pleasure: hack radio, amateur astronomers, computer clubs, and so on. These groups sometimes attain a very advanced level of technical expertise; they do not always resist the temptation to become closed groups with initiates who become "specialists" and refuse the presence of unwanted "ignoramuses" in their midst.

We witness in the growth of these many practices the multiplying of *seminars* offered almost everywhere. They can be for initiation into artistic creation, for art and artisanal activity, or different types of repair (automotive, electric, plumbing, etc.). It would seem that an immense and varied appetite for activities and knowledge exists, which is not satisfied by scholarly institutions and set up by the professional milieu. Objects of personal choice, placed outside of academic or professional hierarchies, and frequented in a rhythm and by impulses of their own, infinite numbers of learning opportunities are available; maybe it is the tactic of ordinary people to get involved in this mobility, in this plurality of knowledge, idioms, and competence that they have been told for so long is needed if they want to be "competitive" in modern society. Everything happens as if the multiplication of received information and known possibilities were awakening in a vast public myriad desires to learn and were pushing them in the direction of an encyclopedism of practices, to endlessly thrust back the limits of their own competence and experience. Thus proliferate all kinds of handiwork, from things sold in kits to artistic creations, from the resurrection of the know-how of tradition—for example, the art of lacemaking—to the practice of new techniques (seriography, video montage, etc.).[10]

We have already underlined the remarkable development of the practices of amateur musicians over the last few years. Less visible but no less significant is that of *writing workshops,* and all the more so because the work done in them is based on poetry, science fiction, or comic strips, that is, on working with written language along the borders of spoken language. In respect to the genre of texts being worked with, these preferences tell much about the conflicted relations or the fears raised over written language, corsetted in scholarly norms but whose manipulation remains a source of trauma that comes with the long-standing fear of "making mistakes," of "not stating things the way one should," of "speaking badly," of "not knowing how to write." Well, every practice of language and, all the more, every effort at writing, constitute an activity of communication. That is why encouraging this kind of practice is also part of a policy of developing social communication, of a "cultural staging of language."

Work needs to be done to destroy the artificial barriers that official discourses of knowledge have erected between written and spoken language. It needs to be explained and shown how the one is always nourished by the other, for example, with seminars of written and oral expression that retain a ludic dimension, writing festivals, slam poetry festivals, and contests of oral rhetoric or written composition concerning the production of varied texts reserved for amateurs and very young professionals (other sites are available for professional writers). Opportunities to practice varied registers of idiomatic expression are needed: circulars with information, fiction and short stories, poetry and theater, comic strips and skits, just as inventive and ephemeral media need to be sustained (amateur journals, small publishing houses) that are sites of experimentation for practices of writing and linguistic performance; for language, both written and spoken, is everyone's commodity, the site par excellence of anonymous practices of creation and circulation, in which a culture, and thus a freedom, is crystallized and concretized.

Chapter 12
Memories

Anyone wishing to grasp the nature of communication in all of its different facets, in the operators, networks, and practices of circulation, must also account for memory and the production of narratives in which the itineraries of life, work, or travel are unfolded and transmitted. Just as a living language is made from the sedimentation of heritages (which are phonetic, syntactic, lexical, or phrasal) set in fragile and provisional figures of equilibrium, the life of a culture and of a society is made of an endless ebb and flow between realities, representations, and their memories. Both the future and the present depend on the archaeology of gestures, objects, words, images, forms, and symbols, a repertory with many entrances from which is composed a landscape of communication and are invented the propositions of innovation.

Culture and communication are nourished by stories, not only in order to conserve piously the great moments of a time past, nor in the vain hope of compiling a complete catalog of a sacred patrimony, but in order to engender the future by reinscribing the present within the past. Thus, in the gestures of work, today we still find these very old uses and habits that sculpted and acculturated the human body, and that have structured its techniques of action. In the constructed order of the city there remain monumental traces of itineraries and forms, of an organization of private and public space, of a way of understanding the landscape and the climate. These are so many material or immaterial memories rent with holes, with incoherences, and with oblivion, just as the idiom of words is at every moment torn by the opposing tension between archaism and neologism. This multiform presence of memory can be found everywhere, even in our most ostensibly theoretical inquiries: thus the interest in astronomy or in the life of the species, two scientific areas that attract many amateurs. They correspond to the need to grasp the meaning of the universe and of life, whose former balances the ecological movement is elsewhere devoted to preserving.[1]

Life Stories

How do individuals use the abundant photographic, cinematic, or video materials that they purchase? To record the fleeting instants of their own history, these great ceremonies of kinship (baptisms, marriages, etc.) or those turning points in the destiny of a family (vacations, moving, the baby's first tooth, the first day of school, etc.).[2] Slides, photos, films, or videocassettes are used to preserve in the form of images these ordinary itineraries, common, intimate experiences among one's closest associates, to detail one's own history. Thus swirls a dust of stories every bit as ordinary and anonymous, and singular for their heroes alone. The latter from time to time reexamine with pleasure the trail of images in long commentary-filled sessions with friends, as if their contemplation and celebration of the past could never become tiring. The repetition of the tale, the attentive return to the commentary, each time renewed by reference to the present and corrected by the voices of the family chorus—all that serves to jointly orchestrate a family legend, to reinscribe the past in the present.

In the same way *life stories* are an old practice of spilling out and giving form to a private memory. Once transmitted by writing and arranged (when the author was a manual laborer) in the secondary category of "proletarian literature"—a movement currently illustrated by the review *Plein Chant*[3]—today their stories often become, thanks to the tape recorder, oral tales composed at the request of a descendant or a family friend, and sometimes of a researcher. The latter awakens and brings forth the speech of the interlocutor, who is often old, sometimes illiterate or barely educated. The researcher helps the person to follow the thread of memory, which easily twists and knots up or gets lost in chaotic or confused repetitions, asks the person to relate one kind of experience or another, or a given moment in his or her life, and helps to clarify the chronology of events in reference to the history of the region or the nation. The recording that results is then transcribed, edited, and published more or less in full.[4]

By moving from a written to an oral form for their research, from a solitary effort to a collaborative labor shared by two participants, these *life stories* (such is the conventional name often ascribed to them) have been enriched in depth and in breadth at the occasional risk of losing in authenticity. Clearly, the presence of the interlocutor, who is generally erased in the product delivered for publication, contributes to broadening the field of memories that are returned to a lucid consciousness. Oral communication retains the vibrancy of speech, its character or style of expression, its traits peculiar to the language spoken, whereas in earlier periods written stories were often stilted in an impoverished language and straightened out by the desire to respect the norms of appropriateness and stereotypes of style. But the quality of transcription and of editing, its honesty and fidelity to the actual narrative depend closely on the person collecting the data. The tape recorder allows for plenty of faking and liberties taken with the narrator's words. Not all researchers are as attentive, respectful, and honest as they ought to be; the gathering of a life story cannot be improvised, and requires a certain method and even a deontology.[5] Often a serial composition is more significant than an isolated episode of the story, which requires perseverance on the part of the collector.

The Past of People Who Have No History

The multiplication of these life stories has the advantage of showing that the introduction of a new technology (in this case, the tape recorder) does not necessarily break all links with the past, but can help to reactivate *the memory of everyday life* and reconstitute the narrative of daily practices and anonymous itineraries hidden in the thick folds of the social fabric, all the more in that these stories—sometimes individual, sometimes broadened to include the dynamics of a group—are also often the object of staging and of community celebrations that thereby reappropriate a common past.[6] In other cases, they will be shown on television and will come to be inscribed in social memory as a whole.[7] Whatever the mode of communication that is selected, these life stories, which are as much the memory of an existence as of a craft, establish a link between generations, transmitting to the youngest members fragments of earlier practices and ways of know-how. Thus they ensure the preservation and transmission of an essential part of tradition. Giving a voice to the memory of "people who have no history," they gather together and compose the polyphonic narrative of anonymous and fragile practices, tell the story of an indefinite proliferation of ways of doing things, and bring it into the common treasure of a cultural memory, as does, in another register and for groups, the animated history of the city and its staging in images.[8]

Life stories are most often the stories of hard work: through the collection of this portion of the oral patrimony, it is also the recognition of a fraction of the culture of work that enters into memory, but with the limitation that often the tools, machines, and gestures of their users have already disappeared. The aged body of the narrator can tell the story with words, but often can no longer mime them, and by then it is already too late for this indispensable visual anthropology.

Chapter 13
Propositions

At the end of this rapid trip through the contrasted landscapes of communication, we should now like to collect our impressions within the symbolic frame of an image, that of the immigrant, the anonymous hero hidden in the infinite crowd, in whom we thought we saw prefigured a portion of our own destiny, because adaptation to modernity also requires us to abandon the security of our traditions and because a necessary, even logical, relation exists in the life of a society between the relation it upholds with the "foreigner" from within and the relation with the foreigner from without.

The Immigrant as a
Social Figure of Communication

A foreigner among us, the bearer of the visible stigma of difference, since he or she moves with the marks of an idiom, a tradition, usages, tastes, and behavior that are not familiar and in which we fail to see ourselves, the immigrant teaches us how to circulate in our language and our customs, and adapts to our material and symbolic universe. So different from ourselves, the immigrant is also the figure who already resembles us, whose destiny anticipates our own. He or she is the exemplary figure imposed by modernity, with the abandonment of our familiar points of reference, the adaptation to other codes, the acquisition of new ways of thinking and acting. The immigrant has already faced this test of imposed change, of obligatory displacement, and has faced it successfully, since immigrants are among us, the recognizable bearers of their original identity, of their *difference*.

Placed at the point connecting two worlds, practicing, with their defending body and in a chaotic way, but practicing two languages and two cultures, the immigrant shows that it is entirely possible to move between the past and the present, between the here and the elsewhere, that one can invent equivalent codes, and organize systems of translation. The immigrant is also the person who puts our society to the test, for it is by its capacity to tolerate that which does not respect its norms and traditions that the tolerance and open-mindedness of a society, and the real quality of its politics of communication, are judged. Here too the situation of the immigrant has exemplary value.

To welcome does not mean forcibly to integrate by erasing all signs of difference, or making things conform to all our customs through a process of obligatory assimilation.[1] It would be both ridiculous and contradictory with the present concern to reestablish, in the national harmony, the specificity of minority cultures, or the play of regional differences.[2] Accepting the real presence of immigrants means in truth to open to them a free space of speech and demonstration in which their own culture can be displayed or offered for the knowledge of others; it means to stop mocking or showing scorn for what makes them different, but to seek to find in it a weight of humanity, a specific creation. For that to happen it must become possible for immigrants — whtever their age or their nation of origin — to follow diverse itineraries within our society. They must be able, as individuals, to choose on their own the trajectory they wish to borrow, between their original culture and the culture in which they are displaced, by determining for themselves the symbolic place in which they wish to settle: at a greater or a lesser distance from one another, preserving a certain number of original traits, and imitating, to a greater or a lesser extent, our own manners and choices in doing things.

It is not up to us to decide for them. Nor can we in any way impose on them, once and for all, a maximal difference with respect to ourselves: this would be a poorly disguised effort at rejecting their presence and their liberty, a fictive way of respecting them by enclosing them within the immobility of a cultural and social ghetto. Nor do we have any right to make them fit the mold of our conformities, to force them to imitate us in everything: that would be to deny the value of their own heritage and their alterity. All we have to do is invent with them a "culture in the plural" and offer them a *plurality of mixed itineraries* that are diverse, changing, and constantly being reshaped. The variety of these passages, the diversity of borrowings and of collages that this plurality will inspire, and the *cultural mixings* that it will promote can only be beneficial to us. They will enrich our own culture. A country with an aging demography is tempted to fold itself gingerly upon itself and its own certainties. These contributions coming from without will bring the good fortune of dynamizing our culture, of expanding its capacity to internationalize, and thus of offering itself as a model and a source of inspiration, a commodity to be consumed. This transformation will contribute to enhancing our attractiveness on foreign markets, at the very moment when an essential battle will be waged with the goods produced by the culture industries. When we have to imagine, compose, promote, astonish, produce, and sell, all experience of cultural *mixing* will be a real advantage.

By becoming more open and more tolerant with regard to immigrants, we would also learn how to relativize our codes of conduct, our way of understanding "high culture," and this change would allow us to confer on anonymous inventions the arts of practical creation and everyday culture, and on what is made by practitioners of everyday life their own cultural role. The opening of a multiplicity of cultural and social itineraries must not remain purely hypothetical; rather, we must create the real conditions that permit the potentialities of imagination and creativity to perform as best they can. Immigrants are in a "privileged" situation as borderliners who find themselves at the line of contact between two symbolic realms. In particular, children of the second generation can exercise a marvelous influence as mediators and translators by materializing, in the world of image and sounds, the diversity of their cultural mixings. Creation is never born of a scrupulous respect for received codes, but of the radicalism of conflicts that tear to shreds received images and of the existential impatience that inhabits these social tensions.

That requires us to change our ways of treating immigrants, to give them the means of constructing a *positive image* of themselves, to give them a *visibility* in our cultural and social space, other than in the features of negative stereotypes (violence, neighboring feuds, delinquency, failure in school, etc.). We have to attend to everything that might revalorize their status, their ways of doing things, as, for example, the Christian churches quite consciously did for the Jews after 1945. In this area, we would do well to draw inspiration from programs directed at "minorities" in the United States: led in a systematic way, in a spirit of voluntarism, these programs have helped to improve, both in reality and in the mirror of public opinion, the status and the cultural image of a fraction of the Black or Latino (Chicano, Puerto Rican) population.

Nothing can be gained from preaching occasional "morality lessons" through advertising campaigns, as was tried a few years ago, unless, at the same time, we carry out a coordinated and stubborn action in every direction. Only that might slowly gnaw away the hard core of age-old and tenacious prejudices that make the foreigner an undesirable and menacing intruder. This bitterness and prejudice must be replaced by other types of information, other images of reference, which, taken together, will finally give a new form of representation to the other. The media has a crucial role to play in this type of action, for if it reflects the state of public opinion with its presuppositions, it also contributes to forming it by furnishing a good portion of its raw materials. There is no social fatality here. Tolerance is learned; the mind opens itself by being educated. To struggle against social stigmatization means working toward *reestablishing communication* throughout the social body by having circulate within it an inventive and vibrant form of polyphony and polyculture, a plurality of information and of propositions. Treating the stranger better from within means preparing us to be better able to meet the stranger from without; learning how to take interest in other peoples and other cultures is still one of the best ways to persuade them, in turn, that we are interesting interlocutors and generous hosts.

General Orientations

What role should the state play in this? It should not take charge of the deficits of communication. That would be to replace an absent social dynamics with the rigidity of an administrative orthodoxy that, despite its good intentions, would further contribute to the atomization of individuals. Communication is nourished by the vitality of different social networks, by the interlacing of transverse itineraries, all levels that escape the power of an administration. The state should, rather, strive to sustain social formations that are an exception to its own institutions, hence to promote differences instead of jumping on the pretext of what is lacking in order to extend its technocratic hegemony. With its limitations, the FIC (Foundation for the Intervention of Culture, created in 1971) in order to aid local experiments in cultural innovation seems to us to offer a strong model that places responsibility on the local level and possibilities for taking initiatives to associations, and allows for the invention of happy alliances between the social and cultural sectors. In this area, stimulation might invigorate the generally disinherited areas (population of old persons, rural life, the culture of labor) by putting imposed themes up for competition, as the National Center for Scientific Research (CNRS) did in collaboration with its Program of Actions on Themes (ATP), of a limited duration and with a defined objective.

The general orientations that we are proposing concern *local* action, a site of differentiation, experimentation, and innovation on a reduced scale; the *associative movement* as the motor force of this experimentation, as the producer of small workshops of apprenticeship and innovation that are coordinated with local milieus, their codes, and their needs; *ordinary culture,* a rubric under which we group what relates to practical knowledge, traditions, and habits of everyday life, such as the "culture of labor," according to Pierre Belleville, and "extended patrimony," in the words of Max Querrien.[3]

But the essential component of our analysis tends to underscore the importance of the *intermediary levels* of culture. In our view, this notion envelops the generative role played by go-betweens and mediators, those pivotal characters who animate the transversal networks of communication and transmit new cultural content by translating it into a form that can be assimilated by those who are part of the network. It also concerns the media and commodities, for example, secondary arts such as comic strips or whatever is extracted from the language of advertising. Finally, it refers to the necessary articulation of oral over written communication, language over the image, the invention of ideas and forms over the creativity of gestures and the everyday arts of doing things. In all these areas, recourse to the technologies of communication, to means of recording and transmission furnished by their apparatuses, is of decisive importance. Thanks to them, a visual anthropology can be constituted, and thus an archive of oral records. This labor of recentering intermediary levels and ordinary practices must not be done in the absence of their own actors: the collation of data, their study, and their formulation ought to be made in collaboration with the practitioners who are their inventors, so that they can witness their own restitution, critique, explanation, and reappropriation, and so that the gaze of others does not succeed in transforming them into objects of study and of curiosity for observers of social facts.

Proposed Measures

The preceding chapters have argued certain points in detail.[4] Here we review the results by dividing them into six broad areas of action.

1. *Minorities and regional cultures.* They must be given visibility and assistance to help them gain a positive image in public space by the production of cultural goods that make their specificities both known and appreciated (film, video, radio, television, recordings, documents, etc.). Here a regional endowment of strong funding placed at their service is indispensable. Their presence in the administrative apparatus must also be ensured, perhaps through a method of quotas of slots reserved for a limited time: recruiting from among their members functionaries who would play a privileged role as intermediaries and translators for their social groups of origin is a way of integrating the evolution of minorities and neglected regional groups into the social body and avoiding the constitution or maintenance of "lower castes."

2. *Transversal networks and mediating go-betweens.* The specificity of the functions of these networks must be respected, and their mediator animators must be given the means to increase their effectiveness: by direct access to databases with possibilities for interactivity (without the control of the intervening institution); editing of informational documents in everyday language (contemporary graphics, vocabulary in the spoken language, expressive techniques borrowed from comic strips or advertising); opening of relay sites of information and documentation (such as the centers of social documentation that have already been used), for which the production of an adequate documentation is sought.

3. *Orality and intermediary cultural levels.* Orality must be returned to its fundamental role (conversation, information, diverse learning experiences, etc.) and, through reference to it, the production of intermediary texts on practical knowledge, the circulation of scientific knowledge, new techniques, and so on, must be encouraged. For that we suggest that places in cities be set aside for speech making, that festivals of orality and writing be created, that questions be opened to competition (for the production of texts or cassette recordings),

that the circulation of recordings as a means of social exchange be developed, and so on. Similarly, the collection and archiving of oral patrimony should be stimulated, by associating with it what pertains to gestures and techniques of the body, for which programs of regional or local action could be launched in liaison with the associative movement and "spontaneous researchers" in the given areas (to use the terms of the Godelier mission).

4. *Experimental workshops established on the local level.* It would be necessary to multiply such workshops as places where new technologies of communication can be imparted, as places for cultural miniproductions (small reviews, local editions, independent radio stations, etc.) and as poles of local animation that in particular hold the attention of young adults. This would also be a testing ground for materials and a place that would train animators from each local area. These workshops should be hooked into the existing associative social fabric and not appear as products coming directly from or being imposed by the will of the state.

5. *Studies and research on overly neglected points.* An entire group of analyses and research would have to be done (through calls for offers, contests, and so on) on the role of the media in the construction of the identity of social groups, on the ways that knowledge is acquired in the context of different modes of learning (in particular, by setting aside the official scholarly models), on ordinary practices and the activities of practitioners (in matters of reading, self-documentation, self-education, the use of broader media channels, etc.).

6. *Council on culture and communication.* It would be desirable to create a permanent office of consultation concerned with questions of culture and communication, at once autonomous and transversal in relation to the big ministerial bodies responsible for these sectors. Its role would be one of stimulating research and critical analysis in these areas, of acting on hypotheses under discussion, by moving toward specific projects, by having access to official dossiers of information, by making public the results of its analyses, by confronting them with the choices made abroad in the same areas, and so on.

Part IV

Ethnic Economies

Chapter 14
An Interethnic Encounter

The abundance of statistical and sociological works relating to cultural and linguistic diversity (minorities, particular kinds of behavior, immigration, etc.) and to the educational policies implemented to "manage" it allows us to wonder about the very *problematics* that inspire these works or that, judging from their results, they might imply.[1] This will be the task of the observations that follow. Therefore, I will not directly consider the conflicts opposing minority groups to national academic institutions, nor the massive data that form the basis for the demands of these groups or that make clear the shortcomings of these institutions. By "problematics" I mean the ways in which the problem that springs from the violence of the facts is treated, the way of raising it, the ideological system in which it is articulated so that solutions can be offered. It is a matter of asking what social coding the *way of thinking* all these facts refers to, and if, by themselves, they do not invite us — if they do not require us — to change the frame of reference for management.

One could foresee a priori that the problem of minorities leads one to think about the very way of dealing with it — or of reflecting on its problematics — since it calls into question the ways in which the system invested in educational policy is confronted by another or other sociocultural groups. With immigrants or minorities, other practices are laid out within the dominant order. An "alterity" needs to be recognized. If we do not stick to "solutions" that are imposed by relationships of forces, how can we envisage that in this process one of the present parties might treat the others according to its own criteria and credit itself with representing universalism? According to protocols that are unfortunately much more complex, the meeting

143

of different cultures in the field of education belonging to one of them cannot fail to threaten the axioms of a particular pedagogy. Hence the intensity of the reactions it provokes.

A return to the problematics that are at stake appears necessary from a historical angle. It has often been emphasized, for example, with regard to migratory movements toward richer, more open, or more liberal regions, that the fact is hardly new; on the other hand, the world in which it is now taking place is entirely new. It is inscribed in a different political, economic, or cultural configuration that treats it with another meaning on every register of political struggle, economic change, and collective consciousness. It is no longer the same "fact." The continuity is in large part illusory, even when it might be found in the statistics of displacement. We have to wonder, therefore, in what terms these movements are currently being effected, and to what problematics we have recourse in order to think through the new functionings.

For about fifteen years, the progress or the resurgence of an ethnic consciousness can be seen throughout the whole world and is signaling important changes. The spread of ethnic revival movements has also surprised scientific observers, who were formerly inclined to take racial, ethnic, or religious protests as survivals, and are led from now on to take them seriously, to which many recent publications bear witness, from the much-debated thesis of John Bennett to the creation of specialized journals, such as *Ethnicity* in 1974.[2] A great deal of work is in progress that will allow "ethnic" reality — having long been postulated, marginalized, or eliminated from our disciplines — to be constructed as a scientific object. This renewal is of special interest for studies on "nation" and "nationalisms," phenomena that, despite a majority tendency still reigning in France, cannot be dissociated from the problems posed by minorities or migrations, and which by and large slip through our analytic grids.[3]

The approach of interethnic situations that have become structural (although for a long time they were assumed to be transitory) thus calls for a revision of our points of view.[4] It is clear, however, that by its very nature, it excludes the hypothesis of a neutral analysis that would overcome the equivocation or the opposition among heterogeneous groups. From what place could these differences be dominated or integrated? Every effort to take up the problem, even the most scientific, refers to a particular system that has its own postulates, rules, and logic, such that ultimately only its success, its spread, and the forces that sustain it would legitimize its universal magistrature. From the outset—and this is a first aspect of the question—a wager must be tendered that is not equivalent to a "realpolitik" that has already fomented many historical renewals, namely, that the law of the stronger does not have the last word and that, in any case, the alterity of the least human community has no less *right* to be recognized than that of the most powerful. That there ought to be, between migrants and minority groups on the one hand, and citizens of the host nation or members of the dominant group on the other, a slate of common interests; that there ought to be transversal jurisdictions admitted by the participants (by means of what ruses!); that necessary networks of agreements among interested powers might already permit recourse and modifications in the existing situations— these are facts that can indeed be used for the defense of this irreducible right of useful instruments but not as its basis. If this right is admitted, the result is that the problematics relative to the interethnic encounters would not be able to overcome the heteronomy among collectivities. In a perspective analogous to that which aims at a compatibility among nations, it is only possible to analyze the conditions of new sociopolitical *contracts,* and in particular to make clear, as a precondition, the *inner* transformations that a dominant group's meeting with others produces or requires.

Such is the point of view that I would like to envisage in turn: first, a critical examination of the conceptual apparatus to which we appeal in order to think and manage ethnic pluralities; and second, a location of a few of the new forms, or at least those that have become determinant forms, that "belonging" takes in the current immigrant or minority experience. From these reciprocal effects of the encounter— the ones calling into question the epistemological framework of a dominant policy, the others relative to changes brought about by a marginalization or by a diaspora—we can induce a few prospective propositions concerning secondary education. In fact, schools reproduce the norms of a society. In our nation, have they not assumed the role played by initiation in traditional societies? Thus schools will not be ruled by diversity unless the interethnic meeting itself becomes a school for diversifying society as a whole.

Chapter 15
Conceptual Assimilation

An Ideological Eclecticism

Categories of highly varied origin punctuate and organize studies on the educational strategies devoted to cultural differences. The working notions, which are taken to be more or less obvious, are rooted in historical and ideological traditions. In France, the ideas of "nation," "patrimony," or "identity" belong to a centralizing political register (of Jacobin origin but often taken up in nationalist perspectives that weigh heavily on reactions with regard to "foreigners" and "autonomists"), while the notions of "equality of rights," "social ties," or "social needs" pertain to a repertory of liberal ideas, to a federalist style. An ideological moat also separates "universalism," a cosmological and nonhistorical concept, from "internationalism," a political, socialist, or juridical concept. The terminology of "deficits" (either cultural or mental) or of "handicaps," like that of "resistances" and including that of "minorities," refers to an ideology of progress, which originated in the Enlightenment and is translated in scholarly or medical ways through a hierarchization of capacities ranked according to a presupposed order of progress. Among these marks of an "enlightened" philosophy—dominant for a long time in pedagogical conceptions—are categories that come from cultural anthropology: "identity," "difference" (which has replaced the "theory of deficit"), "social imaginary," "subculture," and so on. Issuing from the idea that culture is a coherent totality in which individual experiences find their places and symbols are discourses dramatizing the "area in between," as if there had merely existed a void "between" stable things and as if a choice had to be made between two identities. Travel would be nothing more than a loss in expectation of a harbor...

The vocabulary follows a rocky road of heterogeneous references. If I leave aside "national ideology" or the antinomy between "culture" and "economy" (to which I shall return), this elementary list already shows the multiplicity of successive ideologies and different disciplines that are amassed, in fragments, in the discourses that analyze the relations that a system of education has with other cultures. This observation, which could easily be enriched, is not a judgment. Nor could it pass for an effect of chance. It is the result of a dual process: on the one hand, the erosion of intellectual certainties along the borders where they meet other cultural observations; on the other hand, the rapid succession of appeals to new intellectual or scientific references with a view to shoring up this erosion and, each time, the insufficiency of these recourses. A moving eclecticism is produced along the borders where, in increasingly numerous places within the educational grid itself, the often dramatic failures of educated immigrants (or anyone belonging to different linguistic groups) undermine pedagogical certainties. The ideological framework is not autonomous with regard to phenomena whose study it determines. It undergoes their reincarnations. It carries marked upon it the symptoms of the strategies — displacements or ossification — of the social institution on which it depends and which is most often the educational institution itself. The analysis is in ideological solidarity with the particular group to which it pertains.

A few current working concepts are worth noting. That of "particularism," first of all, which has meaning only in relation to its supposed opposite, that is, the existence of "universalisms" that everyone ought to recognize. But can mass-produced products be held to be "universal," for example, those purveyed through the media? We often forget the singularity of the historical conditions of their production and, furthermore, the extreme diversity of their appropriation on the part of those who deploy them, that is, the particularities of the uses to which they are put. Or can we assume that values such as "liberty" or "equality" are universal? But we forget that many groups are based on different principles, such as honor, fidelity, contractual allegiance, and so on, and that, depending on the societies, liberty or equality inherits such diverse — indeed, heteronomous — modalities that we can wonder if, wherever it is accepted, it is a question of the same values.

The concept of "identity," so often held to be obvious, is no less strange. Whatever its juridical, administrative, or controlling expectations may be, it supposes that a group (or an individual) can be assimilated into a representable *object* (a system of beliefs and practices, a place in an order, a type of idiom, etc.) and that, as a result, it becomes both for itself and others an object of knowledge. If this concept were taken literally, we would no doubt discover within it the definition of alienation, since it thus eliminates from a group (or an individual) his or her field of play in a plurality of networks and forces the person to become a *subject* of his or her history in a reciprocity of determining relations. Identity is what an ethnology or a psychosociology makes of the group by turning it into an object of knowledge, according to a process that has first specified juridical status before defining scientific entities.[1] Into this melting pot of definitions must be added the effects of new situations. Thus evolution leads a hyperindividualized society to compensate for the progressive erasure of its inner symbolic hierarchies by an increased stigmatization of the foreigner. The immigrant, the minority group member, indeed, the marginal person, inherits the role of furnishing an antinomical figure for a mass that is increasingly stripped of images of its own. The identity of "others," in turns dramatized as a dangerous instability or frozen in a heterogeneous system, serves as a point of reference for an undifferentiated population. The immigrant becomes the antidote to anonymity. But whatever social role the identification of the "foreigner" may play, the questions posed by the interethnic encounter hit the nail on the head: foreigners living among the citizens of the dominant society challenge not only an identity imposed from without but the very idea of identity, especially when they claim the right to be themselves and follow a path of their own in the midst of diversity.

Other cases can be called to mind, such as the uses to which the notion of "difference" are put. A few examples are enough to suggest the degree to which the confrontation touches on strategic points in a culture and stirs up or transforms a conceptual machinery.

Culture or Economics?

Many analyses have underscored the failure of programs of scholarly action based on the single problematic of the social milieu and on the economic interpretation of status or promotion. They have led to a keener definition of cultural coefficients, such as lifestyles, forms of sociality, feelings of belonging, language, awareness of one's own history, religion, types of habitat, and so on. It would be impossible, in fact, to take up the difficulties of Catholics in Ireland, Jews in Los Angeles, Gypsies or Basques in France, in terms that are limited to their socioprofessional levels. Even if, in the best of all scenarios, there exists no antimony but an accumulation of cultural and economic elements — cultural and linguistic difference being added to an unfavorable cultural status in order to explain the extent of failures in education — one is generally led from an essentially economic approach of the problem to an insistence on its cultural aspects.

The orientations of interested groups also attests to an oscillation between the two poles and proves the difficulty of reconciling them. Thus, for a long time, the Chicano movements in California were divided between those who analyzed their situation in terms of an agricultural proletariat and those who saw their situation as the alienation of a prestigious tradition going back to the Aztecs. Different policies flowed from these two interpretations — one economic, the other cultural. How can an analytical grid be drawn that would favor relations of classes and erase cultural differences over the other, which valorizes symbolic genealogies and anthropological structures?[2] In many cases, moreover, history shows an opposition between them. Thus, a strong desire for national assimilation among immigrant workers in the United States has held back class consciousness and oriented unionization toward corporatisms.[3] In the same way, in post-1970 Quebec, the priority the Parti Québécois gave to defending Francophone culture has, for several years, increasingly limited demands based on class. In other circumstances, the same opposition gives way to inverse reactions. Thus, against the governmental measures that had the effect (or the objective?) of marginalizing the "case" of twelve million foreigners living in Western Europe, immigrant organizations, through their charter of 1979, affirmed the primacy of their solidarity with the working class as a whole.[4]

This tension refers back to the disparity of situations and linkages, but it also is a barometer of our technical and scientific difficulty in reconciling the two types of analysis that, for the past three centuries, Western society has progressively separated and specialized for reasons pertaining to its particular way of being structured: one, *historical*, concerns the dynamic relation of this society to itself, and privileges recourse to a socioeconomic codification; the other, *ethnological*, relating to "different" societies, aims at exhuming the forms of unbending anthropological coherence among ethnic systems. Today, the confrontation of cultures on the very turf of our "developed" societies appears to juxtapose these two types of analysis without uniting them, as if the apparatus organized as a function of an inner historical development was unable to be adjusted to the apparatus seeking the knowledge and domination of greater and more stable configurations existing outside of our world.

The presence of "foreigners" among us slowly inverts the ethnological or colonizing relation and allows us to reexamine the grounding axioms. Are we going to treat it as an internal given in "our" history, on an economic mode, or as a "foreign body" depending on an ethnological analysis? The alternative cannot be sustained, although it is quite frequent: it obliges us to rethink Western categories of knowledge. Immigrants are in a reciprocal situation. Inhabitants of our epistemological territories, they have been led to internalize our codes and, most often, to distribute their very experience of the country of origin according to a division that, by opposing economic and cultural elements, or productive operations and symbolic representations, transforms their traditions into a past that is still present but that remains unthinkable and silent. But they can also house these heterogeneous regimes of sociality in distinct places (such as, on the one hand, the family or the café, and, on the other hand, the office, the factory, and the administration), and insinuate into dominant codings a different practice whose effect is one of unveiling in them unique requirements and hidden functionings. Even if, obviously, its impact is inscribed in a broader framework, I believe that the interethnic experience blurs the clarity of our ethnic distinctions (both intellectual and administrative) and that we are only at the beginning of revising what it brings into our conceptions.

Individual Rights and Collective Rights

In particular, the opposition between a historical or socioeconomic conception of our societies (in terms of progress) and an "ethnological" conception of the others (in terms of cultural structures) appears to be tied to a more fundamental determination: since the eighteenth century, following events and for reasons that cannot be adumbrated here, modern Western society has been conceived as the combination of *individual* units and distinguished as such from traditional societies (medieval, classical — or "primitive") regulated by the principle of a priority of the *group* over its members.[5] This conception was progressively developed and defined through a liberal economy (defined by the competition among productive individuals), a democratic politics (granting one vote to each person with a view to producing collective representation), a mathematical science of society (whose unit of calculation is the individual, all the way from Condorcet up to the statistics of the INSEE [National Institute of Statistics and Economic Studies]), a juridical elaboration of individual rights (assumed to be equal for everyone), and so on.[6] In schooling, the official progressive discourse thus formulates the social imperatives in terms of rights and individual duties, and it is on the turf of an equality of these rights that the vanguard battles are fought.[7] It would be useless to underscore how the extension of an informational treatment of social problems generalizes this way of thinking and managing groups according to the analytical and combinatory mode of formations composed on the basis of elementary units.

The former collective right, arguing for the privilege that the family, the "house," the ethnic group, the client network, and the "nation" have over their members has been driven out of legitimate discourse, or thrown outside in order to become, in the "ethnological" figure of "primitive" or "peasant" societies, the very index of a regime long past—the sign of the other or of former times.[8]

This regime of sociality has been repressed, if not crushed, to the point that in France the collective expression of "families," of "houses," and so on, has been theoretically and practically wiped off institutions and national representations or left to a conservative opposition, and that, where it could not be erased, it was labeled with the value of a "survival," a "resistance," or an opaque and stubborn irreducibility (Basque, Breton, Corsican, etc.) to the democratic law of progress. Whenever possible, it was retranslated and transformed into problems relating to individuals in groups. An enormous labor—an obscure and fundamental hundred years' war—has "reduced" the collective right either through its assimilation into an individual right or through a process of ethnologation.

In so brutally summarizing a very complex history (and one that is also fundamental to the sciences that have assigned themselves the task of rethinking social life on these new bases), I merely wish to underline the difficulty that we experience today in situating, within the dominant logic of individual rights, a right that belongs to collectivities themselves (insofar as they are not reducible to the product of associations among individuals). Each time, the collectivity is brought back to elementary units whose combinations and correlations can be analyzed by political economy or sociology. It is hardly surprising that the inadequacy of these calculations increasingly promotes a recourse to ethnological or anthropological models that are extracted from their function outside of Western society and replanted (with difficulty) in the field of "studies" and programs devoted to the inner nation.

Migrants or members of so-called minority societies clearly reintroduce into juridical, economic, or scholarly administrations, under the rule of the equality of individual rights, the rights of collectivities that cannot be each identified with the sum of their national citizens. Under the sign of one language, one configuration of practices, one common history, a social totality precedes the variants that its members present, and on that very account they seek to be identified. Before outlining a few of the forms that this situation now imposes on "belonging" in the migrant or "minority" experience, it would be worthwhile to specify the figures — more or less masked — whereby these rights of collectivities are conveyed in the apparatuses that deal with social life in terms of individual units. These disguised forms, if they refer to the way in which our history leads *us* to advance the problems concerning *other* types of belonging, if they result from a politics of assimilation that determines our way of thinking, nonetheless furnish instruments of analysis pertaining to our situation and openings for different policies.

Masked Figures

If we are really dealing with a heteronomy between two paradigms (the one founded on the priority of the collective, the other on that of the individual), it is not surprising that the formulation of the social experiences depending on the first give way to bizarre forms of camouflage in the codings of the second. As examples and hypotheses, I will only indicate a few of these paradoxical figures in which communal experiences are presented in our midst, masked in and by our social discourse: the "cultural," the "private," the "customary," and "noncommunication." These "translations" trace a groove of figures or metaphors of another language within our own language.

First of all, a good deal of what appears to us of a *cultural* nature — or what we have transformed into "cultural" activities and expressions — corresponds to these areas of social life that the individualistic bias of our modes of analysis and management have make unthinkable in economic terms. We are calling "cultural" those configurations or fragments of *economies* that conform to criteria other than ours. The term highlights in a different group (or in one of our own) what our instruments only allow us to think in the form of exotic expressions, symbolic structures, or customary practices that are not connected with the law of the marketplace.[9] In fact, studies devoted to this other sociality designated by the "cultural" increasingly reveal systems of exchange, but systems whose rules refer back to the preeminence of the group, its honor, its transmission, its spiritual body, the allegiance owed to its "chiefs" by a clientele, and so on. Conversely, since the work of Joseph Schumpeter, it has been possible slowly to disengage from economic "rationality" even the "cultural" orientations that subtend every system, the historical forms of credibility that it involves, the impact that noncommercial relations have on it. The dividing line between an economic text and cultural margins appears less and less certain, even porous. What we are calling "symbolic" (goods, a language, etc.) is no more symbolic than money or financial writing and signatures. Nor is it less rational. But it is a question of an economy and a reason different from those that have prevailed in our world.

It is equally remarkable that psychoanalytic investigation, directing ethnological inquiries that were formerly oriented toward a "primitive" exteriority toward a "savage" interiority of Western life, is discovering, precisely in the lower depths of our societies, "economy" itself, in its relational, "familial," and collective inflections, whose place is claimed to be occupied by a productivist and individualist order. In this regard, émigrés are bringing back our own "unconscious," the very material we have used to fashion our repression! All the same, our institutions and legitimated knowledges no longer conform to this collective law. But, if we recognize ethnic economies under the "cultural" mask that is the effect of their rejection by our own history, we have before us an initial means of measuring the stakes.[10]

The translation of a type of sociality into the framework of the other produces a second paradox: the right of a collective totality sees itself impose, in the grid of duties and individual rights, the figure of the *private*. What belongs to the community here wears the mask of *private* life. Belonging to social bodies ("aggregate corporations," in the terminology of British law, or "families" of every stripe, ethnic communities, linguistic formations, etc.) was formerly treated in terms of contracts regulating alliances or wars between groups, and not between individuals. Today, it appears only able to penetrate our official rules in the name of prerogatives or charges given to private persons—unless it is possible (a recourse that has the preferences of political bodies vis-à-vis émigrés but that is excluded for many, such as Gypsies, Basques, Catholics, and so on) to provide a diplomatic solution to these problems of belonging. Thus if we make an exception for the conventions passed between states concerning "foreign nationals" (agreements that short-circuit the relations of the groups themselves with the host country), the general administrative tendency consists in treating ethnic appurtenances on a case-by-case basis, in a way that is in turn ethical (the rights of conscience), scholastic (talents and remedial situations), medical (handicaps, the right to Social Security), and so on, and to envisage the community as an "association" (endowed with representatives and powers) formed on the basis of status and individual choices. From this angle, the communitarian reality wears away and is dispersed such that the management based on the individual is now only taken up in elementary units and is no longer confronted by another social logic.

Two cases shed strong light on the procedures that turn collective belonging into a "private" form: familial lineage and the religious institution. Despite their differences, they can be compared on the grounds of the relation that they both present for us between a collective reality and private manifestations.[11] There was a separation of social organization (which was productivist) and belonging (which was familial or religious), whereas they were for a long time linked one on the other through protocols of reciprocal balances. To have been isolated (the way a body is scientifically "isolated"), the sociopolitical administration has marginalized domestic economy and religious economy, both reduced from now on to an expression in this new framework in a disguised form: the private sphere has to take charge of this ethnic dimension; it serves as a social metaphor, and often as a symptom and even as a focal point for complaint for whatever in the familial or religious institution had to be erased from public rules in the name of individual *activity* (the true objective of liberal competition and statewide administration).[12] Fortunately, it is not a question of returning to a past that was not less constricting than the present (and probably was more so), but of recognizing in the private sphere one of the current issues of fundamental ethnic economies, and of dealing with this new social figure as the possible disguise of a communitarian form. That the private sphere makes manifest an ethnic revival (most powerfully in matters of familial or spiritual lineage) is shown clearly by current politics, but it would have to be taken seriously as such, including in the relations between secondary schools and the private requests of émigré parents.

Another figure of the collective is found in a juridical order based on the Constitution, in *customary law*. In ways that have often been a topic of debate, habitual conduct that a group takes to be legitimate constitutes, or can constitute, creative facts of law. They can even have a derogatory force with regard to formal constitutional laws. They refer back to a collective law, to the very inner workings of the legislative system based on the representation of individuals. The counterpoint that this customary normativity writes into the margins of our regular practices obviously requires an official habilitation that for the most part has minimized its importance. No less, it introduces — frequently in the name of concessions made to "survivals" — another logic, that is, in fact, the recognition of a diversity of systems coexisting inside our societies, and other principles of sociality than those that prevail among us. Always a bit awry and accepted with difficulty, in our society customary law becomes the Trojan horse of different social regimes; it brings in the principle of alterities that are compatible with a social dynamics. This instrument could be placed in the service of economies in which are recognized not only the past givens of a present time, but the present conditions of a future.

Finally, we need to evoke the figure that the "foreigner" assumes in a problematics of *communication* whose explicit postulates reach back to the Enlightenment. The great *conquista* of communication has used in turn roads, schools, administrative rationales, telecommunications, the media, and cybernetics. It has endlessly been struggling against the opacity of places (local powers, autonomous or different collectivities, etc.), with a view to a universal invisibility creating immediate relations between citizens and with the central power. In France, two presuppositions can be seen at work, one anthropological (communication, which is fine, and even more is needed), the other political, successively royalist and Jacobin (the growth of the state ensures the progress of the nation). The facts have fortunately imposed limits on the development of these presuppositions. Serving to put a brake to this are the collective and opaque experiences of migrants and minorities, from the Gypsies of the past to the Portuguese of today. To the law of transparency, to the endless task of a complete social legibility, they oppose an obscure difference that would be the equivalent of a crime of lèse-majesté against Communication. But in this irritating figure they uphold two essential givens to which the inflationist logic of information obliges us today to return: on the one hand, communication is built only on noncommunication, on the barriers that invent collective intimacies, on a whole series of closures and "secrets" that create inner spaces of exchange; on the other hand, with the effectiveness of democratic life disappearing with local powers (notables, regional groups, etc.) that have long been its historical support, only the recognition and vitality of communities (ethnic, linguistic, or geographical) can resist the leveling thrust (which is ultimately terrorist) generated by the atomization of citizens in the face of state administrations. From this point of view, the pockets of illegible social alterities that appeared to transgress transparency play an increasingly indispensable role, beyond the qualitative threshold in which the success of communication begins to erode it. In our Western countries, what is opaque becomes what is necessary. The opaque is based on the rights of the collectivity, capable of balancing the economy that, in the name of individual rights, exposes the entire social reality to the great universal light of the market and of the administration.

Chapter 16
The Active and Passive
of Appurtenances

Hybridizations

These communities whose representation on our national scene is transformed and masked through the effects of an *assimilation* are in themselves, because of migration and marginalization, changed through their adjustment to unexpected situations, that is, by the effects of an *adaptation*. Many are the coefficients of these inner mutations: estrangement from vital points of reference (a native land, an idiom, local customs, a genealogy, etc.); the obligatory adoption of different administrative codes, including (police, Social Security, working papers, employment conditions, etc.); the expanding patterns of cadres that organize distances or spatial proximities (the media, marketplaces, urban styles, rapid transit, etc.).

The reactions of the group to new sites obviously cannot be dissociated from the effects generated by the "colonization" that it undergoes, but they are nevertheless not of the same order. The capacity *to adapt* that members of this group display, and that, relating to a dynamism, are translated by an entire spectrum of tactics or ways of bending the imposed order to their own ends, cannot be reduced to the *assimilation* of a foreign body on the part of the host nation (an "anthropophagous" phenomenon). By confusing them, one would be reducing adaptation to passive modes of behavior within a context of constraints; once again, the dominant group would be given the dominant role as the essential actor in history (an evil agent if it cannot be a benevolent hero). The return to the creativity to which these tactics bear witness also requires that we reject the paradigm—both ethnological and mythical—according to which foreign societies are essentially coherent and stable systems; that it is necessary and possible to isolate their "authentic" figures (scientifically "pure" bodies); and that the trials, errors, or changes owed to an adaptation are thus the symptoms of a degradation or an alienation. Every group lives by the compromises that it invents and by the contradictions that it manages (all the way up to the thresholds beyond which it can no longer assume them). To identify it as a stable and homogeneous totality is already to treat it as a dead body. The experience of the immigrant and the minority offers an inverse model; processes of adaptation, pushed to an extreme through a sudden acceleration in the transformations of a cultural ground, display a creativity at the limit of its capacities. This "test" of the mechanisms of mobility, because it works at a higher speed than in normal times, reveals possibilities and blockages that belong to a social dynamics at an accelerated pace.

Although it is violent, the confrontation of "foreign" groups with the host country is not a shock between two systems. It does not correspond to the image of heroes or of gods who used to cross swords. It unwinds inside of dominant societies that have become composite, especially in their urban forms. They produce an eclecticism that is the raw material endlessly enriched and manipulated by a commercial, industrial, or media technology. Today, orthodoxies are multicultural. Their stakes are everywhere. The dominant society deals with diversity itself according to methods that make all differences accessible to each and every individual, that detach them from the limited meaning that a particular collectivity ascribes to them, and that thus level all the ethnic heteronomies by submitting them to the general codes of individualized diffusion. Like those that money puts into circulation, every possible social figure has to be mobilized everywhere, thanks to technological networks whose particular historical, economic, and ideological assumptions are camouflaged under universal expansion. This "hybrid monism" thus has its own laws.[1] It transforms, it rewrites, it homogenizes, it totalizes supple shades of content in a hardened grid.

Reciprocally, adaptation is imposed with more violence on minority groups. It involves more rapid adjustments and a necessary selection in matters of belonging. Here I would like to point out the forms taken by the maintenance—indeed, the explanation and reinforcement—of an alterity in the context of a generalized hybridization. There are some strategic points. They map out a geography of the difficulties met in schooling (as in many other places), and the measures that can be proportioned to them. These points correspond to a reinforcement or to an internalization of specific issues under the effect of stimulations or constraints in the process of adaptation to another social landscape. Operations and settlings that in themselves are not new to the group acquire an entirely unforeseen importance with the erosion or disappearance of traditional sites. Two of the elements of belonging to which the new juncture ascribes a strategic and unexpected functioning can be highlighted: on the one hand, *practices,* or traditional ways of doing things that belong to the group, are henceforth deployed in the network of different givens that another order imposes; on the other hand, *collective fragments of memory* constitute, whether consciously or unconsciously, the roots or the "fixed points" by which a collective irreducibility is engraved in individual members. The first might designate the "active" traits of a belonging, while the latter are "passive," if these two terms are understood as styles of production and forms of inscription.

Politicizations

Before examining these two historical processes, we must situate them in the perspective scale that measures interethnic encounters in a broadly defined evolution: the politicization of belonging. What used to function as a site and an axiom, as a sum of received assumptions, now becomes the stakes of debates and political choices. Accepted tradition is transformed into a history to be written. Challenged by others, it is no longer merely the stage of political struggles, but their very object. By "political" I mean the relationships of forces that frame the immigrant or minority experience in search of employment, recognized roles, and normal promotions. From these struggles (of which schooling is clearly also a ground of struggle), many aspects overdetermine the forms that the ethnic reference will take: as soon as its politicization is neglected, it becomes ideologized. A few of these stakes need to be sketched out.

A debate on nationalism. Relations among groups are conflictual in nature. It is thus impossible to subscribe to the idealistic views that assume that conflicts can be resolved by means of mutual "understanding" or merely by a technical improvement in pedagogical methods. In fact, technical improvement conceals the power that one group exerts over others by defining in its own terms the protocols of the encounter. The contested interests require a *political* clarification and expression, the very ones that either directly or indirectly prohibit analyses that favor, moreover, certain, effective aspects — cultural, psychological, or anthropological — of the problem.

Specifically, these conflictual relationships take place in a framework that is fundamentally hostile to them and that could be characterized as an "obsession with unity." The reference to things *national* is today mobilizing this "obsession." It takes its initial form in a politicization of whatever is ethnic. It provides ethnocentrism with the support of public institutions. It organizes a revised and corrected historiography that, in France anyway, "forgets" the Sétif massacres in 1945 or the tortures of the Algerian War,[2] and that, by leading the reader to believe that it depicts what really took place, becomes the agent of a nationalist endoctrination, an efficient instrument in making present-day society conform to an ethnic model of the state.

Everywhere movements that identify the *state* with the *nation* are being born or reborn. As can be seen in many countries (from France to Israel), these movements, linked to the formation of nationalisms over three centuries (a complex phenomenon whose motivations historical analysis has not, with its usual methods, succeeded in uncovering), convey its logic: in relation to nationalism, difference becomes a specter of treason.[3] Nationalist tendencies are, moreover, expressed through contradictions that inhere in every country. Thus, whereas the French Constitution of 1958 refuses to identify citizenship with nationality, juridical practice favors the national law of the nation of origin in matters pertaining to the political rights of immigrants.[4] Even more, while the economic marketplace slowly erases the importance of national borders in favor of multinational societies, ethnic reference to a territoriality ("to be at home") returns in force in the collective consciousness. It seems that economic internationalization calls for the development of political nationalisms (as an antibody?). Immigrants are at once the effects (their flow follows the ups and downs of the market) and the victims (their arrival irritates local chauvinisms) of this chiasm.

An action and a reflection on this *ethnic nationalism* seem to be urgently needed, first of all in the schools, where the "nationalization" of the state — that is, an "ethnicization" of political problems — can be counteracted. A pretty topic for courses on civic morality! An internationalist tradition could furnish bases for research on the compatibility of different nations within the same state — even if, in its French functioning, it has often been an exported product rather than a rule of domestic politics. Insofar as a public and general debate on the "nation" has not taken place, immigrants are the only ones charged with being the witnesses of an internationalism that is perfectly compatible with the state, and thus, through the inequality of the present forces, they are brought back to the role of being the nationals of foreign powers.

Historical interactions. The social existence of a group *is built* from the effect of this conflict. It is reducible neither to a "nature" defined by biological characters, nor to the "system" produced by its anthropological or ethnological representation, nor to the past that historical research (for the sake of a cause) exhumes, selects, or invents. It is fabricated day after day. It pertains to a "historicity," if by that is meant a group's capacity to transform itself by redeploying the means at its disposal for other ends and for new uses. The way that a group also becomes the subject of its history, and not only the product of constraints, concerns the very analysis of data and suggests a few methodological rules.

a) This collective creativity could not be brought back to a problematic of autonomy. It is developed in *a reciprocity of historical exchanges* and is organized and mobilized by factual situations of intercommunication.[5] Thus the special importance of the "interrelational" dynamics that, in a group of immigrants, the passage from the first generation to the second or third generation, generally inscribes. Since Lévi-Strauss, it has often been shown that isolation has the effect of inertia, and confrontation produces stimulation.[6] In this regard, the necessities of adaptation that populations of immigrants or minorities have to confront give them a vanguard role in the application of the means that their group has at its disposal, even if, ultimately, this new use of a heritage works to the benefit of the host over and above that of the country of origin.

Instruments of analysis—and thus of action—are frequently lacking for this interrelational dialectic. Studies are on the horizon.[7] They could find inspiration in problematics developed in feminist analyses, which—after initially believing that they had isolated a feminine "identity"—analyzed the codeterminations of masculine and feminine figures in different historical situations. These mutual transformations, inseparable from relationships of forces, constitute, on a more or less accelerated mode, the daily movement and creative murmur of all living groups. They refer back to this law of history stating that the meeting of collectivities, like that of the two sexes, is the very principle of generation.

b) The ideological, historical, or mythical *representations* that a group confers on itself at a moment in its history also pertain to the struggles that it leads. They are endlessly being transformed, insofar as they are the instruments and the effects of adaptations, protests, losses, or projects that are built on linkages of conflictual relations. Clearly, at every stage these representations are also given the responsibility of expressing a timeless identity, but in fact constant revisions (often bearing on "details" that are more important than the general schemes) mark collective stories with the redeployments and heterogeneous beliefs of which they are the successive evidence. Despite their apparently greater stability, these representations are no less crafty or subtle than the conjunctural tactics that they regulate or legitimize, nor are they more anchored or legible. They belong to history. They serve for combat. To "depoliticize" them, to turn them into monuments of identity, would be tantamount to self-deception over the ways these tools of social historicity are used; it would mean alienating their uses by depriving them of the spaces of play and adaptation that a space of symbolization provides them.

Internal crises. Interethnic confrontation is a test and a decisive moment (a crisis) for traditional representations. It unveils inner contradictions that were "held together" by the relative stability of the territory, the language, and the group itself. A common "ground" ensured the compatibility of all the heterogeneous elements that a symbolic process gathers together and that allow for a mobility in the field of the same tradition. If it happens to be lacking, this heterogeneity unleashes its explosive force. Even more, the social hierarchies (the "authorities") that were formerly accepted lose their legitimacy with members of the group who move and meet other types of social structure. In these and many other forms, the conflict with other groups is not the most important. In the minority community, it entails inner struggles concerning the modalities of adaptation or resistance. Different strategies reveal or exacerbate tendencies that an autonomous collective policy had previously been able to regulate. Traditional criteria are opposed to unexpected choices that have to be made. Solidarities that up to that point had been silent suddenly break.

This inner alteration surprises many immigrant or minority communities. It requires entirely new research on selections in the past, contracts in the present, and common projects that are still possible. Often, to be sure, personal itineraries of adaptation slowly remove the violence and even the interest from these crises. In many cases, successful assimilation causes individuals to forget the collective problems of their original community of immigrants. It is a solution, but it cannot be the only one and be based on an avoidance of the interethnic question. In fact, for many different reasons (growth of immigration, political affirmation of a double belonging in the second generation, and so on), it appears less frequent. In any case, analysis also needs to be made of strategies that might be called *"diaspora" policies,* capable of undoing the constraint imposed by an alternative between assimilation and the return to the native country and that consigns the collective experience itself to the transitory void of an "in-between."[8]

The same struggle for Algerians and Bretons? Finally, questions must be asked concerning the delicate problem of relations that can exist between the social forms that ethnic alterity of foreign origin (for example, the Portuguese, the Maghrebians, etc., in France) takes in the same country, and ethnic alterity relating to an internal history (for example, the Bretons, the Basques, the Corsicans, etc.). Administrative and juridical logic tends to separate them on the basis of a simple distinction: are you French citizens or not? This classification is not so clear and is not self-evident. The diverse communities living in France present obvious ethnic and social differences that cannot be confused, from the point of view of their own economies. But, from a political point of view, the problem acquires a different cast: the legal recognition of *collective* rights also pertains to these communities and can provide a common ground of political solidarity. In this perspective, no obstacle is posed by the privilege of citizenship—which is, besides, rather liberally granted in France (the Italian or Maghrebian community residing in France includes members who are "naturalized" and others who are not)—nor "cultural estrangement" (Basque society differs more from the Île-de-France than does Piedmontese society), nor the geographical displacement supposedly typical of immigration (in Paris are also Corsican, Basque, or Breton immigrants who have been separated from their local origins for one or more generations), nor even the historical fact of having different pasts (that is also the case in France for two hundred thousand Basques as it is, too, for nine hundred thousand Portuguese). Furthermore, an Upper Volta and a Vietnamese are no closer to each other than they are to a Parisian, and the welcome they receive in Paris separates them even more: to pigeonhole the former two into the category of "foreigners" means effacing their heterogeneity; conversely, to assign them naturalization as the only means of access to political rights (and, above all, the right to vote) means granting them political legitimacy at the cost of a procedure that usually signifies an erasure of their specificity.

Preferable to the policy of fetishizing foreigners by isolating them, or fetishizing citizenship by positing it as the only solution, would seem to be an alliance between collectivities that have in common the demand for rights recognized in the very name of their belonging to an ethnic group and of the role that it already plays in political life. We would thus have a slogan such as "Algerians and Bretons, the same struggle!"—a slogan that rejects, for the former, enclosure into the ghetto of a "foreign" label, and, for the latter, the domination of national ideology.[9] Written into the logic of decentralization or of federalism, this alliance might procure for every ethnic community the political means of developing its own specificity without, however, being a third path imposed on all of its members.

Lists of Practices

Styles. The experiences of migrants take very different forms depending on the stages of implantation in the host country. Thus the "immigration of labor" (adult jobs, especially for men, in workplaces) is qualitatively distinguished from the "immigration of population groups" (families that move into the life of the city). As in the case of the Beurs, the second generation, playing on a double belonging, are detached from the "first generation," separated from a primary belonging that is still tied together by an entire network of economic and familial solidarities.[10] The same holds for minority collectivities, according to the levels where their difference can still be affirmed: an economic power, a linguistic unity, a collection of customs, local institutions, their own means of expression. The minority sociality varies with the different registers that it can use.

Added to these disparities are the internal distortions precipitated by the impact of the surrounding society. For example, if a *collective* consciousness is increased in the group through the immigration of families, it is contradicted among its members through the *individualistic* ambitions and behaviors that are called for by a participation in the socioeconomic logic of the host country. Or else — another paradox — in French minorities, the intensification of *"cultural"* demands is tied to an *economic* and political slackening, such that the communities increase their requirements at the very time when they depend more on means conceded by the central power.

It is thus very difficult to discern common forms and stable types in the variety of channels traced by adaptation or resistance. Defining the situations in terms of socioprofessional categories, "households," administrative status, budgetary or demographic figures, we proceed to static schemes that omit the very operations (strategies, tactics, protocols) whose effects are being calculated. If, thanks to comparisons and correlations, statistical analysis makes it possible to measure developments, it still fails to grasp what motivates their dynamics.

One can attempt to add to the analysis some of the very *procedures* by which "minorities" appropriate, change, and improve the situations imposed on them. No longer are the *conditions* in which they are found a major concern. At issue, rather, are the *operations* by which they construct their history, not of states, but of actions and specific "styles." The few studies devoted on the different styles of procedures and writing that are nonetheless also scientific can serve as a model;[11] examination must be extended to the styles that also characterize — in the arduous hubbub of a schoolroom, a factory, or a street — the operations produced by the members of different communities. A few remarks about them will make clear the "active" quality of belonging.

Ways of speaking. A first indication of the importance that must be granted to these ways of doing things concerns the relation that a group maintains with its language. According to recent research in "ethnography of communication" or "ethnography of speaking," a group has as its own less the language that it speaks (the dictionary and grammar as linguistics defines them) than the *uses* it makes of it, its ways of using it socially, the applications, protocols, fine points, and "wit" adjusting the language to a labyrinth of concatenated exchanges — in short, an interrelational economy of language.[12] These uses are obviously built on the characteristic structures of the language, but they are endlessly generating new lexical or syntactic forms. They add to the "thesaurus" of the language unforeseen possibilities. Furthermore, they easily appropriate foreign linguistic contributions that they "sketch out" (as in painting) according to "manners" or styles of their own. They even survive the language in which they played a role; they can be used outside of the "maternal" or local space, in foreign languages whose unknown resources they develop through a proliferation of new "twists" that often look like verbal or grammatical "errors."[13] Far from the fact that a group can be identified with its language (that is, finally, with the system by which our linguistics represents it), far from the fact that its autonomy may have as a yardstick conformity to a "purity" (decided by whom?) of its language, it is characterized by these operations, carried out first of all in the field of a linguistic heritage and likely to be used elsewhere, in other regions.

Orality is probably the most immediately recognizable and the most favored mode of these operations. It is distinguished from scriptory protocols by the virtuosity with which the uses of spoken language are adjusted to a multiplicity of unique situations. Its "performances," which are executed with a mastery that in time is seen in them (after having long judged them with a docility to the laws of written language), attest to the tactical art of adaptation to endless changes. Because of its very mobility, orality joins two characteristics: (1) more than writing, it explains in linguistic practices the style of a group; (2) it depends more on hierarchies (that either valorize or devalorize) that are established by the power relations among groups and hence among their practices (as seen in ways of phrasing, idiolects, accents, and so on). The most sensitive form of verbal communication, it thus unites in itself a greater *inventiveness,* that can easily put to work all the musical and semantic resources of a language as a function of circumstantial exchanges, and a greater *violence,* either passive (as repression) or active (as domination), due to the fact that speech is captured in social struggles. Whereas written language is at a further remove from interlocutory poetics and social stigmatizations, orality makes endlessly manifest the crisscrossing of a style of creativity and situations of conflict.[14] It associates the art of doing with the battles that entail life itself, which is the very definition of a practice.

Specificities of practice. The procedures of a given group thus continue to influence the linguistic matters and places transformed by contact (for example, by new kinds of socioeconomic exchanges). Likewise, the ways that a community shares in living in a space are maintained where the objective conditions of the habitat have changed; they allow the new landscape to be appropriated while adding to it.[15]

There probably exist thresholds beyond which these practices themselves begin to erode, slowly giving way to the uses suited to a new belonging and to the constraints exerted by another sociolinguistic framework. At least we can already retain a few consequences from these sociolinguistic analyses that involve interethnic encounters.

a) If the ways of using a space (linguistic, geographic, etc.) can survive the transformation of this space, and if they are more characteristic and more durable than the spaces in which, for a time, they are inscribed, then, in the situations created by a displacement, these practices, their art, and their combinations must be granted the right and the means to exert themselves in living, caring, teaching, and so on. From this angle also, one can recognize the specific activities that a group uses to invent its history and participate in broader forms of renewal, rather than alienate it by identifying it with its places of origin and in the past theater of its production.

b) The apparent homology among linguistic systems becomes deceptive (as in the case of geographic, anthropological, and other systems). This homology is the effect of coherent and controllable procedures that are refined by a single Western discipline: linguistics. It is produced through a particular sum of practices that are led outside of our original idiom toward a growing number of foreign languages. It results in specific "ways of doing" that are tied to our history and to criteria of our own, just as ethnology extends the style of our procedures to different societies. From this standpoint, linguistics pertains to the capacity (noted earlier) that a society uses to practice other languages according to its way of using its own. Under clearly valuable and effective — and seemingly universal — methods, it camouflages the heteronomy that exists between our practices of a language and other types of linguistic practices.

There is in fact a real heterogeneity among languages according to the ways they are spoken. This fact especially calls into question the pedagogy that often assumes that language, although obeying different rules, is a single reality in all societies. To recognize, on the contrary, that spoken languages are fields organized by different social practices in the Maghreb or in France, in Mexico or in the United States; that they are thus distinguished not only by variations of norms within homologous systems, but by functionings that are qualitatively foreign to one another; that for one group they are the spiritual edifice of a founding reality, while for another they objectify a network of compatibilities and exchanges among individuals; that in one society, they participate in the bodily staging of acts of language and, in another, they assure the distribution of the value of speech acts, is tantamount also to perceiving in the errors or the innovations of a way of speaking the marks traced in a language by a practice that originates elsewhere, "signatures" of different uses, gestures relative to other ways of doing things and acting. Only then can we seek how to develop a tactical diversity in a given language that will enrich it without destroying any of its effective procedures.

No matter how fundamental it may be, language corresponds to only one regime of these practices. Law, marriage and family, heritage, criminality and penal codes, medicine and cuisine, body care, the uses of day and night hours, the organization of space and time — all these essential "places" of a society are affected with a specificity less through the objects, tools, or concepts with which they are furnished than through ways of appropriating, using, or thinking these totalities of elements. One cannot be sure that these different ways of doing things are coherent in respect to one another. Their combinations result from a multitude of historical compromises and, as a result, they make possible future adaptations and selections. But one can be sure that in extracting from these labyrinths of tactics the objects or the expressions that seem topical to us, we would have in our midst only the inert — and, moreover, nonpertinent — fragments of this different social body, even if their collection induces in us the most brilliant constructions. It is thus better to return to these unassimilable practices that "act on" a specificity.

But here they introduce themselves to us. The immigrant experience brings into our world this tactical economy. Procedures that yesterday were exoticized or replaced through our own practices are implanted inside of what we *are doing with* the space in which we live. Thus it is hardly surprising that by a kind of lucidity about the true nature of ethnic confrontations the most violent allergies are made manifest in opposition to the foreign "ways" of reusing our space and against the "errors" or the "barbarisms" that indicate, among our ways of doing things, these different uses of our territory.

Fragments of history. This very violence sheds light on what is at stake. The confrontation with these different ways of practicing our space initiates a renunciation of property. For "proprietary" individuals it involves a loss that will appear even more threatening when the conflict takes the figure of ravished statutes and stolen goods and when every promotion of the "foreigner" seems to dislodge a "natural being." Whatever the case, the encounter will not leave the majority intact. Reciprocal collisions and transformations insinuate everywhere, with the debris of former exclusivities, a danger that cannot be dissociated from a common renewal.

But for minorities the cost is much higher, prorated with greater risks. In particular, the immigrant has much more at stake: he or she loses more, but in order to gain a higher return. If we stick to the aspects of this defiance inherent in belonging, the loss first of all concerns the need to pursue a history outside of the territory, the language, and the system of exchanges that sustained it to that point. We have seen that practices develop on the basis of this loss. Because of this distance, a representation of everything that happens to lack forms a representation: tradition is turned into the imaginary regions of memory; the implicit givens of life as it is lived appear with a strange lucidity that often rejoins — in many facets — the foreign perspicacity of the ethnologist. Lost places are transformed into fictional places offered to the mourning and reverence of a past.

But, as a phenomenon that is more visible because it is more determinant, adaptation to another social site also inspires the shattering of former references and, among the debris that clings to the voyagers, certain ones begin to play an intensely silent role. These are fragments of rites, protocols of politeness, vestimentary or culinary practices, codes of gift giving or of honor. They are odors, quotations of colors, explosions of sound, tonalities...These relics of a lost social body, detached from the whole in which they played a part, now acquire a greater force, but without being integrated into a totality. They are isolated, inert, planted into another body, like the "little bits of truth" that Freud specifically located in the "displacements" of a tradition.[16] They no longer have a language that symbolizes or reunites them. They no longer form an individual history that would be born of the dissolution of a collective memory. They are there, but they seem dormant. Their sleep is, however, only apparent. If they are touched, unforeseen violence will be unleashed.

These fragments refer to another, more widespread, "cultural" model. Embedded in practices, latent and disseminated like the familiar statuettes that used to be crammed into every corner of the house, mute spirits of the place, but "spirits" that are only material details, they have the common feature of no longer being capable of organizing social, professional, administrative, or familial life; they *punctuate* it with sites that seem insignificant and yet decisive.

A notorious example is provided by what survives from a religious tradition (Islamic, Protestant, and Catholic) among émigrés who no longer practice their faith and no longer even consider themselves believers. This tradition nonetheless remains determinant, but in the form of fragments that pertain to collapsed or abandoned systems. Certain gestures, certain objects, expressions, birthdays, and perfumes in fact retain in the text of daily activities and work the capital function that punctuation has in a written text. As signs that have nothing to do with the letters organizing the meaning of the text, they punctuate the practice of the lexical and syntactic order imposed by the dominant society. These are "signifiers," but we can no longer be sure what they signify. These material markers are called "superstitions," coming from a word designating what exceeds (*super-stare*) and transgresses assimilation. They play a role that is *metonymic* (they express the part for the absent whole), *historical* (they represent the site of the defunct), *elliptical* (one no longer knows the meaning or the reference of these quotations), and *poetic* (they induce and inspire invention).

Through them, an ethnic alterity is kept—obstinate, fragmented, silent, escaping every seizure. This form of belonging, which is traced into the social practices as might be worthless family jewels, is probably no less suggestive than was formerly conformity to sociocultural orthodoxies, for we slowly discover the degree to which this conformity is crafty, tactical, and playful in the space that a system of beliefs gives to it. With these ostensibly trivial relics, the amount of play is reduced; they oblige, even if it is in silence and with punctuality; they bring back into the field of what we "know for sure" the irruptions of a "but all the same..." They represent what is passed over in the teachings that naively invest their faith in the contents of knowledge and that fail to perceive the scansions of materials by which a group defends, unbeknownst to its teachers, its present relation to a dispersed patrimony.

Chapter 17
The School for Diversity

Whether in the representations that we make of them, or in the changes caused by an exile outside of the native country, these figures of different groups can allow us to locate a few possible ways of proceeding in the educational field of their confrontation.[1] A prerequisite is necessary. The experience of this encounter is above all *for us* a school for diversity, an initiation into social "economies" whose secret we can never grasp (they are foreign to the paradigms that have officially become our own) and that nevertheless reveal in our societies themselves aspects destined to illegitimacy by our own criteria. Our pedagogical methods would stand to gain from a few of their more explicit orientations.

1. Exhume from acquired knowledge the real *procedures* that produce it. In fact, teaching often conceals them by exposing their results. At the different levels of the technical labor of their past or present history, these practices belong to the general category of ways of know-how and going about tasks, and procedures and techniques that also pertain to the social practices of other cultural or ethnic groups. By making them clear, we would improve our acquaintance with selected operations that provide access to our disciplines. We would also allow members of minorities to better locate the different "styles" that distinguish operations favored by the host country from their own, and, through a sort of pragmatic polyglottism, to be able to develop a diversification of practices according to milieus and objectives.

2. Make manifest also the relation of knowledge with social formations that still respond to an *ethnic or familial* type. Teaching frequently furnishes the representation of a complex system of disciplines being imposed on "strangers" as a homogeneous whole. This

pedagogical theater is an excellent classification of the existence of a coherent minimum of rules that ensure the verification or falsification of knowledges. But it is nonetheless fictive. It papers over conflicts, often savage but muffled, between "families" (genealogies, clienteles, associations of old people) whose ethnic character our official, democratic, and scientific discourse prefers not to "know." The goal is not one of demystifying the credibility of knowledge (this would be ridiculous, dangerous, and false), but of investing back into the discourse that masks it the existence of collective competitive forces, and hence to provide minorities who live their own situation in terms of belonging with instruments of analysis. While ideology conceals the "ethnic," hence impeding it from being thought, and risks handing it over to racist passions, it would be wise to clarify the tacit laws, initiations, rules of honor, allegiance, and solidarity that belong to these "families," in collaboration with the members of the groups who can better master the subtle and ferocious play than we can. It would be to stop furnishing them with an image that deceives them about the society they inhabit as marginals and that finally deceives them about themselves.[2]

3. Promote in secondary school a *management of social practices*. Teaching often oscillates between a problematic of intersubjective relations and a problematic of the objective contents of a discipline. Between the two would be situated a knowledge and an apprenticeship of the protocols and social contracts. In certain establishments—for example, in high schools in the United States—this apprenticeship seems to be favored over knowledge. Nonetheless, it constitutes laboratories in which experiments are carried out, by trial and error, on the objective and regulated forms that competitions can locate. These ways of proceeding are what make a society operate. They produce the society. It is no longer a question of expressing subjectivities but of undertaking the hard task of social practice.[3] The tensions and conflicts that are especially responsible for agitating interethnic relations would call all the more for these exercises, analogous in the social field to what translation is in the linguistic field: a true school for diversity.

Afterword
The "Events" and Their Erosion

A casual reader of most of the essays in *The Capture of Speech* will probably discover a vocabulary that seems anachronistic, dated, even out of sync with words surrounding the themes of race, class, and gender. Substantives such as *struggle, commitment, labor, ethic,* and *practice,* and others of similar grist, are reminiscent of existential idioms of times past. The words we encounter in this volume are staked, as Luce Giard reminds us with prophetic elegance in her Introduction, on a future that harbors promise for a better tomorrow. A future that, in her words, is "already being born," seems far less probable at the threshold of the twenty-first century than it had been on the eve of the 1970s. In returning to Michel de Certeau's political and journalistic writings of three decades ago, we surely do not want to elucidate the history and the aftermath of 1968 from one historian's point of view. The aim, rather, is one of forming a productive relation with the future by displacing Certeau's essays on and after 1968 *into* the present. In doing so, we invariably happen upon one term whose precocious meaning at the time of the writing of the essays has gained resonance: "event." The "events" of which he writes in the early chapters provide a foundation for broader treatment of issues at the center of debates about ethics and action in philosophy, history, anthropology, sociology, psychoanalysis, and religion.

What is an event? If an event takes place, how does it accede to its name, and why? For whom? Under what circumstances? Even if the revolts of 1968 "happened" the way they did, they were for reasons that included growing social contradiction, the perception that the French government was not in touch with its subjects, a sense of the futility of class struggle as a means to improve the human condition, and a feeling of betrayal over the loss of the rights that the Revolution had granted to the fifty million beneficiaries of its heritage. Historians have copiously adduced other proofs, but in any and every case—or event—the conflicts of May 1968 signaled a collective accession to a new and heightened consciousness about communication. New subjectivities were born. It is tempting to say that the idea behind the English reedition of Michel de Certeau's essays on the revolts of 1968 and their aftermath has been conceived, on a minor scale, to promulgate an event of a similar order. The essays in this volume cry out for consciousness. In this respect, their sheer poetic and analytic force, no matter what may be their anachronism, constitutes a timely impetus for action.

Two Approaches to the Events

In the first chapters, Certeau argues that the "events" of May 1968 were not merely occurrences or happenings reducible to chronicle or liable to be pigeonholed in historical compartments. The revolts called into question the very essence of what scientists and philosophers have pondered about variation, change, shift, and rupture in the fortunes of social groups. He understood that what was being called the "events" was an imperfect name applied to something felt in the streets and on the barricades. Its effects were so pervasive that the resulting enthusiasm and euphoria could not be contained in the hundreds and thousands of instant histories and chronicles capitalizing on the occasion to write about and reflect on them. What happened took place in a dialogic world, of speech and imagination, in interlocution and in debate, that could not be translated into writing. Certeau showed that if what happened in and about May 1968 was being called a series of "events" (*les événements de mai 1968* was a common label that has since stuck in manuals of recent history), they belonged to a broader historiographical tradition. *The Capture of Speech* and its companion volume, *Culture in the Plural*, discern how the consciousness of the nature of an *event*, which had been inaugurated by Fernand Braudel, pertained to May 1968. For Braudel and his school, history consists of different temporal speeds. A *longue durée*, an almost eternal condition of a time of near permanence, akin to what is known as structure in anthropology, provides a background to a *conjointure*, a duration that lasts, roughly, from a decade to a century, that delineates a rhythm of social change. On the horizon of history, an *événement*, by striking contrast, is a scintilla, or a "surface oscillation," that stands in a problematic relation to the other terms.[1] An accumulation of events can allow the historian to chart the outlines of a "conjuncture" against a horizon of seeming permanence. Even though the revolts qualified as the third and least significant term in the series, their relation to the experience of social contradiction showed that the heightened consciousness that resulted from the moment made the "events" resemble minor rifts in a continuum that reached back to 1789 and before.

Certeau describes what happened from a standpoint of admiration and detachment. From the standpoint of an ocular witness, he initially shows how "the August rains" doused the "fires of May" and flushed the ashes and embers of revolt into the city sewers before the French nation returned to work in September. In the first four chapters, he notes how the events were "retaken," not only in the return to law and order over the ensuing year, but also—and more insidiously—in the way that they so quickly became history. In chapters 5 and 6, he reviews the treatments of the events amassed in tons of newsprint, ink, and paper accumulated in the passage of a year. No matter what was made of the revolts, they struck to the quick of the entire nation and bore analogies with similar expressions of protest in Poland and North America.

What happened could have been assimilated to a religious experience, but the effects refused to evaporate into abstraction. And when they did disappear, they did not return, as might have been predicted, a need for a rite of intensification. If they were to be explained in theological terms—which Certeau, despite his training in the history of European religions, refused to do—they could be tied to dialogue, desire, eros, and fantasy, that is, to the imagination that remains a glue of social cohesion. In this way, the initial pages of *The Capture of Speech* show that an informed reflection on events and on "event-theory" was needed to understand what took place. Here we find the first and most extensive consideration of the social ramification of the relation of the notorious "month of forty-four days" to the structure of experience prevailing in industrial societies.[2]

His views become clearer when compared to the way that their concept and practice are studied throughout the philosophical essays of Gilles Deleuze.[3] Two points are worth recalling. First, at the end of a study of the political aspects of Michel Foucault's "cartographical" vision of history, Deleuze compares Herman Melville's spirit of adventure to the events of 1968.

> Chacun témoigne de la façon dont se tord la ligne du dehors dont parlait Melville, sans début ni fin, ligne océanique qui passe par tous les points de résistance, et qui roule, entrechoque les diagrammes, toujours en fonction du plus récent. Quelle curieuse torsion de la ligne fut 1968, la ligne aux mille aberrations! D'où la triple définition d'écrire: écrire, c'est lutter, résister; écrire, c'est devenir; écrire, c'est cartographier.

> [Everyone attests to how the line from the outside, of which Melville spoke, is bent, with neither beginning nor end, an oceanic line that cuts through all points of resistance, that rolls, that jostles diagrams, always in respect to the most recent. What strange torsion there was in the line of 1968, the line with a thousand aberrations! Hence the triple definition of writing: to write is to struggle, to resist; to write is to become; to write is to map out.][4]

Deleuze saw in 1968 a sign of infinity, of a continuous and unending struggle against everything that denies élan and affirmation. For the author of these lines, the "8" of 1968 is infinity turned on its side, a graph of torsion, a form plotting a Moebius-like twist of surfaces that can *only* be perpetual, that forever opens the future to new political and affective spaces.

Second, in Deleuze's views on language and schizophrenia, the vision of the moment is materialized with broader consequence for subjectivity. In an essay on Louis Wolfson, he remarks that the poet is someone who mixes the two idioms that every person inherits from the point of birth. One of these is a "mother tongue," associated with life, nourishment, and an affective rapport with communication. The other, a "father tongue," refers to knowledge or a thousand different jargons culled from every imaginable science. The heroes in Deleuze's pantheon are those who commit a healthy sin of incest. In the failure to distinguish the two, the poet or schizophrenic inaugurates an "event" in which life and knowledge are no longer opposed.[5] Suddenly dissolved are boundaries habitually charted along genealogical, individual, and national lines. If Deleuze's highly literary inflection of the term—which here draws on the experience that Antonin Artaud describes about how he became totally assimilated into and dispersed about the landscape of the Tarahumara of Mexico—can be applied to 1968, we can see how and why Certeau wrote with the detached tenor of a historian.

By both documentary and aesthetic means, Certeau sought to produce reflections that would not be clouded by any aesthetic interference. As is implied by Deleuze's oceanic vision of Herman Melville's itineraries through the filter of 1968, or by the schizo who uses poetry to inspire a new consciousness of space, the events of May risked becoming utopian fictions.

It is an ironic fact that by many of the same *literary* models at his disposal, Michel de Certeau tells us that 1968 was not a moment ripe for utopian literature. At stake was the quality of life on the globe in general and, in particular, the plight of students and workers. What happened was not a collective mobilization that right-wing observers reported to be evidence of more Marxian farce, in which the playacting of July 1789 in May 1968 offered left-wing intellectuals the leisure of two good months to intone tragically about the disturbances in bookish jars of freeze-dried coffee crystals of "instant history" published in September. Nor were the riots an improvised performance or a mere commemoration of the revolution.[6] Rather, the events dissolved individuals into a collective awareness of crushing contradiction. Without having a language that could express their plight in their own words, masses pondered about what indeed lay ahead both for French institutions and the world at large.

The events, then, caused individuals to feel themselves diffused and disseminated into extensions of time and space that could be approximated — but only approximated — by the vocabularies describing the oceanic boundlessness of religious experience.[7] The events took "place" by producing an effect of a commanding "nonspace" in which, paradoxically, there ruled a regime of exclusion. Therein a revolutionary sense of the ground of communication was born. Students and workers did not have to spell out or to elucidate the particulars of their "situations" to each other. There prevailed what Certeau elsewhere calls a "you, too?!" phenomenon characteristic of mystical communication in early modern times. In a dazzling study of Nicolas of Cusa, he shows that in a pure sense an event anticipates, precedes, and sums up communication before any verifiable exchange of signs really occurs.[8] Collectively, irreducible points of view embodied by the players of the theater of May 1968 were coordinated somewhat miraculously, and without a vocabulary to describe its workings. Everyone found in themselves positions that were affirmed by those of others. An unnameable feeling of belief, a strange empathy that could both assimilate and respect the difference of every individual in the nation at large, tied the protesters to what Certeau calls a "dialogic and transcendental process." Positions and languages were being translated across otherwise insurmountable social and physical barriers.

In this volume and the later chapters of *Culture in the Plural*, Certeau relates the political virtue of the mystical grounding in every nation's need to institute a *welcoming of the other*. The other assumes many forms. It is an interlocutor, a fellow protester, or it may be an immigrant. In a more immediate and indiscernible way, it is felt in the anticipation that goes along with what linguists call "phatic" signs, or markers that announce the coming of an exchange before the latter ever takes place. In these moments pregnant with the fantasy of imminent communication, something is about to make manifest the "taking of place" in which, suddenly, among a collectivity of participants, a "space" becomes invented. In it circulated the affirmative interrogative, "you, too?!" that gives cause to solidarity.[9]

Certeau's writings on the mystical experience inform, I would like to stress, the way that in *The Capture of Speech* he studies the relation of speech to the apprehension of social contradiction. At the outset of chapter 3, he recalls the dilemma, in *The Gold Rush*, that Charlie Chaplin experiences in a cabin teetering on the edge of a snowy precipice. The tramp has to move, but he faces the peril of sending the cabin off the cliff. He needs to go outside, but if he moves toward the door, the building will plummet into the valley below. In a similar way, Certeau notes, the impact of May 1968 showed how industrial nations imposed conditions of life that were *impossible both to inhabit and to leave*. An entire cultural "floor" began to vacillate. But, he added, the instabilities on which capitalism thrives were being shrouded by the imminence of a return to business as usual in the months of September and October seen on the far edge of the horizon of July and August. He underscored the global nature of what took place and how much the events summoned the very structures of Western society. "The whole order is at stake and, first of all, it seems to me, a system of representation, what grounds both knowledge and politics."

The very coherence of everyday life in the age of flexible capitalism was shaken, its fragility brought forward. Different social organizations, he argued, were needed if a productive rapport of citizen and nation were to be fostered. The French subject would have to use the events to engage new but — in view of the configuration of a centralized government holding a tentacular grip over the country — *invisible* orderings of social life. It would be a "union" of coordinated differences, "but only if this union is based on the new structuring that is called forth by the event." Certeau's desire was to legitimize differences in a collective view of society, in which each and every subject could murmur, "you, too?!" such that an affirmation could be made of the pleasures taken in the recognition of multiple alterities. A broadening and a pluralization of the French cultural and post-colonial horizon would thus be the aftermath of 1968.

The rich substance of Certeau's reflection on the religious quality of the experience of the events can be seen when contrasted, again in dialogue with Gilles Deleuze, to the theological orientation of the philosopher's views on potentiality. In 1992, in a text on Samuel Beckett, Deleuze inverts the idealism of his 1986 apostrophe to the "line of one thousand aberrations," in which utopia could be traced along a line of flight that would perpetually turn and reverse itself. Six years after the essay on the spatial force of Foucault's concept of mapping and struggle, Deleuze shows how an event is in fact tantamount to an eradication of the idea of potentiality. All of a sudden, what had invested promise in the future in the reflections on 1968 was cast to put an élan vital in the service of the destruction of the world.[10] A spectator of Beckett's plays discovers that the effect of their performance comes from the ways that the dialogue of space and language *exhausts* whatever potential we might have invested in them. In Deleuze's Beckett, an event amounts to an annihilation of possibility.

If potentiality can be equated with possibility, and if either is a sign of the presence of God, then an event has to be understood as that which scatters and obliterates the place in which it is given.

> D'un événement il suffit largement de dire qu'il est possible, puisqu'il n'arrive pas sans se confondre avec rien et abolir le réel auquel il prétend. . . . Il n'y a d'existence que possible.

> [About an event it broadly suffices to say that it is possible, since it does not happen without being confused with nothing and abolishing the real to which it lays claim. . . . Existence can only remain as possible.][11]

Deleuze's readings of May 1968, when seen in light of his reflections on Beckett's theater, affirm that something went sour. It could have been that what had shown so much promise about reducing social inequality had been lost in the years in which the dominance of multinational and "flexible" forms of capitalism intervened. The idea that capitalism would cannibalize itself (dear to Walter Benjamin) was simply erroneous. An "event" was now interpreted as that which might sketch out a destruction of the world, a dissolution of the self, and a general disintegration of collective and individual bodies. A new dystopia prevailed in Deleuze's reflections on subjectivity.

Here the ostensibly anachronistic views of *The Capture of Speech* are especially timely. Certeau's observations about the events coordinate Christian and Marxian means to renew social consciousness. Recalling what every subject sensed in the euphoria of April and May, he felt that the revolts held within their aura an effect of "you, too?!" The participants did not ask grandiose questions about salvation or the future of the planet but about what social causes were inspiring new collective cohesion. In the "you, too?!" exchanged among students and workers, could there be detected a common plight as much as a communal experience? One answer is found in the unique way that Certeau approached the issue of *language* and the protests.

Turning About: A Revolution of Speech

The title of the book provides a hinge about which most of the content turns. Speech was "captured" in the events of 1968, its silencing coming in the ensuing months, after being "recaptured" several months later. In the shift was opened a cleft that required elucidation. In the first four chapters, Certeau puts his finger on what made speech so central to the protests and strikes in faculties and factories. A *need for language* cut into the continuum of everyday life. "We have to force ourselves to grasp the meaning of what happened in the event itself," he remarked, adding that we must not fall victim either to the lyrical illusion of a communal project or to a desire to monitor the forum of exchange being created. All of a sudden it became clear to the author that in the "dissociation between power and language," between violence and song, or in the space separating "the cobblestone and the poem," a gap opened up between what was being said and *what could be said.*

The events of 1968 became the realization that, amid given idioms and discourses, no adequate language was available for French citizens either to describe the malaise as it had been experienced, to find a cause, or, in reaction, to draft a program of social change. "Métro, boulot, dodo": the famous slogan, saying as little as it did, said more about the one-dimensionality of everyday life than could volumes of statistical sociology. But it was a graffito that had no symbolic efficacity. In a general way, then, the protesters were forced to use inherited vocabularies and rhetorical procedures to formulate unknown relations that were being formed in concert with the events. Speech and effective power — places where one could speak — were lacking. The protesters and strikers could only respond to the admonitions of the reigning powers in the terms dictated by those powers. The "retaking" of speech in the summer and fall amounted to an inquisition. The dissidents were destined to fail to outline a program of social change because any formulation had to be cast in the idiolect printed on the agendas of the controlling powers. The situation begged Certeau to inquire, beyond the egalitarian tradition of an equal right to speech that had been the substance of the French Revolution, about *who indeed possessed what was needed to be heard.* If, too, we reflect on Certeau's enduring admiration of the writings of Marguerite Duras, in which the narrative core of the novels and plays is built around a passing encounter with the unknown or an outcry that cannot describe the plight that causes its distress, the events of 1968 were a shriek or a scream, easily mistaken for hysterical outrage, when, indeed, they were a consummate reaction to overarching social blockage.[12]

What Luce Giard underlines as Michel de Certeau's unflagging drive to "elucidate" social problems was centered in his study of different languages of contestation. He showed that what could *not* be said precisely constituted the space that language attempted to create. Communication about inequality or an inadequate state of the world was exchanged, but in view of the stasis that followed, it amounted to nothing more than an acting out. Transmission of specific agendas for change was impossible either because no words existed to convey them, or else, in the conflicts in general, those owning power readily granted response in the terms they set forward. What Certeau uncovers in the discursive struggles of May 1968 is crucial to the architecture of *The Capture of Speech*, especially in Part III, where "ordinary communication" sums up the hidden music, the oral innuendo, the ethnic voice, and the hybrid types of exchange that go unseen or unnoticed in life in general. The awakening of consciousness in the events (in Part I) or the study of the ways indigenous groups seek to gain agency in otherwise oppressive regimes (studied in Part II) are shown to exist in the beauty of quotidian "micropractices" that sift through the webbings of strategic control. The design of the book suggests that if May 1968 ended in the very failure that was written into its project, it nonetheless led, as it did among situationists, to an inventory of ways of coping with the colonizing effects of dominant languages and public policies.

Certeau makes clear that one of the consequences of the relation of the "capture" of speech in respect to what preceded 1968 has been a wholesale shift in the relation of language to subjectivity. The trajectory of this volume shows that the speech born of 1968 was understood as something not conveying any truth or abstraction existing "prior" to the event of enunciation. The act of enunciation makes clear the conditions of expression and reception that are being imposed or performed. Exchange, therefore, needs to be cleared of the democratic illusion that the "right" to speak carries with it an unimpeded expression of a principle. Meaning becomes secondary to the power relations inhabiting any exchange. As in oral cultures based on rhetoric, truth as a function of force is gained through mastery of technologies that fabricate a "forum" of exchange.[13] A traditional institution, Denis Hollier astutely notes, "is able to tolerate any message, including the most subversive ones, so long as they remain messages and do not call its code into question."[14] In Certeau's words, "The *event* engages the *structure*," summoning the very social bases on which any and every statement is performed. Here is where *The Capture of Speech* revives a politics of speech capable of addressing the vital issues concerning who and what agencies acquire—or are given the right to control—what can be said and heard in a social milieu.

The book serves as a history and as a mapping of the shock waves that came from the revolution of speech "captured" as if it were liberated from the Bastille. Certeau's appeal to nonviolent approaches to loathsome practices of murder and pillage in the Americas is based on what he took to be the momentary creation of productive social space in the time of the events. After leading research in Latin American countries, he showed that class conflict between the armed, ruling orders and the indigenous populations required, above all else, the creation of micropractices or "techniques of action" elucidating the conditions of oppression, if, for nothing else, to parry knee-jerk reactions that would lead to bloodshed, reprisal, or the "retaking" of populations under the yoke of nationally imposed laws and languages. A politics that might be compared to Melville's "Bartleby," the figure who "would prefer not to" conform to imposed practices, served as a first step. "A tactic of *no,* which corresponds to the first form of a new consciousness, mobilizes the social group and displaces the geography of legality by replacing it with a more fundamental reference." Thus are opened spaces where "laboratories" can test relations of power without recourse to armed conflict. Clearly, a *belief* in a possibility or potentiality of change comes with the elucidation of the relations that institute effects of authority and impose power. In the chapter on Latin America (chapter 7) and in the subsequent studies of the same types of tactics in the first world, we witness the creation of a spatial analysis of social contradiction. Its foundation is most visible in what may seem to be either the most impertinent or least-engaging chapters of the book, the annotated bibliography of chapters 5 and 6, which sums up dozens of studies of the events of 1968 that today's librarians have dispatched to the paper shredders.

A Form of Content: Certeau's Inventories of May 1968

Two of the greatest moments in modern literature are bibliographical fantasies. One tells of an adolescent hero's visit to the Saint-Victor bookstore in chapter 8 of *Pantagruel.* Another, in chapter 6 of the first part of *Don Quixote,* recounts a priest's and a barber's visit to the hidalgo's library. In the former, the reader follows the gaze that the giant casts upon the 130 titles of every grist, from *Ars honeste petandi in societate per M. Ortuinum* or *La Martingale des fianteurs* to *De patria diabolorum.* In Cervantes's masterpiece, the investigators "halleron más de cien cuerpos de libros grandes, muy bien encuadernados, y otros pequeños" (found more than one hundred bodies of well-framed, big books, and other little ones), sifted through them, and tossed the majority out the window for immediate immolation, as had been done with living bodies during the Inquisition and the recent wars of religion in France. Both Rabelais and Cervantes sum up a status of knowledge at the same time that they perform ferocious satires about political economy. For his humanistic ends, Rabelais appeals to Folengo, while Cervantes recalls the grisly heresy trials of the fifteenth and sixteenth centuries.

"The Publishers' Harvest" (chapter 5) is a variation on Rabelais and Cervantes, attesting to an encyclopedic impulse to understand and to hear everything that was printed — but not necessarily spoken or exchanged — about 1968, whereas "A Literature of Disquiet" (chapter 6) turns about a secret, an indicible murmur that is found between the language of the nation and an unnameable interiority living within each of its subjects. Ending his review of a "moving, agitated, indefinite" surface of bookish reflections on the events, Certeau avows:

> Au sortir de cette immense littérature, on est accablé, sans avoir pu en trouver le secret. Mais la clé est au fond du pays, comme au fond d'un puits.

> [In exiting from the library of this immense literature, the reader is overwhelmed, without having been able to find its secret. But the key is at the bottom of the country, as if at the bottom of a well.]

The poetry of Certeau's conclusion meets that of a Rabelais or a Cervantes, for he asks us to *hear* the unspoken but discernible expression of awareness and discontent in the elision between *pays* and *puits*, in which the last term, although designating the depths of a source of water, also echoes the sound of *puis*, the enumerative adverb signaling that reflection and discourse are vital, infinite, and in search of future change.

At the same time, these chapters betray an obsession with a need to produce a "cognitive mapping" of 1968 from its material remainders. It stands to reason that the order of the histories of the moment allowed Certeau to construct an initially synoptic view of everything that was "made" of the events. The reader who juxtaposes the register of all the speech uttered about 1968 gives way to other worlds of conflict that are either on other continents or in other nations or within the everyday practices of life in general. The extraordinary balance of reflection and poetry that plots out the bibliographical section of *The Capture of Speech* brings the reader to an unparalleled creative energy invested in the labor of historiography and sociology.

Aftereffects

We have observed that a historian of religion uses the "events" of 1968 to inaugurate broader reflections on the future. In a first stage, the author looks at the historical moment through the lens of his labors in historiography, in which he assails the ideology of truth as it is conveyed in the operations of mass media. The ulterior stages are those that chart specific ways of practicing everyday life (Part III of *The Capture of Speech* and the remarks on education and schooling, for example, that follow in chapter 4 of *Culture in the Plural*). Especially enthusing for a general reader is the pertinence of the material in the gap that separates the moments of its writing from now. Most of the observations have gained validity with the passage of time.

The strikes that crippled France in December 1995 attest to the validity of Certeau's observations. More than one observer noted that May 1968 was all but forgotten during the upheaval in Paris when news of curtailments of Social Security spread throughout the country. To this assertion, a reader of *The Capture of Speech* might respond both affirmatively and negatively. Affirmatively, because in 1995 there seemed to be no vision of change, no faith in any possibility of a future, no collective feeling, to the effect that anything could be done to change the world for the better, extended among the population. In place of the nonmemory of 1789, 1848, 1871, and 1968 was the image of a deadly continuum of potentiality shrunken and wasted away. "Métro, dodo," but, alas, no "boulot" in a nation assailed by 12 percent of its citizens without employment. All the social services on which the French egalitarian tradition was based were seen eroding under internationalization. Transportation, Social Security, retirement benefits, and socialized medicine—indeed, every benefit that wore the *cocarde*—were targeted for downsizing, for the sake of balancing the budget, for the project of dissolving the nation into the European economic syndicate, but especially, for advancing privatization. With accelerating awareness of the loss of a standard of living that had heretofore been promised to every citizen, and for which the future of millions was staked, little room remained for the future of culture or the planet in general. The vision that fueled the "events" could not be revived in a world in which potentiality, a condition basic for change, had been crushed under democratic capitalism.

But 1968 did return, in ways that Certeau outlined so precociously in this volume, through the irruption of history. By realizing that in fact a founding vision of the French nation had been maculated, citizens of all social classes began to rethink the heritage of 1789 in view of the twenty-first century. Many, it is reported, asked, "How could the democratic ideals of Montesquieu and Rousseau have anything to do with galloping corporatization and globalization?" "What does it mean to be French or Francophone in a unified Europe?" "Can France be a 'power' in the world when, like a child playing with cherry bombs on the Fourth of July, it resumes nuclear explosions in the nearby Pacific?" "How can the nation condone the torture of the Ogoni in Nigeria at the hands of international oil conglomerates that include Shell and Elf-Aquitaine?"

Thus, 1968 came back with the awareness that the nation would not wish to lose what its democratic "state" had been providing to its subjects. It appeared that a defense against the erosion took place in a will to return power to a democratic cause for the purpose of guaranteeing rights and benefits suddenly awash in the international economic picture.[15] In December, a mental defense was erected against the destruction of national and social barriers vital to illusions of identity and subjectivity, and without which, it must be stressed, life in France would be inconceivable. December 1995 did, then, constitute a "capture of speech" through spatialized action.[16] It did not have overt connections with the style of revolt of 1968, but its quietude might have been a sign of a sense of despair where, almost thirty years earlier, there reigned a sense that a future lay ahead.

For that reason, in order not to avow a loss of the belief and hope on which much of *The Capture of Speech* is based, it is possible to map out several tactics based on the anachronism of its contents. Two come forward. Throughout the study Certeau associates the French state, the centralizing government, with an obsolete, quasi-panoptic order of social control that reaches back well beyond the nineteenth century.[17] When internationalized markets are leveling the broader differences between labor in First and Third World countries (downsizing in the former and employing subjects at niggardly salaries in the latter), and when a stupendous gap is opened between corporate and common standards of living (executive officers proudly making filthy salaries whereas the middle and lower echelons of the working classes are unemployed or bereft of any social benefits), the reinstitution of an empowered, regulatory state would be better conceived than one of advocated decentralization. In 1996, the French model of governmental service, weak as it may be, still could not fail to be envied by American citizens. At the same time, the often utopian character of the remarks on collective community points to what could certainly figure in renewed activity on various local levels throughout the world. In place of the construction of human-centered cultures, there is the need to de-individualize in such a way that a collective political and ecological praxis can be achieved.

Understood in terms that include the safeguarding of all the fauna and flora of the world, the capture of speech joins local politics to practices that might begin by "downsizing" exploitative human presence on the globe. Thus (1) a strengthening of democratic process, a reinstitution of dialogue in government, along with (2) a program to reduce human stress on the biosphere (conceivably in long-range planning to reduce population and to produce ideologies that favor "deconsumerism"), appear to be two major items of the political agenda suggested by rereading of *The Capture of Speech* almost two decades after its writing. In every event, the essays argue for any and every kind of education that will foster awareness and elucidation.

Notes

Introduction: How Tomorrow Is Already Being Born

1. Ludwig Wittgenstein, *Tractatus logico-philosophicus*, trans. D. F. Pears and B. F. McGuinness (London: Routledge and Kegan Paul, 1972), 49.

2. Alain Schnapp and Pierre Vidal-Naquet, *Journal de la Commune étudiante. Textes et documents. Novembre 1967–juin 1968* (Paris: Seuil, 1988); Henri Weber, *Vingt ans après. Que reste-t-il de 68?* (Paris: Seuil, 1988). See below chapters 5 and 6, which present an annotated bibliography of everything published between May 1968 and May 1969 on the "events."

3. On this topic, see Luce Giard et al., *Le voyage mystique, Michel de Certeau* (Paris: Cerf and Recherche de Science Religieuse, 1988), especially the complete bibliography of his writings (191–243); Luce Giard, ed., *Michel de Certeau* (Paris: Centre Georges-Pompidou, "Cahiers pour un temps," 1987); the dossier titled "Michel de Certeau historien," *Le Débat*, no. 49 (March–April 1988); Claude Geffré, ed., *Michel de Certeau ou la différence chrétienne* (Paris: Cerf, "Cogitatio fidei," 1991); Luce Giard, Hervé Martin, and Jacques Revel, *Histoire, Mystique et Politique. Michel de Certeau* (Grenoble: Jérôme Millon, 1991).

4. Schnapp and Vidal-Naquet, *Journal de la Commune étudiante*, 102; Weber, *Vingt ans après*, 73–74.

5. Épistémon [Didier Anzieu], *Ces idées qui ont ébranlé la France (Nanterre, novembre 1967–juin 1968)* (Paris: Fayard, 1968).

6. Michel de Certeau, *La Faiblesse de croire* (Paris: Seuil, 1987), chap. 7 ("La rupture instauratrice"), 183–226.

7. Michel de Certeau, *The Mystic Fable: The Sixteenth and Seventeenth Centuries*, trans. Michael B. Smith (Chicago: University of Chicago Press, 1993), especially chap. 1 and 6. See also Michel de Certeau, *L'Absent de l'histoire* (Paris: Mame, 1973), chaps. 4 and 6; Michel de Certeau, *The Practice of Everyday Life*, vol. 1, trans. Steven Rendall (Berkeley and Los Angeles: University of California Press, 1984), notably chaps. 2, 3, and 6.

8. Luce Giard, "À qui s'éloigne," and Marc Guillaume, "Vers l'autre," in *Le Voyage mystique*, 13–15 and 181–86.

9. Michel de Certeau, in Jean-Michel Damian, ed., *Regards sur une révolte. Que faisaient-ils en avril?* (Paris: Desclée de Brouwer, 1969), in which a dialogue is recorded

by students (211). See Michel de Certeau, *Histoire et Psychanalyse entre science et fiction* (Paris: Gallimard, "Folio," 1987), especially chaps. 6 and 8.

10. Certeau, *La Faiblesse de croire*, chap. 8 ("Lieux de transit"), 227–52.

11. Michel de Certeau, "L'expérience religieuse, connaissance vécue dans l'Église," in Giard et al., *Le Voyage mystique*, 27–51.

12. Michel de Certeau, "L'expérimentation d'une méthode: les Mazarinades de Christian Jouhaud," *Annales ESC* 41 (1986): 507–12.

13. Certeau, *The Mystic Fable*, chaps. 4–6; Certeau, *La Faiblesse de croire*, 91–92, 131–32, 157–59, etc.

14. Certeau, in Damian, *Regards sur une révolte*, 204–5.

15. Certeau, *The Practice of Everyday Life*, vol. 1, chaps. 2 and 3.

16. Michel de Certeau, *L'Étranger ou l'Union dans la différence* (1969), rev. ed. (Paris: Desclée de Brouwer, 1991).

17. Luce Giard, "Histoire d'une recherche," Preface to *L'Invention du quotidien*, vol. 1, *Arts de faire* (Paris: Gallimard, "Folio," 1990), xix–xx.

18. Michel de Certeau, "Qu'est-ce qu'un séminaire?" *Esprit* (November–December 1978): 177.

19. Certeau, *L'Étranger*, chaps. 2, 3, and 7; Michel de Certeau, *Culture in the Plural*, ed. and with an Introduction by Luce Giard, trans. and with an Afterword by Tom Conley (Minneapolis: University of Minnesota Press, 1997), chap. 7; Michel de Certeau, Dominique Julia, and Jacques Revel, *Une politique de la langue. La Révolution française et les patois: l'enquête de Grégoire* (Paris: Gallimard, 1975). See chaps. 14–17.

20. Certeau, *La Faiblesse de croire*, 219.

21. Certeau, "Qu'est-ce qu'un séminaire?" 177.

22. Michel de Certeau, *The Writing of History*, trans. Tom Conley (New York: Columbia University Press, 1992), chap. 2.

23. Michel de Certeau and Luce Giard, in *L'Invention du quotidien*, vol. 2, *Habiter, cuisiner*, rev. ed. (Paris: Gallimard, "Folio," 1994), conclusion.

24. Certeau, *The Practice of Everyday Life*, chaps. 7 and 9.

25. Certeau, *The Writing of History*, chap. 6.

26. Certeau, *The Mystic Fable*, chap. 7, 287–308.

27. Ibid., chap. 9 ("Labadie le nomade").

28. Certeau, *The Writing of History*, chap. 1 ("Making History"). With his agreement, this title was lent to a broad editorial enterprise of a flock of historians (mostly the *Annales* and the École des Hautes Études en Sciences Sociales), to which he was also invited to contribute, which gave birth to the "historical operation" (later completed and entitled "The Historiographical Operation"). See Jacques Le Goff and Pierre Nora, eds., *Faire de l'histoire*, 3 vols. (Paris: Gallimard, 1974).

29. Jacques Revel, in *Histoire, Mystique et Politique*, 127.

30. Michel de Certeau, *La Prise de parole* (Paris: Desclée de Brouwer, 1968), 165 pp. Only chapter 4 is omitted, but is included in another work, *La Culture au pluriel* (1964), in which it figures as chapter 8. On this point, I have followed the author's preference and allowed this chapter to continue to circulate under the auspices of culture. [It is chapter 7 of the companion volume, *Culture in the Plural.* — *Trans.*]

31. It first appeared in *Le Monde diplomatique*, no. 266 (May 1976): 16–17. Other elements of Certeau's views on the Americas are included in *La Faiblesse de croire*,

chaps. 5 and 6. [See also Michel de Certeau, *Heterologies: Discourse on the Other*, trans. Brian Massumi (Minneapolis: University of Minnesota Press, 1986), chap. 16, which includes chap. 8 of Luce Giard's 1994 edition of *La Prise de parole.—Trans.*] The raising of political consciousness on the part of the Indians [chap. 16 of *Heterologies*] was in fact designed as a conclusion to a collection of documents assembled and translated by the group DIAL (Diffusion of Information about Latin America), of which Michel de Certeau had been a founder—at the time of military dictatorship in Brazil, I believe—and for which he served as vice president in 1975. Signed with a pseudonym, but whose Afterword bore the name of Michel de Certeau, this collection was widely circulated, notably in partial translation in the United States (Yves Materne, ed., *Le Réveil indien en Amérique latine* [Paris: Cerf, 1977], 139 pp.).

32. [Forthcoming in English translation by Timothy Tomasik (University of Minnesota Press, 1998).—*Trans.*]

Chapter 1. A Symbolic Revolution

1. Épistémon, *Ces idées qui ont ébranlé la France (Nanterre, novembre 1967–juin 1968)* (Paris: Fayard, 1968). The author borrows his pseudonym from Rabelais's *Pantagruel*, from which he drew a quotation in epigraph (but a second epigraph is drawn from Erasmus's *In Praise of Folly*). Épistémon was in fact Didier Anzieu, a former student of the École Normale Supérieure (at the rue d'Ulm), a professor of philosophy in what was then the college of liberal arts at Nanterre, a university known for its many works on group and adolescent psychology and on psychoanalysis [L. G.].

2. A detailed bibliography of the works on May 1968 will be found in chapters 5 and 6 [L. G.].

3. In the Paris that was brimming with rumors in May—and elsewhere, of course—much was made about deaths caused by the "events," but the news of them was kept secret by the political authorities. There was in fact the death of Gilles Tautin near the Renault factory at Flins: this high-school student drowned while attempting to flee a police attack on June 10, 1968 (see Alain Schnapp and Pierre Vidal-Naquet, *Journal de la Commune étudiante*, rev. ed. [Paris: Seuil, 1988], 521–23). There were also, it appears, a very small number of deaths that were more accidental than the result of violence by or against the police, in the provinces (Sochaux, Lyons), during this period [L. G.].

4. Allusion is made here to the bare-handed resistance, founded on free and open discussion and humor, that the Czech population, at the end of the "Prague Spring" in 1968, tried in vain to oppose to the advance of the Soviet army, charged with reestablishing order and orthodoxy in the Eastern bloc [L. G.].

5. The name given to the active kernel of students at Nanterre, where the first strike of the university year (November 17–25, 1967) began, and whose agitation mounted from January to March 1968. On this topic, see Schnapp and Vidal-Naquet, *Journal de la Commune étudiante*, 101ff. and 415ff., who termed the Movement an "anti-groupuscule." Épistémon gives his account of the facts and offers his own analysis of the Movement's actions in *Ces idées qui ont ébranlé la France* [L. G.].

6. Philippe Labro, *Ce n'est qu'un début* (Paris: Éditions Premières, 1968) [L. G.].

Chapter 2. Capturing Speech

1. Victor Serge, *Mémoires d'un révolutionnaire* (Paris: Seuil, 1951), 25–52.

2. The author never indicates what an "analogous crisis" may be. It remains a secret in the text but may refer to the status of popular language that was unable to make itself heard in the aftermath of 1789, a topic of *Une politique de la langue*, coauthored by Certeau, Dominique Julia, and Jacques Revel (Paris: Gallimard, 1975).

3. On the "symbolic" character of places and actions, see chapter 1, the section titled "Symbolic Action."

4. On many occasions, the events of May were interpreted by reference to the American psychologist Carl Rogers's concepts on expression, seen as liberating profound tendencies.

Chapter 3. The Power of Speech

1. Julien Freund, *L'Essence du politique* (Paris: Sirey, 1965), 328–30.

2. It is in relation to this desire that he was speaking of the "disillusion felt in the heart of every student" (in *Un Mois de mai orageux* [Toulouse: Privat, 1968], 63).

3. Léopold Sédar Senghor, *Liberté I: Négritude et humanisme* (Paris: Seuil, 1964), 316–17, in which he takes up a famous passage by Sartre.

4. Alfred Métraux, *Religions et Magies indiennes d'Amérique du Sud* (Paris: Gallimard, 1967), 11–41.

5. Among many others, Pierre Marcilhacy writes: "For at least two weeks, France not only went without essential services and the movement of elements of production, but even without its government, for the one that was in place suddenly saw *its 'consensus' lacking*, without which no political authority can claim to exercise the least degree of power" ("Le chemin de Damas," *La Revue des deux mondes* [July 15, 1968]: 162; Certeau's emphasis).

6. It was with delay, a few days later (on May 28–30), that the political parties envisaged taking power.

7. After the Congo-Kinshasa became independent in 1960, Katanga seceded until 1963. Mercenary soldiers, veterans of the colonial wars led by European powers, enrolled in the ranks of the secessionists. In May 1968, more than one imaginative mind thought they recognized somewhere along the barricades or in the corridors of the occupied Sorbonne the menacing presence (but for whom?) of the "Katangese" who had returned to the country. See the note by Alain Schnapp and Pierre Vidal-Naquet, *Journal de la Commune étudiante*, rev. ed. (Paris: Seuil, 1988), 454, 460, 523, 534–35 [L. G.].

8. A marvelous example of this type of *explanation* is furnished by François Duprat, *Les Journées de mai* (Paris: Éditions Latines, 1968), a work, moreover, rich in information that should not be neglected.

9. Charles de Gaulle, *Le Fil de l'épée* (Paris: Berger-Levrault, 1932), 42.

10. Edgar Morin, "La Révolution sans visage," in Edgar Morin, Claude Lefort, and Jean-Marc Coudray, *Mai 1968: La Brèche* (Paris: Fayard, 1968), 63–87.

11. According to the first polls, it also appears that abstentionism has shifted: those who yesterday voted "left" have increasingly abstained; those who yesterday abstained voted "right" (for the UDR [Union pour la Défense de la République, a

coalition of the right that obtained 358 out of 485 seats in the legislative elections of June 23 and June 30, 1968]). The perplexity would seem to have passed from right to left, immobilizing some and mobilizing others, because the insecurity of the *order* changed the meaning of an opposition to the *government*, which was furthermore divided and uncertain.

12. A study of the elections of June 1968 remains to be done, and without which the real meaning of an almost unique phenomenon in the history of French elections remains subject to debatable interpretations. The works of Jean-Paul Charnay, such as *Les Scrutins politiques en France de 1815 à 1962* (Paris: Armand Colin, 1964) and, especially, *Le Suffrage politique en France* (The Hague: Mouton, 1964), at least allow one to think that a *method*, a normal procedure for establishing political decisions, became on this occasion its own *goal*. There already exists the description of an election, that of the Vendôme region, with Georges Chaffard's amusing chronicle, *Les Orages de mai: histoire exemplaire d'une élection* (Paris: Calmann-Lévy, 1968), a useful document for study of the provinces.

Chapter 4. For a New Culture

1. *L'Express*, no. 880 (July 29–August 4, 1968): 64.

2. See chapters 5 and 6 for more specific information on the bibliography pertaining to May 1968.

3. Philippe Labro, *Ce n'est qu'un début* (Paris: Éditions Premières, 1968), 124–42.

4. Jean-Marie Domenach, *Esprit* (June–July 1968): 1060: "It is too early to bury ideologies . . . ," and so on.

5. The dissociation between language (a system) and meaning—such as several "structuralisms" assume—is in accord with the tension that today opposes order to speech. As for the relation of structure to event, in the work of Michel Foucault, for example, it is far from being constructed in antinomies. See Michel de Certeau, *Histoire et Psychanalyse entre science et fiction* (Paris: Gallimard, 1987), chap. 1; translated by Brian Massumi as "Michel Foucault: The Black Sun of Language," in *Heterologies: Discourse on the Other* (Minneapolis: University of Minnesota Press, 1986).

6. Boris Nicolaïevski and Otto Maenchen-Helfen, *Karl Marx: Man and Fighter*, trans. Gwenda David and Eric Mosbacher (Harmondsworth, England: Penguin, 1976), 120 and 123.

Chapter 5. The Publishers' Harvest: May Seen in September

1. Philippe Labro, *Ce n'est qu'un début* (Paris: Éditions Premières, 1968), 275 pp. For the issue concerning the ORTF, see Claude Frédéric, *Libérer l'ORTF* (Paris: Seuil, 1968), 34–35.

2. This is a general and regrettable fact, despite the few exceptions that will be noted later on. Two articles are nonetheless very interesting: Jean Dubois, "Les grèves: révolte d'hier ou de demain?" *Projet* (July–August 1968): 814–34; and, in a more anecdotal style, Philippe Gavi, "Des ouvriers parlent," *Les Temps modernes* (July 1968): 80–93. Many new pieces of information appear in the August–September 1968 issue of *Esprit* (97–120) and especially *Les Temps modernes* (also August–September), under the title "Problems of the Workers' Movement."

3. For the secondary schools, a basic work is this little masterpiece of humor and lucidity, the letter of the "dunces," written by the students of a private course in Paris, in Sylvain Zegel, *Les Idées de mai* (Paris: Gallimard, 1968), 180–83. See also the beautiful account by a high-school principal: André Rouède, "La révolte des lycéens," *Esprit* (June–July 1968): 1003–14.

4. P. Andro, A. Dauvergne, and L. M. Lagoutte, *Le Mai de la révolution* (Paris: Julliard, 1968), 248 pp.

5. Jean-Claude Kerbourch, *Le Piéton de mai* (Paris: Julliard, 1968), 183 pp.

6. Patrick Seale and Maureen McConville, *Red Flag/Black Flag: French Revolution, 1968* (New York: Putnam, 1968); in French, *Drapeaux rouges sur la France* (Paris: Mercure de France, 1968).

7. *Les Poèmes de la révolution,* ed. Bruno Durocher (Paris: B. Durocher, "Caractères," 1969). Extracts had appeared in *Le Monde* (June 1, 1968).

8. Alain Ayache, *Les Citations de la révolution de mai* (Paris: Jean-Jacques Pauvert, 1968), 106 pp.; and *La Chienlit de Papa* (Paris: Albin Michel, 1968).

9. Ninety-four documents by E. Dejay, P. Johnsson, and C. Moliterni (Paris: SERG, 1968).

10. Walter Lewino, *L'Imagination au pouvoir,* photographs by Jo Schnapp (Paris: Eric Losfeld, 1968).

11. *Les Barricades de mai,* presented by Philippe Labro, photographs from Gamma (Paris: Solar, 1968).

12. "Extraits sonores d'un film réalisé par un collectif de travail animé par Guy Chalon," Accusti-Yuri Korolkoff.

13. Joseph Henz, *Barricades 68,* Le Jas du Revest Saint-Martin (Paris: Robert Morel, 1968).

14. For example, in Alain Buhler, *Petit Dictionnaire de la révolution étudiante,* preface by Georges Conchon and drawings by Cabu (Paris: John Didier, 1968), 48 pp.

15. Hubert Tonka, *Fiction de la contestation aliénée* (Paris: Jean-Jacques Pauvert, 1968).

16. *Le Livre noir des journées de mai* (Paris: Seuil, "Combats," 1968), 94 pp. Hastily put together from newspaper clippings, this dossier is not only incomplete (which was fatal), but also full of inaccuracies.

17. *L'Insurrection étudiante, 2–13 mai 1968,* a critical and documentary collection edited by Marc Kravetz, with the collaboration of Raymond Bellour and A. Karsenty (Paris: Union Générale d'Éditions, "10/18," 1968), 509 pp. Also Marc Kravetz, "Naissance d'un syndicalisme étudiant," *Les Temps modernes* (February 1964): 1447–75; Antoine Griset and Marc Kravetz, "De l'Algérie à la réforme Fouchet," *Les Temps modernes* (April and May 1965): 1880–1902, 2066–89.

18. Jacques Sauvageot, Alain Geismar, Daniel Cohn-Bendit, and Jean-Pierre Duteuil, *La Révolte étudiante* (Paris: Seuil, 1968), 129 pp.; 95. Included here (86–97) is Cohn-Bendit's interview with Jean-Paul Sartre (published in *Le Nouvel Observateur,* May 20, 1968), one of the most revealing documents of the crisis.

19. *Quelle Université? Quelle société?*; texts collected by the Centre de Regroupement des Informations Universitaires (Paris: Seuil, 1968), 223 pp. In May the CRIU represented a rather "moderate" tendency.

20. Alain Schnapp and Pierre Vidal-Naquet, *Journal de la Commune étudiante* (Paris: Seuil, 1969; rev. ed. 1988). See chapter 6, section E.

21. Sylvain Zegel, *Les Idées de mai* (Paris: Gallimard, "Idées," 1968), 249 pp. Especially interesting are the chapters on doctors, city planners, architects, lawyers, and high-school students.

22. *Les Journées de mai 68*. Encounters and dialogues presented by Jacques Durandeaux (Paris: Desclée de Brouwer, 1968), 163 pp.; *Un Mois de mai orageux*, 113 Parisian students analyze the university uprising (Toulouse: Privat, 1968), 163 pp.

23. *Les Chrétiens et la Révolution de mai* (Paris: Témoignage Chrétien, 1968).

24. On this topic, see *Christianisme et Révolution* (a conference), supplement to *La Lettre* (1968); H. Gollwitzer, J. M. Lochmann, R. Shaull, and C. C. West, *Une Théologie de la révolution?* (Geneva: Labor et Fides, 1968), to cite only the material published since May 1968.

25. *Libérer l'ORTF*. Documents and testimonies collected by Claude Frédéric (Paris: Seuil, 1968), 157 pp. Two authors are hidden behind this pseudonym.

26. Jean-Pierre Manel and Alomée Planel, *La crise de l'ORTF* (Paris: Pauvert, 1968), 117 pp.

27. See Roger Errera, "Une liberté surveillée: la radio-télévision," *Esprit* (May 1968): 833–49; and *Liberté à l'abandon* (Paris: Seuil, 1968), especially 44–87.

28. That is the last work of *Libérer l'ORTF*. The "union of television journalists" is leading an information campaign that is very useful in its "Notes and Comments," especially that of July 1968 on "the crisis of the ORTF and the strike by television journalists."

29. March 22d Movement, *Ce n'est qu'un début. Continuons le combat* (Paris: Maspero, "Cahiers libres," 1968), 141 pp., especially 59–74.

30. In addition to those furnished by *Ce n'est qu'un début*, Jean-Philippe Talbo, *La Grève à Flins* (Paris: Maspero, "Cahiers libres," 1968), is more developed, but less theorized.

31. Patrick Ravignant, *L'Odéon est ouvert* (Paris: Stock, 1968). The author also wrote a play titled *La poire* (The pear).

32. Daniel and Gabriel Cohn-Bendit, *Le Gauchisme remède à la malade sénile du communisme* (Paris: Seuil, 1968), 270 pp.

33. Jean Bloch-Michel, *Une Révolution du XXᵉ siècle. Les journées de mai 1968* (Paris: Robert Laffont, 1968), 127 pp.

34. Marc Paillet, *Table rase. 3 mai–30 juin 1968* (Paris: Robert Laffont, 1968), 249 pp.

35. Jean-Jacques Servan-Schreiber, *Le Réveil de la France* (Paris: Denoël, 1968).

36. *Que faire de la révolution de mai?* (Paris: Seuil, 1968), 93 pp.

37. *Projets pour la France* (Paris: Seuil, "Société," 1968), 144 pp. Also worthy of mention is André Barjonet's short, vigorous manifesto, *La Révolution trahie de 1968* (Paris: John Didier, 1968), 45 pp. It is an explanation of his position opposing the policy of the Communist Party and the Confédération Générale du Travail. Along the same lines is Peret and G. Munis, *Les Syndicats contre la révolution* (Paris: Eric Losfeld, [1968]). From the Communist side, a book that deserves more than a passing allusion is René Andrieu, *Les Communistes et la Révolution* (Paris: Julliard, 1968). This apology is also part of history, in the name of one of the determining elements.

38. J. Jousselin, *Les Révoltes des jeunes* (Paris: Éditions Ouvrières, 1968), 272 pp.

39. André Glucksmann, *Stratégie et Révolution en France 1968* (the different heading on the title page — *Stratégie de la révolution* — also specifies that the book is an "Introduction") (Paris: Christian Bourgois, 1968), 131 pp.

40. Edgar Morin, Claude Lefort, and Jean-Marc Coudray, *Mai 1968: la Brèche. Premières réflexions sur les événements* (Paris: Fayard, 1968), 142 pp.

41. Raymond Aron, *La Révolution introuvable. Réflexions sur la révolution de mai* (Paris: Fayard, 1968), 189 pp.; 87.

42. Épistémon [Didier Anzieu], *Ces idées qui ont ébranlé la France (Nanterre, novembre 1967–juin 1968)* (Paris: Fayard, 1968), 129 pp.

Chapter 6. A Literature of Disquiet: A Year Later

1. There are many reading groups, university seminars, and research centers that are collecting or analyzing the literature of May 1968. It is gathered together in the Bibliothèque Nationale, in the Library of the History of the City of Paris, and so on, not to mention the archives set up at the Institute of the History of the Labor Movement at the Sorbonne, at the Popular Pedagogical Institute, and so on. On the archives, see Alain Schnapp and Pierre Vidal-Naquet, *Journal de la Commune étudiante* (Paris: Seuil, 1969; rev. ed. 1988), cited in section E of this chapter. As the memory of May 1968 becomes increasingly bloated, the networks of scientific investigation multiply. Diplomas, and soon doctoral dissertations, will be built with this immense body of material. Could it be that the university is being nourished by the antiuniversity? As of May 1969, among the well-known research groups, it suffices to note those, in Paris, of the CECMAS (Edgar Morin and Bernard Paillard), of the faculty of law (M. Merle), of the Institute of Political Science; in Caen, in the College of Letters (M. Lefort); in Strasbourg, the Theology School, and so on.

2. In many centers devoted to the literature of May 1968 it is asked: do we know how to *think* the crisis, indeed, the social mobility? Elsewhere the question is translated thus: is it *possible* to write a history of contemporary events, given the lack of a perspective that opens a space necessary for the establishment of an order, in other words, for an intelligibility? Another interrogation that calls into question received ideas is formulated thus: is it only *rich* societies (see the eighteenth century) that lead to violent revolutions?

3. Roland Barthes showed with a lot of perspicacity that the stereotypes and the formalization of "news items," as they are presented in the major daily papers, conform to a logic of contrasts (what shocks, for example), but ultimately *eliminate the event,* which here too becomes inaccessible. See G. Auclair, "Faits divers et 'pensée naïve,'" *Critique* 19 (1963): 893–906.

4. The "death of the father" in particular has become a handmaiden for every discipline, sweeping up all the leftover "scraps" — as if the "father" were not only "displaced" and hidden, never eliminated, in the very disciplines that think they are getting rid of his effects!

5. We need only note Frédéric Bon and Michel-Antoine Burnier, *Les Nouveaux Intellectuels* (Paris: Cujas, 1966); Manuel de Diéguez, "Les clercs et la nouvelle lutte des classes," in *De l'idolâtrie: Discours aux clercs et aux derviches,* 208–32; André Philip, "Le rôle des intellectuels dans le mouvement socialiste," in *Mai 68 et la Foi démocratique,* 71–77 (for complete references to these two books, see the Annotated Bibliography in the next section). See also the whole experiment of the journal *Politique,* founded in January 1969; J. Julliard, "Questions sur la politique" (a working paper), *Esprit* (February 1969): 337–40; the issue of *La Nouvelle Critique* on intellectuals, and so on. On

this increasingly thorny issue many earlier studies can be noted, especially with regard to the Communist Party, such as David Caute, *Le Communisme et les Intellectuels français (1914–1966)* (Paris: Gallimard, 1967); the special issue of the *Revue française de science politique* (June 1967), and so on.

6. Henri Lefebvre casts light on this challenge in his *Introduction à la Ville* (Paris: Anthropos, 1968), which connects philosophy to several problems of urban planning. Also, Françoise Choay, in *Preuves* (September, October, and November 1968), and so on.

7. To be complemented by a useful and polemical "glossary" titled "The Masterwords of the Month of May," *La Nouvelle Critique* (June 1968): 30–33.

8. Alain Geismar, Serge July, and Erlyne Morane, *Vers la guerre civile* (Paris: Éditions Premières, 1969), 442 pp., has just come out. The book, at once vigorous and lyrical, carries important analyses of "the phantasm of conspiracy" (229–51) and on Belleville (337–64). The first chapter clarifies in detail previous "leftist" positions.

9. See the discussion of Marcuse in chapter 7 of this volume.

10. See Michel de Certeau, "La loi Faure, ou le status de l'enseignement dans la Nation," *Études* (December 1968): 682–89 [L. G.].

Chapter 7. Violent Mystics and Nonviolent Strategies

1. See Renato Ortiz, *A morte brancha do feiticeiro negro: Umbanda, integração de uma religião numa sociedade de classes* (Petropolis, Brazil: Editora Vozes, 1978).

2. Robert N. Bellah, "Civil Religion in America," in *Beyond Belief: Essays on Religion in a Post-Traditional World* (New York: Harper and Row, 1970), 168–89.

3. Michel de Certeau, "Les chrétiens et la dictature militaire au Brésil," *Politique d'aujourd'hui* (November 1969), 39–53. On Latin American ecclesial positions, two important dossiers have been published in Lima by the Comisión Episcopal de Acción Social: *Signos de Renovación* (1969); *Signos de Liberación. Testimonios de la Iglesia en América Latina, 1969–1973* (1974).

4. Michael McKale, "Nestor Paz: The Mystic Christian Guerrilla," *Radical Religion* 2.1 (1975): 36–44; Nestor Paz Zamora, *My Life for My Friends* (Maryknoll, N.Y.: Orbis Books, 1975); Walter Broderick, *Camilo Torres: A Biography of the Priest-Guerrilla* (New York: Doubleday, 1975), is the best biography of Camilo Torres.

5. *Noticias Aliadas* (Lima), July 25, 1970.

6. Nicole Bonnet, "A guerrilha dos cristãos," *Estado de São Paulo* (January 3, 1971).

7. *Noticias Aliadas*, December 20, 1973. Father Lain is the author of a call to revolution addressed to "the priests of Colombia" (the text is in *Nadoc* [Lima, September 8, 1971]) and of a study titled *El sacerdote y la Revolución* (1973).

8. P. G., "De plus en plus de prêtres dans la guérilla," *La Croix*, January 11, 1974.

9. *Noticias Aliadas*, February 2, 1972.

10. Ricardo Antoncich, "El tema de la liberación en Medellín y el Sínodo de 1974," *Medellín* 3 (1976).

11. An important dossier is *Frei Damião e os impasses de religião popular* (Recife, December 1971). [On this topic see Michel de Certeau, *The Practice of Everyday Life*, vol. 1, trans. Steven Rendall (Berkeley and Los Angeles: University of California Press, 1984), chap. 2 (L. G.).] Many other analogies pertain that have been put together by teams composed of researchers, militants, workers, and so forth.

12. Since 1960–70, a whole literature has come out on the topic. Thus, for Catholicism: A. Büntig, S. Galilea, J. Monast, et al., *Catolicismo popular* (Quito, 1969); P. A. Ribeiro de Olivera, *Catolicismo popular no Brasil* (Rio de Janeiro, 1970), and *Catolicismo popular na America Latina* (Rio de Janeiro, 1971), which includes an important bibliography (77–79); S. Galilea and M. Gonzalez, *Catolicismo popular* (Quito, 1972); ITER, *A Fé popular no Nordeste* (Salvador-Bahia, 1974), among others.

13. Thus, in Brazil, the FUNDIFRAN experiment (Fundação de Desenvolvimento Integrado do São Franciscão) in the São Franciscão Valley, in Barra (in the state of Bahia); see the dossier of the *Cadernos do Ceas* (Salvador), August 1973; Freddy A. J. Servais, "Un projet de développement au Brésil," *Demain le monde*, February 18, 1974; or, in Peru, the CIPCA, in Piura.

14. Worth noting in this respect is Roberto da Matta, *Ensaios de Anthropologia estrutural* (Rio de Janeiro: Vozes, 1973), especially 121–68 on "carnival as a rite of passage," which renews methods according to the classic studies of Luis da Camara Cascudo, *Folclore do Brasil* (Rio de Janeiro: Harper and Row, 1967), *Tradição, Ciência do Povo* (São Paulo: Harper and Row, 1971), *Cultura de massa e cultura popular* (Rio de Janeiro: Harper and Row, 1973), etc.

15. On the messianic movements, I refer to the well-known works of Maria Isaura Pereira de Queiroz, and also to the well-documented *Miracle at Joseiro* by Ralph Della Cava (New York: Columbia University Press, 1970). Here I am referring to the research seminars on popular and religious language in which I have been taking part at Recife since 1973.

16. On the remarks of Monsignor Camus (secretary of the Episcopal Conference) during a meeting with journalists in Santiago and the affair that ensued, see *Mensaje* (Santiago) (November 1975): 489–90. A communiqué from the Episcopal Conference in Chile (October 10, 1975), moreover, estimated these remarks to conform in general with the episcopal declaration "Evangelism and Peace" (September 1975) that forbade struggle in the defense of "rights" and indicated its "gratitude" to the armed forces for their "services rendered to the country" and for "having freed us from a Marxist dictatorship" (the complete text is document 247 of the Diffusion of Information about Latin America).

17. For Proaño: "L'engagement politique du chrétien," a radio message broadcast on January 24, 1975 (see the Diffusion of Information about Latin America, document 210). Casaldaliga was threatened with expulsion (as a Spaniard) for having defended marginalized rural populations and small-scale expatriate farmers. He was defended by the entire episcopate (Diffusion of Information about Latin America, dossier 249).

18. Diffusion of Information about Latin America, documents 183 and 203.

19. The general coordinator, Adolfo Pérez Esquivel ("Servicio para la acción liberadora en América Latina. Orientación no violenta," Peru 620, 5° P. Dpt 19, Buenos Aires, Argentina), publishes a bulletin, *Paz y Justicia* (España 890, San Isidro, Buenos Aires Province, Argentina), providing information and theoretical reflections. For the Medellín meeting of February 1974, see *Paz y Justicia*, nos. 10–12 (January–March 1974 and July 15, 1974).

20. A good analysis of the repression can be found in *Sic* (the review of the CEAS of Caracas), September 1975.

21. Thus, created in 1973 and theoretically dissolved by the junta in November 1975, the "Cooperative Committee for Peace in Chile," or Pro Paz, which is inspired

by Christian principles, works for the "liberation" of prisoners, and had a brush with the DINA (Dirección de Inteligencia Nacional), the central police department of Chile.

22. For an analysis of the techniques and the experiments of nonviolence, see Jean-Marie Muller, *Stratégie de l'action non violente* (Paris: Fayard, 1972), and especially the excellent journal, *Alternatives non violentes* (Lyons).

23. *Alternatives non violentes*, no. 4, 12; no. 12, 38.

Chapter 8. A Necessary Music

1. On these questions, see Armand Mattelart and Yves Stourdzé, *Technologie, Culture et Communication* (Paris: La Documentation Française, 1982).

2. Pierre Drouin, "L'autre économie," *Le Monde*, August 22–23, 1982.

3. Luce Giard, "Espaces privés," in Michel de Certeau, Luce Giard, and Pierre Mayol, *L'Invention du quotidien*, vol. 2, *Habiter, cuisiner*, rev. ed. (Paris: Gallimard, "Folio," 1994).

4. Colette Pétonnet, *Espaces habités. Ethnologie des banlieues* (Paris: Galilée, 1982), 29.

5. That is, if Jürgen Habermas's thesis about "public space" is entertained, as it is studied in his *The Structural Transformation of the Public Sphere: An Inquiry into a Category of Bourgeois Society*, trans. Thomas Burger with the assistance of Frederick Lawrence (Cambridge: MIT Press, 1989).

6. *Communications*, no. 30, titled "La Communication" (1979).

7. For an overall view, see Jean-Pierre Courtial, *La Communication piégée* (Paris: Robert Jauze, 1979).

8. Gregory Bateson, *Towards an Ecology of Mind* (New York: Ballantine Books, 1970); Paul Watzlawick et al., *Une Logique de la communication* (Paris: Seuil, 1972), along with *Changements* (Paris: Seuil, 1975), and *La Réalité de la réalité* (Paris: Seuil, 1978); William Labov, *Sociolinguistique* (Paris: Minuit, 1976); Erving Goffman, *Les Rites d'interactions* (Paris: Minuit, 1974).

9. D. Sudnow, ed., *Studies in Social Interaction* (New York: Free Press, 1972); Jeremy Boissevain, *Friends of Friends* (Oxford: Basil Blackwell, 1974); Edward O. Laumann, *Bonds of Pluralism* (New York: John Wiley, 1973); and so on.

10. Jean-François Barbier-Bouvet et al., *Communication et Pouvoir. Mass media et médias communautaires au Québec* (Paris: Anthropos, 1979).

11. Pétonnet, *Espaces habités*, 30–35; see also Pierre Mayol, "Habiter," in *L'Invention du quotidien*, vol. 2.

12. Michel Vovelle, ed., *Les Intermédiaires culturels* (Aix-en-Provence: University of Provence, 1981); Claire Krafft Pourrat, *Le Colporteur et la Mercière* (Paris: Denoël, 1982); Françoise Parent-Lardeur, *Lire à Paris au temps de Balzac* (Paris: École des Hautes Études en Sciences Sociales, 1981).

13. Isabelle Benjamin and Jacqueline Mengin, *Innovation culturelle des nouveaux ensembles urbains* (Paris: Ministry of Culture [SER], 1982), 6–20, 63, 67–68.

14. Pierre Clastres, *La Société contre l'État* (Paris: Minuit, 1974).

15. Problems in the audiovisual domain will be taken up only indirectly, for lack of competence in the material, especially in that earlier studies have provided strong analyses: Mattelart and Stourdzé, *Technologie, Culture et Communication*; Raymond Bellour's and Marc Piault's contributions in Maurice Godelier, *Les Sciences de l'homme et*

de la société en France. Rapports complémentaires (Paris: La Documentation Française, 1982). See also Louis Quéré's general summary in *Des miroirs équivalents. Aux origines de la communication* (Paris: Aubier, 1982).

16. Pierre Drouin, "La fin du jacobinisme électronique?" in *Le Monde,* October 31–November 1, 1982; Michel Picho, "Télématique en Provence profonde," *Le Monde-Dimanche,* January 9, 1983.

17. Marie-Claude Betbeder, "Casse-croûte à Sandouville," *Le Monde-Dimanche,* December 5, 1982.

18. Pierre, in the broadcast, *Nous tous chacun,* October 27, 1982 (France-Culture, 12–12:30 P.M.), produced by Jean-Claude Bringuier.

19. Claire Brisset, "Les 7 ans de David dans un placard," *Le Monde,* August 24, 1982; Patrick Benquet, "Le retour à la vie de David, l'enfant martyr," *Le Monde,* August 27, 1982.

Chapter 9. Priorities

1. Abelmalek Sayad, "Les trois âmes de l'émigration algérienne," *Actes de la recherche en sciences sociales,* no. 15 (June 1977): 68.

2. Michel de Certeau, *The Practice of Everyday Life,* vol. 1, trans. Steven Rendall (Berkeley and Los Angeles: University of California Press, 1984); but also the new edition in French: *L'Invention du quotidien,* vol. 1, *Arts de faire* (Paris: Gallimard, "Folio"), xl–xlii, 40–43, 63–68; George Lakoff, *Linguistique et logique naturelle* (Paris: Klincksieck, 1976); *Communications,* no. 32, *Les Actes de discours* (1980); *DRLAV,* no. 25 (1981) and no. 26 (1982); and Pierre Bourdieu, *Ce que parler veut dire* (Paris: Fayard, 1982). [Paul Zumthor, *Parler au Moyen Âge* (Paris: Minuit, 1980). — *Trans.*]

3. The vocabulary of limits here is drawn from sources of unquestionable authority: Gerald Holton and Robert S. Morison, eds., *Limits of Scientific Inquiry* (New York: W. W. Norton, 1979); Patrick Suppes, *Logique du probable* (Paris: Flammarion, 1981).

Chapter 10. Networks

1. Alain Giraud et al., *Les Réseaux pensants. Télécommunications et société* (Paris: Masson, 1978); *Le Courrier du CNRS,* no. 39 (January 1981); *Traverses,* no. 13, under the theme of "Networks: The Model of the Railway" (December 1978).

2. Guy Arbellot, "La grande mutation des routes de France au milieu du XVIIIᵉ siècle," *Annales* 28 (1973): 765–91.

3. Henri Giordan, *Démocratie culturelle et Droit à la différence* (Paris: La Documentation Française, 1982).

4. Lucien Sfez, ed., *L'Objet local* (Paris: Union Générale d'Éditions, "10–18," 1977).

5. Pierre Grémion, *Le Pouvoir périphérique* (Paris: Seuil, 1976).

6. Giordan, *Démocratie culturelle et Droit à la différence.*

7. Gérard Bauer and Jean-Michel Roux, *La Rurbanisation* (Paris: Seuil, 1976).

8. John Gumperz and Dell Hymes, eds., *Directions in Sociolinguistics: The Ethnography of Communication* (New York: Holt, Rinehart and Winston, 1972); and the works of W. A. Stewart, C. Ferguson, William Labov, and Sylvia Ostrowetsky.

9. Michel de Certeau et al., *Une politique de la langue* (Paris: Gallimard, 1975). [This remark was written in 1983, before regionalization became a national policy in France (L. G.).]

10. Gérard Noiriel, *Vivre et lutter à Longwy* (Paris: Maspero, 1980), 10; David Charrasse, *Lorraine Cœur d'Acier* (Paris: Maspero, 1981).

11. For leisure groups, see Paul Puaux, *Les Établissements culturels* (Paris: La Documentation Française, 1982), 20. Questions of patrimony are taken up in Max Querrien, *Pour une nouvelle politique du patrimoine* (Paris: La Documentation Française, 1982), 7–8.

12. Maurice Godelier, *Les Sciences de l'homme et de la société en France* (Paris: La Documentation Française, 1982), 73–74, 78.

13. Colette Pétonnet, *Espaces habités. Ethnologie des banlieues* (Paris: Galilée, 1982), 49–55; 105–14; Oumar Dia and Renée Colin-Noguès, *Yâkâré. Autobiographie d'Oumar* (Paris: Maspero, 1982); Abdelmalek Sayad, "El Ghorba: le mécanisme de reproduction de l'émigration," *Actes de la recherche en sciences sociales* (March 1975): 50–66, and "Les trois âges de l'émigration algérienne," no. 15 (June 1977): 59–79.

14. Abdemalek Sayad, "Les enfants illégitimes," *Actes de la recherche en sciences sociales*, no. 25 (January 1979): 61–81, and "Hakim Ghanem le doux," *Le Monde de l'éducation*, no. 90 (January 1983).

15. Catherine de Seynes, *On n'a pas le temps. Création collective en milieu ouvrier à Saint-Nazaire* (Paris: Maspero, 1978).

16. Noiriel, *Vivre et lutter à Longwy*, 116.

17. Geneviève Breerette, "Les véhicules de la peinture," *Le Monde* (September 26–27, 1982).

18. Michel de Certeau, *The Practice of Everyday Life*, vol. 1, trans. Steven Rendall (Berkeley and Los Angeles: University of California Press, 1984), 24–28.

19. Claudine de France, ed., *Pour une anthropologie visuelle* (Paris: Mouton, 1979), and *Le Film documentaire: options méthodologiques* (Paris: University of Paris X-Nanterre, 1981).

20. Ministry of Culture (SER), *Pratiques culturelles des Français, évolution 1973–1981* (Paris: Dalloz, 1982).

Chapter 11. Operators

1. Saul Alinsky, *Rules for Radicals: A Practical Primer for Realistic Radicals* (New York: Vintage Books, 1971 [repr. 1989], 3.

2. Ministry of Culture (SER), *Les Publics du festival d'Avignon* (Paris: La Documentation Française, 1982), 188.

3. See Michel Vovelle, ed., *Les Intermédiaires culturels* (Aix-en-Provence: Presses de l'Université de Provence, 1981); Robert Muchembled, *Culture populaire et Culture des élites dans la France moderne (XVe–XVIIIe siècles)* (Paris: Flammarion, 1978), 355–56; Françoise Parent-Lardeur, *Lire à Paris au temps de Balzac* (Paris: École des Hautes Études en Sciences Sociales, 1981).

4. Oumar Dia and Renée Colin-Noguès, *Yâkâré. Autobiographie d'Oumar* (Paris: Maspero, 1982).

5. Jack Goody, *The Domestication of the Savage Mind* (Cambridge: Cambridge University Press, 1977), 57–58, 68–69.

6. Bernard Pingaud and Jean-Claude Barreau, *Pour une politique nouvelle du livre et de la lecture* (Paris: Dalloz, 1982), 275–78. For the Centers of Social Documentation, see Marie-Claire Vitale, *Les Centres de documentation sociale. Bilan d'un an de fonctionnement* (Paris: Ministry of Culture [SER], 1982 [May]).

7. Michel Castaing, "Les campagnes publicitaires du gouvernement. Un marché de 150 millions de francs en 1982," *Le Monde*, October 12, 1982, and "Publicité et information gouvernementales. Fin de campagne," *Le Monde*, November 11, 1982.

8. We know that over time commercial conformity and the weight of the economy have won out over the associative movement and local initiatives, which are incapable of competing with the received model of local stations [L. G.].

9. Vitale, *Les Centres de documentation sociale*, 10–11.

10. Jean-Pierre Foron, "Des dentelles pour les émirs," *Le Monde*, January 19, 1983.

Chapter 12. Memories

1. The success of Steven Spielberg's *Jurassic Park* (1993) and the attraction of historical fictions staged by Euro-Disney convey the same themes [L. G.].

2. Francis Rousseau, "Confidences familiales en V.H.S.," *Libération*, February 11, 1983.

3. Michel Ragon, *Histoire de la littérature prolétarienne en France* (Paris: Albin Michel, 1974); and *Plein Chant* (Georges Monti and Edmond Thomas, Bassac 16120 Châteauneuf-sur-Charente), notably the dossier titled "Paul Feller et les écrivains prolétariens," assembled by Jérôme Radwan (spring 1980).

4. Jean-Claude Bouvier et al., *Tradition orale et identité culturelle. Problèmes et méthodes* (Paris: Centre National de la Recherche Scientifique, 1980). A somewhat condescending discussion appeared in *Cahiers internationaux de sociologie* 69 (1980–82) under the title "Histoires de vie et vie sociale."

5. Fanch Elegoët, "Le recueil d'une histoire de vie," *Tud Ha Bro. Sociétés bretonnes* (Plouguerneau), no. 2, titled *Les paysans parlent* (1979): 141–70.

6. Mathilde La Bardonnie, "Aline en Poitou. Les échos du bal," *Le Monde*, August 17, 1982.

7. For example, Hubert Knapp, *Les pique-chalosse*, on TF1, six episodes, beginning February 24, 1983 (10:15–11:15 P.M.).

8. Jean-François Lacan, "La vidéothèque de Paris: les images des mégalopoles," *Le Monde-Dimanche*, January 9, 1983.

Chapter 13. Propositions

1. See part IV, "Ethnic Economies," chaps. 14–17 [L. G.].

2. See Michel de Certeau, *Culture in the Plural*, ed. and with an Introduction by Luce Giard, trans. and with an Afterword by Tom Conley (Minneapolis: University of Minnesota Press, 1997), chap. 6, "Minorities" [L. G.].

3. Pierre Belleville, *Pour la culture dans l'entreprise* (Paris: La Documentation Française, 1982); Max Querrien, *Pour une nouvelle politique du patrimoine* (Paris: La Documentation Française, 1982) [L. G.].

4. In addition to the chapters that Michel de Certeau and I prepared for the report submitted to the Ministry of Culture (reprinted in this book) are added four dossiers, prepared under our guidance, and dealing, respectively, with childhood (Anne Baldassari), immigration (Philippe Mustar), the suburbs (Jacques Katuszewski and Ruwen Ogien), and regional cultures (Fanch Elegoët specifically dealt with the case of Brittany) [L. G.].

Chapter 14. An Interethnic Encounter

1. Synthesis published by the Organization for Economic Cooperation and Development (OECD), "The Education of Minority Groups: An Enquiry into Problems and Practices of Fifteen Countries" (Paris-Hampshire: Gower, 1983).

2. Erick Allardt, "Implications of the Ethnic Revival in Modern Industrialized Society: A Comparative Study of the Linguistic Minorities in Western Europe," *Commentationes Scientiarum Socialium* 12 (Helsinki: Societas Scientiarum Fennica, 1979). For the United States, see Michael Novak, *The Rise of Unmeltable Ethnics* (New York: Macmillan, 1972). See John W. Bennett, *The New Ethnicity: Perspectives from Ethnology* (Saint Paul: West Publishing, 1975). Especially important are the ethno- and sociolinguistics of Joshua A. Fishman, *Advances in the Sociology of Language*, 2 vols. (The Hague: Mouton, 1972). On *Ethnicity*, Wsevolod Isajiw, "Definitions of Ethnicity," *Ethnicity* 1 (1974): 111–24. Worth noting also is the older journal, *Plural Societies* (The Hague).

3. French research on this topic is presented in *Pluriel*, nos. 32–33 (1982–83), titled *Minorités. Ethnicité. Mouvements nationalitaires* (colloquium held at Sèvres by the French Association of Ethnologists). In this publication, Jean-Pierre Simon notes the "repugnance for interethnics and those in the minority" that characterizes the French ethnological tradition, with the exception of a few "oases" (Bastide, Balandier) (ibid., 13–26). The absence of a specific field (still obvious in the Godelier Report, *Les Sciences de l'homme et de la société en France* [Paris: La Documentation Française, 1982]) is probably rooted at once in a centralizing tradition, in the antirepublican past of minority demands, and in the structuralist or Marxist orientation of research until very recently.

4. In this regard, see especially the sociopolitical works of Nathan Glazer (*Ethnic Dilemmas, 1964–1982* [Cambridge: Harvard University Press, 1983]) and the comparative studies of Jerzy Smolicz on ethnolinguistic practices ("Is the Monolingual Nation-State Out of Date?" *Comparative Education* 20.2 [1983]: 265–86; "Multiculturalism and an Over-Arching Framework of Values: Some Educational Responses for Ethnically Plural Societies," *European Journal of Education* 19.1 [1984]: 11–25).

Chapter 15. Conceptual Assimilation

1. The concept of "identity" is the object of an ongoing debate. See *L'identité*, seminar directed by Claude Lévi-Strauss (Paris: Grasset, 1977); M. Oriol, "Identité produite, identité instituée, identitée exprimée...," *Cahiers internationaux de Sociologie* 6.6 (1979): 19–28; C. Camillieri, "Identités et changements sociaux," in *Identités collectives et changements sociaux* (Toulouse: Privat, 1980), 331–44; S. Abou, *L'identité culturelle. Relations interethniques et problèmes d'acculturation* (Paris: Anthropos, 1981); G. Grandguillaume, "Langue, identité, et culture nationale au Maghreb," in *Peuples méditerranéens*, no. 9 (1979): 3–28.

2. Rodolfo Acuna, *Occupied America: The Chicano's Struggle toward Liberation* (New York: Harper and Row, 1972). A more recent example: a growing number of North American blacks, whose upward mobility has detached them from an increasingly impoverished black proletariat, are now led to consider the race question in the United States to be "obsolete" or "archaeological." For them, economic competition is the essential rule.

3. See especially Stanley Aronowitz, *False Promises: The Shaping of American Working Class Consciousness* (New York: McGraw-Hill, 1974).

4. Françoise Biot and Gilles Verbunt, *Immigrés dans la crise* (Paris: Éditions Ouvrières, 1981), 171–81.

5. On the appearance and development of Western individualism (a highly debated problem), see C. B. Macpherson, *The Political Theory of Possessive Individualism*, 7th ed. (Oxford: Oxford University Press, 1977); and Alan Macfarlane, *The Origins of English Individualism* (Cambridge: Cambridge University Press, 1979).

6. Thus, for Hans Kelsen, founder of the Austrian School (*Théorie pure du droit*, trans. C. Einsenmann [Paris: Dalloz, 1962], 438), the base of law is "the postulate of sovereignty of the individual and his or her liberty." Similarly, for John Rawls (*A Theory of Justice* [Cambridge: Harvard University Press, 7th ed., 1976]), the "concept of a well-ordered society" has as its basis the category of "everyone" (453ff.) and the notion of "the unity of self" that defines the society on the basis of individuals and their associations (560–67). Hence the two principles on which justice is based: (1) every person must have an equal right on the grounds of the most extensive freedom compatible with a similar freedom for others; (2) social and economic inequalities must be organized so as to be simultaneously (*a*) reasonably apt to be to everyone's advantage, and (*b*) attached to positions and charges "accessible to everyone" (60).

7. Lucien Sfez, in *Leçons sur l'égalité* (Paris: Fondation Nationale des Sciences Politiques, 1984), submits what he calls the "theology of the equal" to a critical appraisal of its historical figures.

8. For the notion of "house" and societies with "houses," see Claude Lévi-Strauss's review of courses taught from 1976 to 1982 in *Paroles données* (Paris: Plon, 1984), 189–241.

9. These practices (reciprocal services, hospitality, exchanges of gifts, etc.) obviously have an economic value, and they do escape careful social control, but they do not figure in the law of the market, which is based on the general equivalent of money. Thus they cannot be accounted for in financial and budgetary calculations.

10. Generally speaking, "cultures" would be *economies* vanquished or misconstrued by others, or else transversal and minor, or still again in reserve in relation to dominant economies and being developed suddenly when the time is ripe (in France, during the Occupation). Neither more nor less symbolic than the others, they represent different types of "commerce" that are perfectly compatible in a single territory, but are hierarchized. In French society, for example, supposedly "cultural protests" (carnival, the village banquet, and even the family reunion) constitute economies (provisionally?) repressed by history: even as these islands are progressively occupied by a touristic technology, they continue to puncture the territory of sites organized through heterogeneously *economic* principles (collective property, exchange of gifts, familial allegiance, etc.).

11. Corresponding to the collapse of paternal power (the law of July 24, 1889), which allows an increasing number of interventions on the part of the judge and the state in defense of the individual rights of the child is, moreover, "the separation of church and state" (the law of December 9, 1905). The synchrony has its logic.

12. See Françoise Héritier-Augé's conclusions in "Famille," in *Encyclopaedia Universalis, Supplément,* vol. 1, *Le Savoir* (1985), 534–38, as well as those of Claude Lefort, "L'individu," *Passé présent,* no. 1 (1982).

Chapter 16: The Active and Passive of Appurtenances

1. "Hybrid monism" is the term J. Smolicz uses in "Culture, Ethnicity and Education: Multiculturalism in a Plural Society," in J. Megarry, S. Nisbet, and E. Hoyle, eds., *World Yearbook of Education 1981: Education of Minorities* (New York: Nichols, 1982), 19.

2. Suzanne Citron, *Enseigner l'histoire aujourd'hui. La mémoire perdue et retrouvée* (Paris: Éditions Ouvrières, 1984). [In 1945, the town of Sétif in northeastern Algeria witnessed a revolt against French rule. More than a hundred Europeans were murdered, and, in response, the French massacred, according to Algerian sources, more than six thousand Muslims. — *Trans.*]

3. For the current forms of nationalism, see Franjo Tudjman, *Nationalism in Contemporary Europe* (New York: Columbia University Press, 1981). In France, the relations among "Republic," "Homeland," and "Nation" need to be sorted out; see, for example, Charles Renouvier, *Manuel républicain de l'homme et du citoyen, 1848* (Paris: Garnier, 1981). For the history of "national ideology," some essential books include Jean-Yves Guiomar, *L'idéologie nationale* (Paris: Champ Libre, 1974); and G. Weill, *L'Europe du XIXᵉ siècle et l'idée de nationalité* (Paris, 1938). The identification of the state with the nation calls for a reflection on their distinction and on the political forms of national autonomies that exist inside the same state. Examples and hypotheses are found in *Les Autonomies en differents Estats. Experiences i perspectives* (Barcelona: Publications de l'Abadia de Montserrat, 1979). An opposite problematic is developed in Michael Hechter, *Internal Colonialism: The Celtic Fringe in British National Development, 1536–1966* (London: Routledge and Kegan Paul, 1975), which valorizes nationalism.

4. Article 77 (paragraphs 2 and 3) of the Constitution of 1958, however, clearly lagged behind the Constitution of June 24, 1793, of which article 4 admitted certain foreigners to an exercise at all levels of their "rights as French citizens," but it was never applied. See Jacqueline Costa-Lascoux and Catherine de Wenden-Didier, in *Les Droits politiques des immigrés,* Cahiers de la pastorale des migrants, nos. 10–11 (1982): 47–58.

5. See the studies that develop a "situational" conception of ethnicity, and that underlie ethnic adaptability, its developments, or its stiffening, and so on, since John W. Bennett, *The New Ethnicity: Perspectives from Ethnology* (Saint Paul: West Publishing, 1975); L. A. Despress, *Ethnicity and Resource Competition in Plural Societies* (The Hague: Mouton, 1975); A. L. Epstein, *Ethos and Identity: Three Studies in Ethnicity* (London: Tavistock, 1978).

6. Claude Lévi-Strauss, "Race et histoire," in *Anthropologie structurale deux* (Paris: Plon, 1973), 377–422.

7. In North America, for example, there is already the entire "interactionist" current inaugurated by the founding studies of Frederik Barth (1969).

8. See, for example, Jacques Katuszewski and Ruwen Ogien, *Réseaux d'immigrés* (Paris: Éditions Ouvrières, 1981), on the successive "disconnections" and "reconnections" of a network of kinship and on the evolution of traditional rules applicable to matters of alliance.

9. In this perspective, exemplary is the experience of the professor who knows well how to recognize the common formality of problems posed by Gypsy, Portuguese, and Breton pupils. French experiments, of which there are far too few analyses, are in *Migrants formation,* organ of the CEFISEM. Also the *Cahiers de l'Éducation nationale,* no. 26 (June 1984), in particular on intercultural projects for action in education (PAE), for example [in Paris], in the eleventh arrondissement (research on short stories) or the fifteenth arrondissement (sister school relationships with African schools). For many instructors, as for those of Douai, the results from these experiments show that "the difficulties met by children of immigrants are not specifically related to problems of teaching" and thus that ghettoized classes need to be avoided (16).

10. Abdelmalek Sayad, "Les trois âges de l'émigration algérienne," in *Actes de la recherche en sciences sociales,* no. 15 (June 1977): 59–79; also "De 'populations d'immigrés' à 'minorités', l'enjeu des dénominations," *Rapport à l'OCDE* (January 1985).

11. G. G. Grander, *Essais d'une philosophie du style* (Paris: Armand Colin, 1968), in which the development of a "stylistics" of scientific writings is more central for the work here than the will to discover within a "principle of individuation."

12. Dell Hymes, "On Communicative Competence," in J. B. Pride and J. Holmes, *Sociolinguistics* (Harmondsworth, England: Penguin Books, 1972). "Communicative competence" means knowing when, how, and to whom a given linguistic form can be directed, and it sets out the rules for using the language. Following John Gumperz and Dell Hymes, eds., *Directions in Sociolinguistics: The Ethnography of Communication* (New York: Holt, Rinehart and Winston, 1972), and Richard Bauman and Joel Scherzer, *Explorations in the Ethnography of Speaking* (Cambridge: Cambridge University Press, 1974), one can call attention to the works of C. A. Ferguson, William Labov, P. Watzlawick, and so on, as well as Uli Windisch, *Pensée sociale, langage en usage et logiques autres* (Lausanne-Vienna: L'Âge d'Homme, 1982). Also important in this regard is research in pragmatics: *Langue française,* no. 42 (1979), "Pragmatics"; *Actes de la recherche en sciences sociales,* no. 46 (March 1983), "The Uses of Speech."

13. In this regard, "errors" are marks of elocution in the regular system of expression. They locate the speakers' "modes of expression." In a related perspective that deals with the "functions" of language, see Henri Frei, *La Grammaire des fautes* (Geneva: Slatkine Reprints, 1971).

14. An example is in Geneva Smitherman, *Talkin and Testifyin: The Language of Black America* (Boston: Houghton Mifflin, 1977).

15. A wealth of studies are found on the art of reusing and bending the products of another economy thanks to practices of one's own. For the book, the telephone, or the radio, see Catherine N'Diaye's astute observations in *Gens de sable* (Paris: POL, 1984), or the model developed by Francis Affergan, in *Anthropologie à la Martinique* (Paris: Fondation Nationale des Sciences Politiques, 1983). A general approach is taken in Michel de Certeau, *The Practice of Everyday Life,* vol. 1, trans. Steven Rendall (Berkeley and Los Angeles: University of California Press, 1984). Two enlightening cases: reading (in *The Practice of Everyday Life,* chap. 12), which Wolfgang Iser has shown to be very much determined by the practices of the reader (*The Act of Reading* [Baltimore:

Johns Hopkins University Press, 1981], 107–34); television, whose generally "colonizing" programs (e.g., *Dallas*, the target and the favorite for sociologies of communication) can be "used" in a thousand different ways (Elihu Katz and Tamar Liebes, "Once upon a Time, in Dallas," *Intermedia* [May 1984]: 28–32).

16. Sigmund Freud, *Moses and Monotheism*, in *The Standard Edition of the Complete Psychological Works of Sigmund Freud*, vol. 23, trans. and ed. James Strachey (London: Hogarth Press, 1961), 1–137. Freud analyzes the "particular power" (*Macht*) of "little bits" that are dispersed from an abandoned origin.

Chapter 17: The School for Diversity

1. The conclusion drawn from a pilot project at the Jules-Guesde II secondary school (Argenteuil, 1982) can be applied here: it is a question "giving to children the *necessary tools* for understanding the culture of the other and, as a consequence, their own" (quoted in *Cahiers de l'Éducation nationale* [June 1984]: 12).

2. In particular, a history or an institutional analysis would have to show not only workers' struggles and social movements whose progress in law is the effect, but also the role played in past or present struggles by "appurtenances" (of a quasi-"clannish" or adapted form) that official discourse covers over. In France, the ever-difficult relations between the *school* itself and *families* still pertains to this problem and can allow for a better clarification of social reality.

3. In a related perspective, on the topic of the teaching of young Gypsies, Jean-Pierre Liégois wonders if they are being given the "negotiating tools" that include technical practices as well as elements that allow them to understand the non-Gypsy environment (the "gadgé") and its institutions. See Jean-Pierre Liégois, *Formation des enseignants des enfants tziganes* (Donaueschingen, June 20–25, 1983) (Strasbourg: Council of Europe, 1983), 4–5.

Afterword: The "Events" and Their Erosion

1. Emiko Ohnuki-Tierney sums up Braudel and projects his conclusions onto anthropology, a science built on time understood as permanence, in her "Introduction: The Historicization of Anthropology," in Emiko Ohnuki-Tierney, ed., *Culture through Time: Anthropological Approaches* (Stanford, Calif.: Stanford University Press, 1990), 7ff.

2. A remarkable piece of postrevolutionary theater, both faithful to the spirit of the events and graphic in its reconstruction of their duration—and not included in Michel de Certeau's bibliography in chapters 5 and 6—is Jean Thibaudeau, *Dix-neuf soixante-huit en France*, with a preface, "Printemps rouge," by Philippe Sollers (Paris: Seuil, 1970). Thibaudeau's script puts forward the experience of time at once compressed (the revolt in its totalizing flash) and extended (over a calendar of forty-four days).

3. What follows recoups one point in François Zourabichvili, *Deleuze: Une philosophie de l'événement* (Paris: PUF, 1994), on the question of *belief* and the feeling of "exhaustion" experienced in the affirmation of immanence, a condition in which new forces and new signs (and political actions) can be engaged (69–70). Zourabichvili echoes a Certellian note when he states, "Croire en ce monde-ci, c'est affirmer l'immanence" (68) (To believe in this world is to affirm immanence).

4. Gilles Deleuze, "Un nouveau cartographe?" in *Foucault* (Paris: Minuit, 1986), 51; my translation. Certeau's relation to this text and the practices it advocates are seen in *Heterologies: Discourse on the Other,* trans. Brian Massumi (Minneapolis: University of Minnesota Press, 1986), 197.

5. Gilles Deleuze, "Louis Wolfson, or the Procedure," in *Essays Critical and Clinical,* trans. Daniel W. Smith and Michael A. Greco (Minneapolis: University of Minnesota Press, 1997), chap. 2.

6. Two recent studies take different paths to show why. Priscilla Parkhurst Ferguson, in *Paris as Revolution* (Berkeley: University of California Press, 1993), studies how the entire nineteenth century, from the July Monarchy of 1830 to the Commune of 1871 and beyond, upheld the belief that democratic action needed to be staged in the nation's capital. The construction of the Eiffel Tower tended to put a lid on that tradition by using an image of the future (and its emblem in the movement of modernism) to forget the force of revolutionary struggle. Whatever happened *after* the installation of the tower could not arch back to events that had taken place before. In *Logics of Failed Revolt: French Theory after 1968* (Stanford, Calif.: Stanford University Press, 1995), Peter Starr notes that Americans often fail to understand French social action because of a tendency not to relate the tradition of 1789 to that of theory. In North America, decentralization, a pragmatism in matters of education, an economic structure ("commodity terrorism," 201), and other causes make the willful *failure* of May 1968 difficult to grasp. Starr affirms that the theoretical dimension of the events precluded them from any association with the French past.

7. The prevailing slogan was "Au-dessous des pavés, la plage..." (Beneath the bricks, the beach...).

8. " 'You, too?' — 'Yes.' ... [T]he particular point of view is not denied; it is changed from within, or rather revealed to itself, restored to the 'impossible' that inhabits it, while recognizing that other undertakings are being constructed around the same secret" ("The Gaze of Nicholas of Cusa," trans. Catherine Porter, *Diacritics* 17.3 [fall 1987]: 29).

9. Two essays by Jean-François Lyotard especially capture what May 1968 "meant" for its participants in ways consonant with Certeau's reflections. In "Unbeknownst" (originally "À l'insu"), he shows that the Revolution had success when it showed how much "politics will never be anything but the art of the possible" (in Miami Theory Collective, *Community at Loose Ends,* trans. Georges Van den Abbeele and James Creech [Minneapolis: University of Minnesota Press, 1991], 46), and that its own identification with childhood determined how much "May 1968 clearly showed a scrupulous fidelity to a state of dependency more immanent to the mind than its state of mind" (47). With "childhood" came a sense for everyone that we are "dropped into a situation whose meaning is unknown to us," in which we "have to learn what it is to live, what it is to die, what it is to be male for female" (Jean-François Lyotard, "Oikos," in *Political Writings,* trans. Bill Readings with Kevin Paul Geiman [Minneapolis: University of Minnesota Press, 1993], 102). The feeling for the relation held to the world at large is constitutive, adds Lyotard, of the ecology of May 1968, a theme and a practice that may be its most important legacy.

10. On the position of this theme in Deleuze's writing, see Daniel A. Smith, "A Life of Pure Immanence: Deleuze's 'Critique et clinique' Project," preface to Deleuze, *Essays Critical and Clinical.* Following Leibniz's monadology, Deleuze notes that in this precapitalistic sphere we are "beyond any lived experience," where the world "exists

only in thought and has no other result than the world of art," in which both thought and art also upset the applecart of the world's reality, morality, and economy.

11. Gilles Deleuze, "L'épuisé," Afterword to Samuel Beckett, *Quad* (Paris: Minuit, 1992), 59; my translation.

12. See Michel de Certeau, *The Mystic Fable: The Sixteenth and Seventeenth Centuries*, trans. Michael B. Smith (Chicago: University of Chicago Press, 1993), 42–44.

13. In a telling conundrum, Jacques Derrida makes the same point. When he speaks of "les formes et normes" (forms and norms) that legitimize communication, he puns on their presence as "formes énormes" (enormous forms) ("Où commence et comment finit un corps enseignant," in *Du droit à la philosophie* [Paris: Galilée, 1990], 114ff.; originally printed in D. Grisoni, ed., *Politiques de la philosophie* [Paris: Grasset, 1976]).

14. Denis Hollier, "Actions, No! Words, Yes!" in *A New History of French Literature* (Cambridge: Harvard University Press, 1989), 1040.

15. Articles in *Le Monde* in December 1995 stressed the point. Reporters for the *Atlantic Monthly* (September 1995) predicted that strikes would occur if political decisions exacerbated the social contradiction that the French felt in their own midst (in view of unemployment and immigration) and before the world at large (in respect to the absence of social benefits in other industrialized nations, especially the United States).

16. The spatialization of action is a leitmotif in all of Certeau's politics. A succinct treatment of their virtue is available in Ian Buchanan, "Heterophenomenology, or de Certeau's Theory of Space," *Social Semiotics* 6.1 (1996): 111–32.

17. Certeau studies the pedagogical architecture of the state in "Culture and the Schools," chapter 5 of *Culture in the Plural*. The spatial mechanisms of statecraft are outlined in his "Micro-Techniques and Panoptic Discourse: A Quid pro Quo," in *Heterologies*, 185–92.

Index

213

Before his untimely death in 1986, Michel de Certeau had authored numerous articles and books, including *The Writing of History, The Mystic Fable, The Practice of Everyday Life, The Stranger: Union in Difference,* and *Heterologies* (1986, University of Minnesota Press). A historian of religion and a student of ethnography, Michel de Certeau was a professor at both the École des Hautes Études en Sciences Sociales, Paris, and the University of California, San Diego. The second volume of his *Practice of Everyday Life,* coauthored with Luce Giard and Pierre Mayol, is forthcoming from the University of Minnesota Press.

Tom Conley is professor of French at Harvard University. He is the translator of *The Writing of History,* by Michel de Certeau; *The Fold,* by Gilles Deleuze; and *The Year of Passages,* by Reda Bensmaïa. Conley is also the author of *Film Hieroglyphs* (1991) and *The Self-Made Map: Cartographic Writing in Early Modern France* (1996), both published by the University of Minnesota Press.

Luce Giard is a research fellow at the Centre National de la Recherche Scientifique, affiliated with the Centre de Recherches Historiques at the École des Hautes Études en Sciences Sociales, Paris. Since 1988, she has taught one quarter of each year as a visiting professor in the Department of History at the University of California, San Diego. Giard's studies focus on the history of science and philosophy of the medieval and Renaissance periods. Michel de Certeau left Giard the editorial responsibility for his works.